Keywords
in Qualitative Methods

Keywords
in Qualitative Methods

A Vocabulary of Research Concepts

Michael Bloor and Fiona Wood

SAGE Publications
London • Thousand Oaks • New Delhi

First published 2006

The format of this book was originated by Eugene McLaughlin and
John Muncie and was first used in the *SAGE Dictionary of Criminology*
(Sage, May 2001).

 SAGE Publications Ltd
1 Oliver's Yard
55 City Road
London EC1Y 1SP

SAGE Publications Inc.
2455 Teller Road
Thousand Oaks, California 91320

SAGE Publications India Pvt Ltd
B-42, Panchsheel Enclave
Post Box 4109
New Delhi 110 017

British Library Cataloguing in Publication data

A catalogue record for this book is available
from the British Library

ISBN10 0 7619 4330 7   ISBN13 978 0 7619 4330 3
ISBN10 0 7619 4331 5 (pbk)   ISBN13 978 0 7619 4331 0 (pbk)

Library of Congress Control Number 2005936298

Typeset by C&M Digitals (P) Ltd, Chennai, India
Printed on paper from sustainable resources
Printed in Great Britain by The Cromwell Press Ltd, Trowbridge Wiltshire

Contents

About the Authors

Michael Bloor is a professorial research fellow at the Centre for Drug Misuse Research at Glasgow University. He has previously worked at the Medical Research Council's Social and Public Health Research Unit (first in Aberdeen and then in Glasgow) and at Cardiff University's School of Social Sciences, where he was Director of the Health & Social Care Research Support Unit. His research interests are in substance misuse, risk behaviour, health services research, research methods and occupational health and safety. He has more than 150 academic publications, including *Focus Groups in Social Research* (Sage, 2001) and *The Sociology of HIV Transmission* (Sage, 1995).

Fiona Wood is a lecturer in the Department of General Practice at Cardiff University. She is a medical sociologist with considerable experience in health services research. Her current interests include lay and professional views of antibiotic prescribing and patients' experiences of chronic disease. She also teaches qualitative research methods to medical undergraduates. Previously she has worked in the School of Social Sciences at Cardiff University and the Department of Public Health Medicine in Gwent Health Authority.

Introduction

A 'vocabulary' is concerned primarily with communicating the meanings of terms and concepts so that the reader may use those terms and concepts in his or her own everyday life and work. A vocabulary is therefore not concerned first and foremost with authoritative definitions or with etymological origins (though both of these have their place), but rather is concerned with the pragmatic meaning-in-use of particular terms and concepts. Accordingly, our main purpose in this vocabulary is to assist the reader in his or her use of qualitative research concepts by giving the reader a firm grasp of how these concepts are used in everyday research practice. To reiterate, our aim is to provide some practical assistance, not (emphatically not) to pronounce in a final and imperious manner on all matters methodological. Our refusal of The Mantle of Authority owes nothing to shrinking modesty, or commitment to postmodern poly-vocalism, and everything to the fact that the library shelves are already replete with encyclopaedias and handbooks which aim to provide syntheses and overviews of up-to-date thinking in the methods field. Let the encyclopaedias and handbooks function as Courts of Appeal.

But rather than dwell on what this book is *not*, we should state at some length what functions this vocabulary is meant to fulfil, and this leads us on to describe the structure of the individual vocabulary entries. Each entry begins with a short *definition* or explanation of the term, for example 'taxonomies are systems of classification used by collectivities to order and make sense of everyday experience'. But bald definitions, without elaboration, can be somewhat opaque. So each entry has a second section, *distinctive features*, which seeks to flesh out the bones of the earlier definition by use of handy comparisons (for example, the similarities and differences between ethnomethodology and symbolic interactionism) and associated principles (for example, the rejection by a postmodernist methodology of authorial authority). However, even the provision of comparisons and associated principles cannot always provide sufficient context for unequivocal understanding, so we further flesh out each entry with an *examples* section. We hope this is sound pedagogy: any methodological text would be rather dull and monochromatic without the colour provided by illustrations of actual studies that used the techniques under discussion, but sometimes illustration is necessary to convey the true flavour of a technique or principle. The enormity of the betrayal that may be occasioned by the (rather abstract) practice of 'covert research' can only be fully appreciated when we read of how the covert researcher, Laud Humphreys, tracked down the men he observed engaging in anonymous gay sex in public lavatories ('Tearoom Trade') by noting down their car license plates, obtaining their addresses from police files, and then posing as an interviewer in a community health survey in order to collect data on their occupations and marital statuses.

In his original '*Keywords*', that inspirational forerunner of this vocabulary, the late Raymond Williams noted that:

> Anyone who reads Dr Johnson's great Dictionary soon becomes aware of his active and partisan mind as well as his remarkable learning .... [and] ... the air of massive impersonality which the Oxford Dictionary communicates is not so impersonal, so purely scholarly, or so free of active social and political values as might be supposed from its occasional use. Indeed, to work closely in it is at times to get a fascinating insight into what can be called the ideology of its editors. (Williams, 1976: 16)

An underlying commitment to certain values, as Williams rightly observes, is an inevitable corollary of all scholarship, this book included. But where one is primarily concerned, as we are in this vocabulary, with the meanings of particular concepts, rather than with matters purely philological and etymological, then it is most important that a falsely consensual picture is not drawn. The reportage of definitions, distinctive features and examples should provide the reader with a grounded understanding of qualitative research principles and practices, but qualitative methods are nothing if not disputed. So we also provide an *evaluation* section, summarizing so far as we are able the reported strengths and weaknesses of different methods and approaches. Thus in the entry on 'naturalism' we reprise briefly the criticisms of naturalistic studies – their lack of generalizability, their alleged failure to recognize the provisional nature of all scientific claims, a naïve romanticism, and their covert attempts to persuade the reader by rhetorical authorial devices. But we also refer to the lifeboats offered to naturalistic studies by 'subtle realism' and by 'reflexive' authorship, and to the abiding warrant offered to naturalism by 'the postulate of intersubjectivity' on which all social intercourse is based, namely that one human being can imaginatively place him or herself in the position of another.

All our entries cross-refer. Where terms used in a vocabulary entry are themselves the subjects of entries, then those words are highlighted in **bold** text. Towards the close of each entry, a section listing *associated concepts* allows the reader to extend his or her understanding of, for example, postmodern criticisms of 'naturalism', by referring the reader to companion entries, for example that on 'postmodernism'. And finally, the *key readings* provide the references to citations in the text of the foregoing entry and provide a guide to further reading. One of the key readings attached to each entry is asterisked* as our particular recommendation for further study.

So each entry aims to define a method, to elaborate that definition through a discussion of the method's distinctive features and through illustrative examples, to provide a balanced assessment of strengths and weaknesses, and to furnish a guide to further reading. To reiterate, we have sought to be helpful rather than authoritative and, in pursuit of that aim, we have valued brevity over exhaustiveness.

Our choice of subjects for entry has also involved selectivity rather than exhaustiveness. While we think we can justify the inclusion of 'Delphi groups', but the exclusion of 'consensus conferences', and the inclusion of 'citizens' juries', but the exclusion of 'peoples' parliaments', we recognize that there is a degree of arbitrariness in our selections. But better a degree of arbitrariness than the production of a doorstopper volume, cluttered with entries of interest only to small coteries of specialists.

Nevertheless, the arbitrariness of our choices for inclusion has been tempered by the wisdom of our interdisciplinary panel of advisors: Amanda Coffey (sociology), Stephen Gorard (education), Gabrielle Ivinson (psychology), Mike Maguire (criminology), Roisin Pill (anthropology), Derrick Purdue (geography) and Srikant Sarangi (linguistics). Our thanks to them for their advice, but the responsibility for decisions on selection of entries and on their content remains ours alone.

In making our selections, the reasons for choosing many of our entries (for example, 'ethnography') are self-evident. Other entries (for example, 'autoethnography') were chosen because of a contemporary popularity. And just a few entries (for example, 'meta-ethnography') were chosen because of a suspected future popularity. In selecting our entries and our illustrations, we have drawn from the full range of academic disciplines in which qualitative research is found: anthropology and sociology first and foremost, but also education, geography, linguistics, management science, psychology, public health and nursing studies. Having a broad range of reference carries with it a danger of occasional interdisciplinary confusions. For example, 'cognitive mapping' is a term which means quite different things to operational researchers/management scientists on the one hand, and to urban planners/geographers on the other. So where these interdisciplinary confusions do occur, we have simply stated the different disciplinary positions.

Qualitative research, of course, has increasing commercial applications: Intel, the computer chip company, currently employs more than a dozen ethnographers. We have included some entries on topics (for example, 'group interviews')

3

used primarily by commercial rather than academic researchers. But where commercial and academic research practice diverges, most notably in the conduct of focus groups, we have chosen to elaborate on academic rather than commercial research practice.

A vocabulary is a work of reference not a focus of study in its own right, and we have written this book to be a work of reference for students (on undergraduate and postgraduate methods courses) and for practising academic researchers. We do not claim that the practising conversational analyst will learn much that is new to him or her from our entry on 'conversational analysis', but if he or she wishes to obtain a quick overview of techniques with which they are *not* conversant, such as 'rapid assessment', then we hope this book will prove its usefulness. To reiterate, we have aimed to be useful, rather than authoritative.

We could have upped the authority quota by making this an edited work, with contributions from acknowledged experts in their fields. Co-ordinating the activities of a large number of senior academics is a singularly unattractive task (sometimes likened to that of herding cats), but there are also positive reasons for making this book a work of authorship, rather than a work of editorship. A common structure and purpose is easier self-imposed than externally imposed, and vocabulary entries, self-evidently, must be all-of-a-piece. But also we felt there was some intrinsic merit in writing all these entries from a common perspective, from that of the experienced, jobbing researcher.

Between us, we have about 45 years of research experience, most of it in full-time research posts. This does not mean that, taking us together, we have comprehensive personal experience of all the research techniques, situations and perspectives referred to in this volume, although our joint coverage is pretty good. But it does mean that we naturally have a pragmatic, journeyman's take on these issues. This is *not* to say that we subscribe to the idea that qualitative research is a craft skill that must be absorbed incrementally through long practice and cannot be communicated: such a view would be self-defeating for a methods writer. But it *is* to say that we ourselves put a premium on *useful* knowledge: on pointing out ready applications, practical difficulties, and pitfalls for the unwary.

Viewing qualitative research from a standpoint of pragmatic utility implies certain judgements. For example, if it be correct, as we claim, that 'grounded theory' is more properly described as an approach to analysis than a technique of analysis, then its practical utility is thereby diminished. But we hope that readers will forgive these implicit judgements, knowing that they emanate from modest practitioners simply wishing to be helpful.

Reference

Williams, R. (1976) *Keywords: A Vocabulary of Culture and Society*. London: Fontana.

Access Negotiations

Definition
The process by which researchers obtain admittance to research settings.

Distinctive Features
Different research settings vary in their ease of access to social researchers. Hornsby-Smith (1993) suggests that it is useful to consider access in terms of a framework of two factors: the openness of access and whether the research involves overt or **covert** methods. Generally, the greater the degree of openness, the easier it is for the researcher to make contact with potential respondents. Closed access groups therefore typically involve a greater challenge for researchers and could include research on powerful elites such as politicians or deviant or marginalized groups such as drug users or romany travellers. Open access groups may typically include open institutions such as churches. This does not mean the admittance to open access groups is a foregone positive outcome. The distinction between open and closed access may in reality be blurred: each research setting has its own particular problem of access and furthermore access may be hampered or eased by the biography of the researcher (their gender, age, ethnicity, accent, social background).

Traditionally there has been a tendency for social researchers to study marginal or less powerful groups (patients, prisoners, school children), although research on powerful elites (doctors, scientists, lawyers, civil servants) provides interesting insights into the extent of their powers and privileges within society. Gaining access to elites can be difficult as such groups have the ability to resist the scrutiny of social researchers. However access can be eased if the researcher has contacts in the field, prior experience and an understanding of the culture.

Access negotiations should not be viewed as a one-off event but as an on-going process which is required during research planning, data collection, analysis and writing (Burgess, 1991). Cassell (1988) draws a distinction between physical and social access. Achieving access therefore involves both getting in (achieving physical access to the setting) and getting on (achieving social acceptability among the respondents). Good **fieldwork relationships** are particularly crucial to the latter of these as this will improve the **trust** and consequently the data that the researcher is allowed to observe and record. As well as having personal and professional integrity, researchers often require highly developed social skills which may include social sensitivity and charm. How researchers dress, speak and the social values which they outwardly support will need to mesh with the presentation and values of the research subjects. Indeed in some research settings continued access depends on performance and conduct from prior sessions of data collection.

Social researchers initially approach their research setting via a 'gatekeeper' who controls access to the setting. Of course the nature of the gatekeeper will depend on the research topic: he or she may be a head teacher, hospital consultant, prison warden, chief executive or priest. Thus the gatekeeper may not always be a member of the study population but has the responsibility for allowing access and will often become a champion to protect the interests of the (usually less powerful) study population. It is with the gatekeeper that much of the access negotiation is conducted. For example the researcher will need to explain the purpose of the research, what it will entail for the gatekeeper and others in the group, and how **ethical** issues such as protection of identities will be dealt with. Some social groups might view the research as a threat. At the very least it is likely to involve inconvenience and disruption to their organizational routine. During the negotiations the researcher and gatekeeper should consider how the research may benefit the research subjects. For example the research may raise the profile of the social group or raise awareness of a problem faced by the subjects therefore potentially increasing external resources which may alleviate the problem. However raising awareness might not necessarily be a desired outcome for some groups and institutions. For example a school may not thank a researcher for highlighting problems of bullying to the outside world. Gatekeepers may also seek assurances about how the research is to be conducted and how it will be presented to the outside world. Normally these are reasonable requests such as minimized disruption, protection of identities and prior sight of published material. There may be occasions where researchers feel they are not able to meet the requests if, for example, they feel their academic freedom is being controlled. In such circumstances researchers would do well to consider another research setting. If the gatekeeper has been convinced of the merit of the research they will be able to facilitate access to other members of the group. In cases where access proceeds well, the gatekeeper then may take the role of informal sponsor of the research and the researcher. It is also worth bearing in mind that after negotiating formal access with a superordinate gatekeeper (for example, a prison governor), it may be necessary to negotiate informal access with subordinates (prisoners) who may be suspicious of persons and projects endorsed by superordinates.

Researchers may want to consider forms of reciprocity that could be offered to the gatekeeper and/or members of the social group. Although this does not necessarily involve huge financial costs, there is perhaps a lesson to be learnt from pharmaceutical companies: that gaining access to elites often means attracting them with social events and lavish meals. Some professionals may expect an honorarium to be offered to them for giving up their time to participate in the research. Payments, charitable donations or, at the very least, out-of-pocket expenses may be offered to non-elite research subjects.

Examples

Smith and Wincup (2000) provide an overview of their access negotiations both in terms of getting in and getting on while conducting their doctoral research on women in prison (Smith) and in bail hostels (Wincup). Institutions such as these are perhaps among the most closed to the researcher and therefore required lengthy access negotiations. In the case of Smith's research, the gatekeepers were officials within the Home Office and prison governors. Wincup also had to negotiate numerous levels of gatekeepers particularly at the local level: the area Chief Probation Officer, Senior Probation Officer in charge of the hostels and the hostel managers. The fieldwork conducted in 1994 came at a sensitive time in penal policy which reflected an increased punitive approach to crime control following the Criminal Justice Act of 1991. Due to heightened sensitivity from the gatekeepers and research subjects in the light of this legislation, the authors discuss a number of strategies they employed and concessions they made in order to maximize their chances of access: presenting themselves to their gatekeepers as non-threatening, agreeing to provide periodic research reports and prior sight of publications, referencing their supervisors who had long histories of prison research and agreeing to take responsibility for the emotional effects of their research on the research subjects. The authors also describe how, once in the prisons and hostels, they were faced with problems of social access in their fieldwork relationships. In these institutions they found themselves out of place, anxious and alone among what they admit were at times intimidating research subjects. The authors report how they felt they were being continually 'sussed out' and consequently they spent considerable time at the beginning of their fieldwork getting their faces known and explaining who they were and why they were interested in the lives of these women. The authors also reflect that being naïve can have research advantages as they projected an image of themselves as earnest, sympathetic and grateful to learn. The fact that they were female researchers undoubtedly facilitated access to the women prisoners and residents (indeed it would have been almost impossible for a male researcher to

7

conduct research in the women's hostels), as many of the prisoners' and residents' relationships with men had been characterized by violence and abuse. At times the research subjects (both staff and prisoners/residents) were suspicious of their research and at other times dismissive, brushing it off as 'just another student project'. Throughout their social access to the institutions the authors describe how they were cast in a number of roles: student, spy, social worker, ex-nurse and counsellor.

Whitty and Edwards (1994) provide a **reflexive** account of accessing and researching the powerful in their evaluation of the Assisted Places Scheme. The scheme, introduced under the Thatcher government, provided government assistance with fees to enable children from poorer backgrounds to attend academically selective independent schools and attracted strong support and strong opposition from clearly identifiable interest groups. The political sensitivity of the scheme led to difficult access negotiations at both national and local levels as it engendered both hostility and loyalty from the institutional gatekeepers. At the national level the researchers became aware of conflicts between the trained caution of civil servants and the enthusiasm of policy advisors. While one policy advisor provided the research team with documentary data on the scheme, the civil servants were appalled by such disclosures and put pressure on the research team to return the documents unread. The research team attended difficult conferences and lunches with educational advisors and headmasters in order to develop more support. Such meetings tended to develop into detailed cross-questioning of the research team and an opportunity for the research team's pedigree to be evaluated. At the local level, the generally Labour-controlled education authorities were opposed to the scheme and viewed participation in the research as implying support for the scheme. In reflecting on the difficulties of access, the authors admit that at times they were tempted to resort to subterfuge to achieve their aims and to persuade informants that they were on the same side as their respondents. In fact they suggest that being viewed suspiciously by one side helped them to gain access to the other.

Evaluation

For some methodological approaches, for example ethnography, it is difficult to determine the exact aims, duration and direction of the study during the planning stages. Qualitative researchers who use inductive methods may therefore find it difficult to convince a gatekeeper and other members of a social group of the value of the research if there are no settled aims, objectives and outcomes.

Where access to a research setting is deemed to be unlikely through negotiation with a gatekeeper or its members, researchers may consider conducting covert research. Covert methods of research have been employed in studies of closed organizations. Researchers may also forego access negotiations if they consider the study could not be conducted openly, perhaps if they consider the behaviour of the research subjects would alter in the knowledge of being observed. But the ethical case against covert methods is strong and covert methods are rarely justified.

Associated Concepts: Covert Research, Ethics, Fieldwork Relationships, Reflexivity, Trust.

Key Readings

Burgess, R.G. (1991) 'Sponsor, gatekeepers and friends: access in educational settings', in W.B. Shaffir and R.A. Stebbins (eds), *Experiencing Fieldwork*. London: Sage. pp. 43–52.

Cassell, J. (1988) 'The relationship of observer to observed when studying up', in R.G. Burgess (ed.), *Studies in Qualitative Methodology*. Greenwich, CT and London: JAI press. pp. 89–108.

Duke, K. (2002) 'Getting beyond the "official line": reflections on dilemmas of access, knowledge and power in researching policy networks', *Journal of Social Policy*, 31(1): 39–59.

*Hornsby-Smith, M. (1993) 'Gaining access', in N. Gilbert (ed.), *Researching Social Life*. London: Sage. pp. 52–67.

Smith, C. and Wincup, E. (2000) 'Breaking IN: researching criminal justice institutions', in R. King and E. Wincup (eds), *Doing Research on Crime and Justice*. Oxford: Oxford University Press. pp. 331–350.

Whitty, G. and Edwards, T. (1994) 'Researching Thatcherite educational policy', in G. Walford (ed.), *Researching the Powerful in Education*. London: UCL Press. pp. 14–31.

Action Research

Definition

Action research is a form of research which pursues action (change) and research (knowledge or understanding) at the same time. In most of its forms it is participative in that the subjects of the research are actively involved in the research process.

Distinctive Features

The origins of action research are usually credited to Kurt Lewin (1946) who argued that social science should be concerned with addressing goals. The method is a socially engaged approach to knowledge generation and can be explicitly political. Rather than aiming to maintain a distance between themselves and the research problem in order to remain free from **bias**, action researchers often find themselves in simultaneous roles as academic and activist.

Combining theories from pragmatic philosophy, critical thinking and systems thinking, the method is popular in environmental studies, community studies and urban planning, but has also been adopted within the disciplines of sociology, education and nursing (Reason and Bradbury, 2000). Action research may be conducted in schools, organizations, or communities, but it does tend to operate primarily in communities that are socially disadvantaged or marginalized. With the research skills of the researcher at the disposal of the community, the purpose is often for the community to identify issues that are of concern to themselves, gather information and explore possible solutions.

A key feature of action research is that it adopts a dynamic, cyclical process which moves through phases of planning, action, observation and reflection. In some situations, members of the community may become competent action researchers themselves, thereby providing potential for sustainability of the project after the researcher has **left the field**. The emergent nature of the process often results in projects being redirected to focus on new issues. In turn, this can mean that the outcomes of the project are not easy to predict in the planning stages.

A further distinctive feature of action research is **public participation** in the project. Although clearly displaying a commitment to user empowerment and the democratization of the knowledge process, a further benefit of community collaboration is that change is usually easier to achieve when those affected by the change are involved. The researcher may encourage the users to identify their own research questions, conduct data collection by interviewing other members of the community and identify practical solutions.

Despite a general consensus towards the key features of action research as discussed above, two broad varieties of action research have been identified. The first type, promoted by authors such as Whyte (1991), is concerned primarily with forms of community development and focuses particularly on the empowerment of marginalized groups. The second tradition uses a problem-solving approach to organizational change (Eden and Huxham, 1996). Examples of both broad varieties are given below.

Examples

Todhunter (2001) describes an action research project in the field of drugs prevention within a community experiencing social and economic decline including drug-related difficulties. Commissioned by the Home Office, the aims of the project were to elicit the community's concerns and residents' perceptions of what drugs prevention should involve. Initially in-depth individual and group interviews were conducted. These were later supplemented by a series of small-scale public meetings and community newsletters which were produced in order to feed back earlier findings and seek future directions. Residents' participation took various forms: developing and conducting interviews with other residents, producing articles for newsletters, developing a community forum to discuss emerging research issues and lobbying local agencies. Although the initial research agenda had been more or less professionally led, as time progressed residents began to change the agenda and started to lead the process through their own actions. In his article, Todhunter discusses problems the project faced, which primarily relate to how the regeneration agency (which was expected to fund any changes) perceived the 'biased' findings of residents and consequently how other statutory and voluntary agencies, unwilling to disrupt their own relationship with the regeneration agency, were unwilling to support the forum. Funding for the researcher expired after a six-month period and residents were either unable or unwilling to continue their activities.

Huxham and Vangen (2000) provide an example of the second type of action research in their 'leadership in partnership' project which aimed to facilitate collaboration between organizations. The research team introduced a number of different interventions such as planning meetings and workshops. The effects of the interventions were evaluated using naturally occurring data generated by observation and documentary analysis (from minutes of meetings or flipcharts), but these were supplemented by interviews with **key informants**. In their article the authors discuss various methodological problems the research team faced. For example they discovered that members of the organization rarely referred explicitly to 'leadership', leaving the research team unsure how they would recognize it in an intervention.

Evaluation

Greenwood (2002) presents a critique of action research, arguing that among its practitioners there is often a fundamental complacency towards research rigour particularly relating to issues of **validity, reliability** and theory. Greenwood's central argument is that 'doing good' is not the same as 'doing good social research' and that action researchers should hold themselves accountable to higher academic standards. Similar criticisms have been levelled at **rapid assessment** techniques, often used in action research in developing countries. As a counter-argument, advocates of the method claim that it prioritizes relevance over precision and, unlike other methods, does not ignore the needs of stakeholders. Furthermore, co-participation of stakeholders in the research process is the most effective way of generating commitment to action (Oja and Smulyan, 1989).

Gibson (1985) argues that action researchers are often naïve about group processes and the ability of action research to truly engage members of the public in research, despite the most well-intentioned efforts.

Perhaps the most frequently cited problems of action research relate to issues of uncertainty and lack of control from the perspective of the community, the researcher and the research funder (Todhunter, 2001). In the short term action research may produce a 'feel good' factor among participants through the processes of consciousness raising, mobilization and instilling a self-belief in ordinary people regarding ther capacity to bring about change. However, in the longer term, real and radical change may not be forthcoming among all local agencies and interest groups. This can lead to bitter disappointment among the community which may result in hostility or cynicism towards other projects. Research funders should remain mindful that action research can be a high-risk strategy, possibly resulting in proposed action that does not sit comfortably with their own ideals.

Associated Concepts: Bias, Key Informants, Leaving the Field, Public Participation, Rapid Assessment, Reliability, Validity (*see* Reliability).

Key Readings

Eden, C. and Huxham, C. (1996) 'Action research for the study of organizations', in S. Clegg, C. Hardy and W. Nord (eds), *Handbook of Organization Studies*. London: Sage. pp. 526–542.

Gibson, R. (1985) 'Critical times for action research', *Cambridge Journal of Education*, 15: 59–64.

Greenwood, D. (2002) 'Action research: unfulfilled promises and unmet challenges', *Concepts and Transformation*, 7(2): 117–139.

Greenwood, D. and Levin, M. (1998) *Introduction to Action Research: Social Research for Social Change*. London: Sage.

Huxham, C. and Vangen, S. (2000) 'Leadership in the shaping and implementation of collaboration agendas: how things happen in a (not quite) joined up world', *Academy of Management Journal*, 43(6): 1159–1175.

Lewin, K. (1946) 'Action research and minority problems,' *Journal of Social Issues*, 2: 34–46.

Oja, S. and Smulyan, L. (1989) *Collaborative Action Research: A Developmental Approach*. London: Falmer Press.

*Reason, P. and Bradbury, H. (2000) *Handbook of Action Research: Participatory Inquiry and Practice*. London: Sage.

Todhunter, C. (2001) 'Undertaking action research: negotiating the road ahead', *Social Research Update*, 34. http://www.soc.surrey.ac.uk/sru/SRU34.html

Whyte, W.F. (1991) *Participatory Action Research*. Newbury Park: Sage.

Analytic Induction

Definition
Induction, in contrast to deduction, involves inferring general conclusions from particular instances. Analytic induction is a procedure for analysing data which both requires the analyst to work systematically and aims to ensure that the analyst's theoretical conclusions cover the entire range of the available data.

Distinctive Features
The procedure of analytic induction requires the researcher, once he or she has formed an initial hypothesis, to search his or her data for falsifying evidence and then to modify his or her theoretical conclusions in the light of that evidence. The centrality of searching for falsifying evidence explains why analytic induction has also sometimes been called 'deviant case analysis'. Since it is a procedural requirement that the end-point of the analysis is only reached when *all* the data are explicable in terms of the analyst's theoretical conclusions, some researchers may prefer the procedural rigour of analytic induction to its close cousin **'grounded theory'**. In grounded theory, despite a commitment to 'constant comparison' and achieving **'theoretical saturation'**, the end-point of the analysis is implicit rather than explicit, leaving the analyst open to criticism that the analysis was insufficiently rigorous and possibly selective in its attention to evidence (see Silverman, 2000: 283–97).

Nevertheless, the distinction between analytic induction and grounded theory should not be overdrawn. It is possible, for example, for researchers using analytic induction to attend selectively to evidence and to neglect deviant cases simply by reclassifying the deviant cases as ones which lie outside the population of cases being studied and theorized: the case is no longer identified as deviant, but merely as irrelevant.

Analytic induction clearly requires that the researcher be readily able to identify those cases in his or her sample which are deviant. This presupposes an

13

early theorization of the research topic (for example, 'Welsh school children perform best academically in schools where Welsh is the language of instruction'). The next requirement is that the researcher is able to identify the cases that falsify this early theory (in the present example, this would be English-speaking Welsh schools where pupils perform excellently, or Welsh-speaking schools with poor academic performance). This presupposes that the data are so organized as to readily allow identification of the deviant cases: in a large dataset, this suggests the need to use **computer-assisted data analysis**. And finally, the researcher should, by scrutiny of the deviant cases, be able to re-theorize the research topic so that no deviant cases occur (for example, 'Welsh children from middle-class homes perform best academically, regardless of whether English or Welsh is the medium of instruction'). This presupposes either that the researcher is able to collect new data on the deviant cases to further his or her new enquiries, or that the dataset is already so rich that all further enquiries can be addressed.

Examples

Analytic induction enjoyed a brief vogue among American criminologists in the 1940s and 50s. Cressey (1953) studied convicted embezzlers and, drawing on more and more deviant cases, modified his initial hypothesis about the reasons for embezzlement four times before he arrived at his final formulation: embezzlement was held to occur when the embezzler found him or herself in a socially unacceptable position or personal emergency, knowing that embezzlement would solve the problem and that the embezzler had the skills to carry it off; moreover, the would-be embezzler retained a self-image of him or herself as trustworthy – he or she was simply making unauthorized use of available money which they might later repay.

Bloor (1978) followed the same approach to work out the decision rules used by different surgeons in outpatient clinics when assessing children for possible tonsillectomy. For each surgeon separately, Bloor was able to classify those decision rules which allowed him or her to list children for surgery, or to keep a child under review, or to recommend that surgery was not indicated.

Evaluation

The philosopher Karl Popper famously argued that the attempt to falsify an investigable hypothesis by the search for contrary evidence was the whole basis of the scientific method (Popper, 1959). And the Polish-American sociologist Florian Znaniecki, who invented the term 'analytic induction', grandly claimed it was *the* method for uncovering universal laws of human conduct (Znaniecki, 1934). However, there is no need for qualitative researchers to accept the overblown claims of Znaniecki, or even the precepts of Popperian positivism, in using analytic induction: as Seale (1999) has argued, analytic induction or deviant case analysis can simply be adopted, without any philosophical baggage, as a pragmatic procedure for the rigorous and systematic analysis of complex qualitative data.

An oft-repeated criticism of analytic induction (first made by Robinson, 1951) is that the procedure fails to distinguish between the *sufficient* conditions for a social phenomenon to occur and those that are merely *necessary* preconditions (for the reader to understand the argument we are making, it is *necessary* for him or her to read the passage in question, but simply reading it is not a *sufficient* condition for understanding it). However, Robinson's argument is not, in fact, a criticism of the method itself, but rather a criticism of the sample to which the method is being applied. Cressey could not distinguish between the necessary and sufficient conditions of embezzlement because he only had a sample of convicted embezzlers, with no control group for comparison. In contrast, Bloor could distinguish between the necessary and sufficient conditions for a given surgeon to decide to remove a child's tonsils because he had data on other children assessed by the surgeon but not offered surgery.

A more serious difficulty lies in the already noted requirement to examine the deviant cases in more detail. Not all researchers will be in a position to stagger their data collection so that deviant cases can be revisited at a later point in the study in order to allow the collection of additional data. In such cases, researchers face the dilemma of collecting a possible superfluity of data on cases to provide for possible later re-scrutiny, or of finding themselves with insufficient data at a later point in the analysis to account satisfactorily for the deviant case(s).

Associated Concepts: Computer-Assisted Data Analysis, Grounded Theory, Theoretical Saturation.

Key Readings

Bloor, M. (1978) 'On the analysis of observational data', *Sociology*, 12: 545–552.

Cressey, D. (1953) *Other People's Money: A Study of the Social Psychology of Embezzlement*. New York: Free Press of Glencoe.

Popper, K. (1959) *The Logic of Scientific Discovery*. London: Hutchinson.

Robinson, W. (1951) 'The logical structure of analytic induction', *American Sociological Review*, 16: 812–818.

*Seale, C. (1999) *The Quality of Qualitative Research*. London: Sage.

Silverman, D. (2000) *Doing Qualitative Research: A Practical Handbook*. London: Sage.

Znaniecki, F. (1934) *The Method of Sociology*. New York: Farrar and Rinehart.

Audio-Recording

Definition
The recording of sound (typically speech) for the purposes of data collection.

Distinctive Features
The recording of audio data through devices such as tape recorders has been a significant development within qualitative research, replacing the researcher's handwritten notes. Over time the devices have become more widespread among researchers and a familiar technology for those whose life or views are being observed and recorded. Audio-recorders are probably most frequently used in interview or focus group settings, but may also be used to record naturally occurring data such as professional meetings or perhaps for the researcher to dictate his or her own **fieldnotes**. The resulting recorded data are usually **transcribed** at a later date.

The quality of audio-recordings has improved over time with advances in audio technology. For example the use of multi-directional microphones attached to the recorder have proved popular in **focus group** research where the researcher is eager to pick up voices from all corners of the room. Since the late 1990s, minidisc players began to replace the tape recorder as the qualitative researcher's gadget of choice (Maloney and Paolisso, 2001) and even more recently digital voice-recorders have become popular. These devices represent a significant improvement in audio quality and also have the advantage of being more discreet than their bulky tape recorder counterparts. **Telephone interviews** can also be recorded through the use of a relatively cheap device that is attached to both the telephone socket and the recording equipment. This allows the voices of both speakers to be recorded.

Prudent researchers will prepare before data collection by familiarizing themselves with the operating instructions of their equipment and ensuring that they have a ready supply of spare batteries and tapes/minidiscs. There are also practical issues to be considered after leaving the field. Tapes/minidiscs or digital media cards should be clearly labelled with a non-personalized identifier as soon as possible after the recording has been made. A separate secure file should then be kept which links the identifier to the respondent's personal details such as their name and address.

Examples
Wilkie (1963) provides an early example of a comparison between audio-recorded data and data in which the interviewer maintained handwritten notes

in the context of social worker and client interviews. Wilkie explains that following such interviews social workers routinely make notes of their inter-actions with the client but inevitably the worker listens selectively and records selectively, resulting in what Wilkie terms 'distortions'. Clients' statements may be paraphrased, amplified, condensed or the facts may be reordered to stress a particular focus. It was only when the social workers' notes were compared to the full transcripts that additional information about the clients' situations emerged. Wilkie also makes the point that by audio-recording the practitioner has an opportunity to reflect on and improve his or her interviewing techniques.

Speer and Hutchby (2003) recorded naturally occurring interaction between counsellors and young children in a study about children's responses to family separation. In their paper they report that the counsellors had initial concerns about whether the children's awareness of the presence of tape recorders would undermine the authenticity and naturalness of the talk produced during the counselling sessions. However, the authors describe how the tape recorder became a resource for the counsellors as, by introducing the equipment to the children, they managed to generate counselling talk.

Evaluation

The obvious advantage of audio-recording is that it frees up the researcher from note-taking thereby allowing them to concentrate on the job in hand: to listen to what is being said and prompt for further responses where appropri-ate. Furthermore, as data are not dependent on the researcher's recall or selec-tive attention, audio-recording improves the **reliability** of data collection. Audio-recorded data have also made possible certain types of qualitative analysis such as **conversation analysis**, which would have been impossible without an exact record of the conversation. Thus recorded audio data can serve a number of purposes from a useful *aide-mémoire* of the respondent's views to a detailed record of the exact speech.

Despite its advantages, the audio-recording of data presents researchers with additional **ethical** issues. The main problem is the loss of anonymity as the respondent's exact words and voice are recorded and consequently there is always a danger that the respondent's identity might be disclosed. Researchers must ensure that respondents are aware of the intention to record before they give their consent, that the data will be anonymized on transcription and that they can request that the recording device be switched off at any time in the discussion.

Respondents' reluctance to speak freely while being recorded will cause **biases** in the data. This reluctance may stem from a fear of loss of anonymity (particularly if the discussion is relevant to their personal or professional life), or the presence of the equipment might distract or intimidate the respondent. In order to counteract this, the recording device should be as unobtrusive as possible (without being deliberately concealed or compromising the quality of the recording) and the researcher should be relaxed about its presence. On a more positive note, the use of recording devices may emphasize to participants that their views are being taken seriously (Fielding and Thomas, 2001). Acceptance of recording devices has also been facilitated by the fact that people are becoming more familiar with the equipment as the technology pervades progressively more aspects of everyday life.

Associated Concepts: Bias, Conversation Analysis, Ethics, Fieldnotes, Focus Groups, Interviews, Naturalism, Reliability, Telephone Interviewing (*see* Electronic Data Collection), Transcription, Video-Recording.

Key Readings
Fielding, N. and Thomas, H. (2001) 'Qualitative interviewing', in N. Gilbert (ed.), *Researching Social Life*. London: Sage. pp. 123–144.

Lee, R.M. (2004) 'Recording technologies and the interview in sociology, 1920–2000', *Sociology*, 38(5): 869–890.

Maloney, R.S. and Paolisso, M. (2001) 'What can digital audio data do for you?', *Field Methods*, 13(1): 88–96.

*Speer, S.H. and Hutchby, I. (2003) 'From ethics to analytics: aspects of participants' orientations to the presence and the relevance of recording devices', *Sociology*, 37(2): 315–337.

Wilkie, C.H. (1963) 'A study of distortions in recording interviews', *Social Work*, 8(3): 31–36.

Autoethnography

Definition
Reportage of the reporter's own personal and emotional life, that is explicitly informed by social science concepts and perspectives, by sociological introspection.

Distinctive Features

Autoethnography is associated with the **postmodernist** turn in the social sciences, with a belief in the inevitable partiality of all accounts of social reality and a celebration of alternative accounts: where there is no final, authoritative version of reality to be captured or narrated, then a poly-vocal social science can be built on multiple personal narratives. Additionally, it is claimed that the autoethnographic writer is freed from the **ethical** dilemmas implicit in the attempt to represent any experience other than his or her own, representations that have sometimes been attacked as a new form of colonialism. Autoethnography may be portrayed as the postmodern successor of both **ethnography** and **life history**.

In effect, autoethnography reverses the traditional epistemology of qualitative methods found in the **naturalist** approach. Whereas authors have traditionally sought an empathic understanding of the other, autoethnographers must report the events of their own lives with scientific rigour.

Examples

There are two major edited collections of autoethnographic writing – Ellis and Bochner (1996) and Reed-Danahay (1997). The most widely discussed autoethnography is probably Ellis's (1995) account of her relationship with her partner, the sociologist Gene Weinstock, through their first attachment, his disablement and finally his death.

Evaluation

As Murphy and Dingwall (2001) point out, the claim is overblown that autoethnography circumvents the ethical dilemmas inherent in the representation of others' lives – many an autobiographer has found him or herself sued for libel by others who believed themselves misrepresented in the autobiographical narrative. There is also the danger that, as one autoethnographer has herself put it, 'this process can, for many, result in nothing more than pointless, self-absorbing, introspective, navel-gazing, excessive subjectivity and self-delusion' (Boufoy-Bastick, 2004).

Associated Concepts: Biographies, Ethics, Ethnography, Life History, Naturalism, Postmodernism.

Key Readings

Boufoy-Bastick, B. (2004) 'Auto-interviewing, auto-ethnography and critical incident methodology for eliciting a self-conceptualised worldview', *Forum Qualitative Sozialforschung*, 5: article 37 [http://www.qualitative-research.net].

Ellis, C. (1995) *Final Negotiations: A Story of Love, Loss and Chronic Illness.* Philadelphia: Temple University Press.

Ellis, C. and Bochner, A. (eds) (1996) *Composing Ethnography: Alternative Forms of Qualitative Writing.* London: Sage.

Murphy, E. and Dingwall, R. (2001) 'The ethics of ethnography', in P. Atkinson, A. Coffey, S. Delamont, J. Lofland and L. Lofland (eds), *Handbook of Ethnography*. London: Sage. pp. 339–351.

Reed-Danahay, D. (ed.) (1997) *Auto-ethnography: Rewriting the Self and the Social*. Oxford: Berg.

*Reed-Danahay, D. (2001) 'Autobiography, intimacy and ethnography', in P. Atkinson, A. Coffey, S. Delamont, J. Lofland and L. Lofland (eds), *Handbook of Ethnography*. London: Sage. pp. 407–425.

Bias

Definition

Any influence that distorts the results of a research study. Bias may derive either from a conscious or unconscious tendency on the behalf of the researcher to collect data or interpret them in such a way as to produce erroneous conclusions that favour their own beliefs or commitments.

Distinctive Features

Bias is usually considered to be a negative feature of research and something that should be avoided. It implies there has been some deviation from the truth either as a consequence of the limitations of the research method or from the data analysis. The term refers to the researcher's inclination to collect, interpret or present data which support results that are congruous with their own pre-judgements or political ideology. Bias is associated with research **validity**: that is, the extent to which the inquiry is able to yield the 'correct answer'.

Bias is a concern of both quantitative and qualitative research. In particular quantitative researchers are concerned with measurement or **sampling** bias, that is, where the results found from the research sample do not represent the general population. However qualitative research is by no means immune to bias, and indeed could be considered to be particularly prone to bias when the researcher is the main instrument of enquiry.

Hammersley's (2000) typological model of error suggests that bias is a type of systematic culpable error that may either be motivated or unmotivated. If the bias is motivated, that motivation may either be conscious (wilful bias) or unconscious (negligent bias). If the bias is unmotivated then the resulting bias will be negligent. The use of the term 'systematic' in such a definition of bias implies that the error is not random, that is, a false result has not arisen by random chance. Unmotivated bias suggests that researchers may be unaware of their own tendencies to collect or interpret data in terms of their own particular commitment. Ignorance of this is little defence as errors which may represent a deviation from the truth should be recognized and acknowledged.

How might bias arise within qualitative research? The response to this is that it can arise from a number of sources and at a number of stages within the research process. Thus it may occur while the researcher is engaged in research design, sample selection, fieldwork, analysis or report **writing**. For example, within interview-based research, bias may occur as a consequence of particular questions being asked in an interview, the way in which questions are being asked, or indeed the **fieldwork relationships** between the researcher and the researched. Some **ethnographers** have warned against the dangers of 'going native', a situation in which the researcher adopts the perspective of their own participants and consequently may also adopt their participants' particular biases. In terms of analysis, researchers may be vulnerable to bias due to their tendency to be particularly vigilant in searching for data that support their favoured theory. Similarly in terms of research design, researchers may be inclined to devise methodological strategies that could favour the generation of particular results.

Bias is not just an issue of concern for individual researchers, but is also an issue that exists within the wider research community. Researchers are generally reliant on patronage from sponsoring agencies such as government research councils. Funding bodies may seek to constrain the autonomy of the researcher by retaining control over the orientation of the research so that it aligns with government policy, or funding bodies may place restrictions on what may be supported or published. Academic journals have also been accused of publication bias in that they may favour research articles that report significant findings (where, for example, an evaluation of an intervention was found to have a positive impact rather than no impact) because such articles are deemed to be more newsworthy.

Examples

Perhaps the best known example of accusations of bias within qualitative social research is Freeman's (1983) critique of Margaret Mead's anthropological study *Coming of Age in Samoa* (Mead, 1928). The charge was that Mead's portrayal of Samoan adolescent culture as sexually permissive was a consequence of her easy access to adolescent girls due to her young age and gender. Freeman attempted to replicate Mead's study in the 1960s and claimed Mead was wrong, that Samoan culture was in fact characterized by aggression and parental monitoring and control. Freeman accused Mead of being biased by her desire to demonstrate the importance of culture over biology in the determination of human nature. Shortly after publishing his own version of Samoan culture, Freeman was accused of making similar errors to those he had himself accused Mead of (Ember, 1985). The accusation was that due to his gender and age, Freeman had not had the same access to female adolescents that Mead had enjoyed but rather had conducted his research among the elders of the community – the very individuals who wished to promote a respectable image of their community.

Evaluation

Debates around bias have sometimes been met with resistance from relativist writers who argue that appeals to facts are misguided, that we live in a world of multiple perspectives, and social accounts of the world will reflect, for example, the cultural or gendered position of the people who produced them. If qualitative research is to be viewed as a dynamic meaning-making process, accounts of the world produced by one researcher should not produce identical results to those of another researcher attempting to replicate the study, as they are produced in different circumstances. In this view there are no such things as biased accounts, only differently situated accounts drawing on different perspectives. One response to these difficulties is the promotion of **reflexivity** whereby researchers are encouraged to remain mindful that they themselves are part of the social world that they study and should therefore consider how their own values or biographical experiences may influence their perceptions of the culture. It is considered good practice for researchers to declare their potential biases to readers of their research. This may include declaring and reflecting upon their gender, age, status, employer and funding source. Some qualitative researchers also seek to minimize accusations of bias by providing their readers or sponsors with detailed justifications of specific decisions that were made during the course of the study. An 'audit trail' of the research process may include specifics of why a particular sample was chosen, why a specific technique was used or why it was considered that a particular research theme emerged from the data.

It has been argued that all social research is ideologically driven and consequently the notion of value-free inquiry is untenable. Most famously Howard Becker's paper **'whose side are we on?'** argued that research is always from someone's point of view and therefore partisan (Becker, 1967). The question therefore becomes not so much one of whether the data are biased but rather whose interests are served by the bias. Becker's question encouraged social researchers to consider whether they affiliated themselves to powerful interest groups such as government funding bodies, or whether their commitment was to empowering the traditionally oppressed groups whose lives were often the focus of social inquiry. This can lead to an **ethical** dilemma for researchers arising from the tension between a desire for objectivity and a commitment to their principles of social justice.

Associated Concepts: Ethics, Ethnography, Fieldwork Relationships, Reflexivity, Sampling, Validity (*see* Reliability), 'Whose Side Are We On?', Writing.

Key Readings

Becker, H.S. (1967) 'Whose side are we on?', *Social Problems*, 14: 239–247.

Ember, M. (1985) 'Evidence and science in ethnography: reflections on the Freeman-Mead controversy', *American Anthropologist*, 87: 906–910.

Freeman, D. (1983) *Margaret Mead and Samoa: The Making and Unmaking of an Anthropological Myth*. Cambridge, MS: Harvard University Press.

*Hammersley, M. (2000) *Taking Sides in Social Research: Essays on Partisanship and Bias*. London: Routledge.

Mead, M. (1928) *Coming of Age in Samoa*. New York: Morrow.

Troyna, B. and Carrington, B. (1989) 'Whose side are we on? Ethical dilemmas in research on "race" and education', in R.G. Burgess (ed.), *The Ethics of Educational Research*. Lewes: Falmer.

Biographies

Definition

The biographic method involves the detailed reconstruction of individual life stories. Inevitably the method overlaps with other qualitative research methods such as **life history**, **narratives** and **oral history**, but biographical research may be used as a generic term to denote work which uses the stories of individuals.

Distinctive Features

Biographies enable the understanding of individual lives set within their social contexts by tracing the circumstances, choices, constraints and decisions that affect people's lives. The purpose of a biographical study is to gain insights into the everyday experiences of individual lives thereby enabling the researcher to reflect on the wider cultural meanings of society. Biographical methods may include the supplementation of the life story, as told by the respondent, with other personal and social artefacts such as **diaries**, photographs and letters (Roberts, 2002).

The biographical approach to the study of lives has been inspired by interpretive approaches such as the **phenomenological** perspective of Schutz and the **symbolic interactionism** of Mead, which emphasized the study of the attribution of meaning in personal lives. As with many other qualitative methodologies, the biographical method emphasizes a commitment to remaining close to the experiences and views of those being researched. The method also stresses a commitment to viewing social life as developmental rather than static by studying how experiences of daily life may change over time.

24

Typically biographical research focuses on a few (or even one) individuals or cases. Data collection is characterized by depth **interviews**, with individual respondents being encouraged to reflect upon their lives and develop their own accounts of them. The interviewer's role is therefore to facilitate the respondent's story being told, but the result is nevertheless a joint action, a collaboration between researched and researcher (Plummer, 2001).

Examples

Thomas and Znaniecki ([1918–20]1958) have produced what is often cited as the classic study of a life history in *The Polish Peasant in Europe and America*. Originally published in a number of volumes, the study deals with issues of immigration and transition into a new society in America, paying attention to the difficulties and adaptations they faced as well as the social values at the time. Of particular interest is the extensively written case of a peasant named Wladek. By providing a 'life-record' of Wladek the authors describe his early life in Poland through to his new life in America. His story is also placed alongside other materials (family letters to and from Poland, newspaper reports, official records from the Polish emigration offices) thus reflecting society and its influences. Wladek is seen as representative of other immigrants to America and the study has been influential in its ability to demonstrate how the selection of individual stories can describe and explain wider ethnic and social behaviour.

A more recent example of the biographical method has been offered by Schiebel (2000) in her biographical interviews with West German youths between 1989 and 1991. Her work aimed to explore the social, familial and biographical factors that attract individuals to far-right politics. In the two biographical cases discussed she demonstrates how personal opinions are formulated within a context of political events during the 1970s and 1980s (protests over nuclear power, debates over immigration), as well as insecurities within the parental home. Schiebel concludes that emotional instability caused the two youths to seek community, security and self-affirmation outside of the family.

Evaluation

The biographical method has received relatively little methodological attention, perhaps because it is often subsumed under other methodologies such as depth **interviewing** or **ethnography**. Becker (1970) has suggested that the previous unpopularity of the method was because it did not produce data that could be tested on pre-formulated hypotheses. However Chamberlayne, Bornat and Wengraf (2000) argue there has been a 'biographical turn' signaling the wider recognition of biographical methods within social science. The traditional criteria of assessment (**reliability, generalizability**) typically associated with quantitative methods are often considered to be inappropriate for qualitative methodologies and thus other criteria of quality may be required. Hatch and Wisniewski (1995) suggest a range of alternative criteria such as adequacy, aesthetic finality, authenticity, persuasiveness and so on. Clearly using these alternative-criteria biographical methods would be considered to be a superior method.

Denzin (1989) has reviewed the debate between realism and constructionism in relation to biographical research. Realism is the view that individuals' stories should reflect a lived reality. In contrast constructionism argues that claims of stories reflecting an empirical truth are too simplistic. Rather respondents' stories and the researcher's interpretation of them are shaped by narrative conventions such as pace, emphasis and a degree of artificial fabrication. As with narratives, biographic interviews may serve a purpose of persuading an audience or making a moral point. A further postmodern perspective is that biographical interviews will generate differing interpretations of the story by the audience and that therefore biographies may be seen as co-constructed between respondent, researcher and reader.

Associated Concepts: Diary Methods, Ethnography, Generalization, Interviews, Life History (*See* Oral History), Narratives, Oral History, Phenomenological Methods, Reliability, Symbolic Interactionism.

Key Readings

Becker, H.S. (1970) 'The life history', in P. Worsley (ed.), *Modern Sociology: Introductory Readings*. Harmondsworth: Penguin. pp. 126–130.

Chamberlayne, P., Bornat, J. and Wengraf, T. (2000) *The Turn to Biographical Methods in Social Science: Comparative Issues and Examples*. London: Routledge.

Denzin, N.K. (1989) *Interpretative Biography*. London: Sage.

Hatch, L.A. and Wisniewski, R. (eds), Life History and Narrative. London: Falmer.

Plummer, K. (2001) 'The call of life stories in ethnographic research', in P. Atkinson, S. Delamont, A. Coffey, J. Lofland and L. Lofland (eds), *Handbook of Ethnography*. London: Sage. pp. 395–406.

*Roberts, B. (2002) *Biographical Research*. Buckingham OUP.

Schiebel, M. (2000) 'Extreme right attitudes in the biographies of West German Youth', in P. Chamberlayne, J. Bornat and T. Wengraf (eds), *The Turn to Biographical Methods in Social Science: Comparative Issues and Examples*. London: Routledge. pp. 214–228.

Thomas, W.I. and Znaniecki, F. ([1918–20] 1958) *The Polish Peasant in Europe and America*. New York: Dover Press.

Case Study

Definition

A strategy of research that aims to understand social phenomena within a single or small number of naturally occurring settings. The purpose may be to provide description through a detailed example or to generate or test particular theories.

Distinctive Features

Case studies are often described as an exploration of a 'bounded system'. The object of the case could therefore be many things – for example, a community, an institution, an individual, an activity or an event. Case studies are often associated with **ethnography** where the purpose is to describe and interpret social groups in their natural setting using a number of qualitative techniques over an extended period of time. The shared preoccupations between case study research and other forms of naturalistic inquiry have made it difficult to provide absolute definitions of case study research and the problem is made more acute by the fact that researchers have not used the term in a standardized way. For example there is debate over whether a case study is a methodological choice (Simmons, 1996) or an object that is studied (Stake, 1995). The term has also been influential within professional practice in the fields of medicine, law, social work and management studies. Within these disciplines the case study is often associated with practical problem solving (Gomm, Hammersley and Foster, 2000). The term 'bounded system' has also been considered unhelpful (Atkinson and Delamont, 1995; Creswell, 1998) as it is often difficult to define the boundaries of a case both in time and space. Indeed, social systems are rarely bounded and, where they are, such boundaries are often constructed by the participants or researcher.

Case studies are considered particularly valuable where the research context is too complex for experimental or survey research. Although a valid research strategy in its own right, case studies may be used to supplement other research methods including quantitative techniques – for example to generate theories before such theories are tested in the main study or to provide details that enable researchers to expand on quantitative findings.

The purpose of a case study is to gain a detailed understanding of the processes involved within a setting, but this can involve studying a single or multiple cases and numerous levels of analysis (Yin, 1994). The size of each case can also vary from single individuals, to groups of people, organizations and whole cultures. The selection of cases is crucial to the purpose of the research. Cases may be **sampled** for their typicality, that is, they are a typical example of a category of cases such as a typical hospital, or cases may be selected purposefully on the basis of theoretical sampling, perhaps for the insights they generate or because they represent polar types. Where a case is purposively sampled because the collection of negative evidence may serve to falsify a particular theory this is termed 'critical case' sampling (Goldthorpe, Lockwood, Bechhofer and Platt: 1960). In addition to these sampling strategies, the choice of cases may also be influenced by more pragmatic reasons, such as their accessibility. However, as Cresswell (1998) warns, it is not always in the researcher's best interests to study sites in which the researcher is already an active participant. Familiarity with a setting can be an asset in terms of access but can also result in raised expectations from subjects. Generally speaking, depth of data decreases with the more cases studied, however this disadvantage may be offset by the temptation to produce more generalizable conclusions.

Case studies often use **multiple methods** of data collection. These can include techniques such as **interviews, observations, documentary methods** and **audio or video recording**. Data collection typically continues over prolonged periods. **Fieldnotes** are also a key source of data. Fieldnotes are the researcher's running commentary to him/herself and members of the research team, in which observations, reflections and emerging ideas are recorded.

Case study analysis usually proceeds by the researcher providing a description of the setting, searching for themes, aggregating data into themes and comparing themes. Even if the research is conducted within a single setting, it is possible to analyse the data at multiple levels. For example, if studying a change of curriculum within a school, analysis might be at the pupil or classroom level. Cross-case comparisons can follow from within case analysis.

Examples

Livingstone, Keane and Boal (1998) offer an example of a single case study in the field of cultural geography. Their work explores the significance of religious space in the city of Belfast, Northern Ireland. The Belfast case confirms other work in the field which draws attention to the importance of space in the processes of social reproduction, but offers insights into an otherwise neglected aspect of cultural space – that of religious space. The selection of Belfast as a case was no doubt partly due to its accessibility (the city in which the authors are based), but it was also selected purposefully for being a city divided into Catholic and Protestant communities.

Salvato (2003) expanded on an already existing theory of firm evolution through a comparative case study of two companies. Data were collected on the micro-processes of each company, particularly relating to the firms' routines and managerial leadership. The study describes each case before offering a descriptive model of the strategy evolution inductively built from the two cases and from cross-case analysis.

Bloor (1986) examines the proposition that formally democratic 'therapeutic communities' for mental patients can be considered a critical case for the hypothesis that all mental health treatment facilities act as institutions of social control. He re-examines Sharp's earlier (1975) analysis of how staff interpret work in a therapeutic community through the 'nihilation' of dissent. Taking data from a similar therapeutic community to that studied by Sharp, Bloor shows how therapeutic work may also be connected with the conscious provocation (rather than the nihilation) of dissent, and with the deliberate toleration (rather than the control) of disruption, indicating that mental health institutions have an occasional, rather than a universal, social control function. Power relations in a therapeutic community may be used both to encourage patient autonomy and to exercise social control: not all treatment institutions routinely maintain manipulative control of their clientele.

Evaluation

Case studies have been advocated as a method on the basis that they can capture the unique characters of people and groups through their ability to generate detailed holistic data (Simmons, 1996), they have the capacity to make surprising discoveries (Platt, 1988) and they produce novel theories (Eisenhardt, 2002).

The main disadvantage of case study research is the problem of **generalization** to larger populations, a problem that questions the value of studying a single case. Consequently although case study theories may be novel and empirically valid, they run the risk of being narrow and idiosyncratic theories which are only relevant to specific phenomena. Advocates of the case study method have responded to this criticism. For example, Yin (1994) points out how the case study method produces results that are generalizable to theoretical propositions rather than to populations, and Gomm et al. (2000) argues that general conclusions can be drawn from case studies by means of theoretical inference through comparative analysis. Others have suggested that it is unnecessary to draw general conclusions and argue instead that case studies provide a depth and richness of description that are indispensable to the social sciences (Lincoln and Guba, 2002; Platt, 1988; Stake, 1995). This view suggests that although case studies may not provide a sound basis for scientific generalizations, they still have a general relevance and are able to generate ideas and produce theoretical conclusions.

Associated Concepts: Audio-Recording, Documentary Methods, Ethnography, Fieldnotes, Generalization, Interviews, Multiple Methods, Observation (*See* Ethnography), Sampling, Video-Recording.

Key Readings

Atkinson, P. and Delamont, S. (1995) 'Bread and dreams or bread and circuses? A critique of "case study" research in education', in M. Shipman (ed.), *Educational Research Principles, Policies and Practices*. Lewes: Falmer Press. pp. 26–45.

Bloor, M. (1986) 'Social control in the therapeutic community: re-examination of a critical case', *Sociology of Health & Illness*, 8: 305–323.

Cresswell, J.W. (1998) *Qualitative Inquiry and Research Design: Choosing Among Five Traditions*. Thousand Oaks: Sage.

Eishenhardt, K.M. (2002) 'Building theories from case study research', in A.M. Huberman and M.B. Miles (eds), *The Qualitative Researcher's Companion*. Thousand Oaks, CA: Sage. pp. 5–36.

Gillham, B. (2000) *Case Study Research Methods*. London: Continuum.

Goldthorpe, J., Lockwood, D., Bechhofer, F. and Platt, J. (1960) *The Affluent Worker: Industrial Attitudes and Behaviour*. Cambridge: Cambridge University Press.

*Gomm, R., Hammersley, M. and Foster, P. (2000) *Case Study Method*. London: Sage.

Lincoln, Y.S. and Guba, E.G. (2002) 'Judging the quality of case study reports', in A.M. Huberman and M.B. Miles (eds), *The Qualitative Researcher's Companion*. Thousand Oaks, CA: Sage.

Livingstone, D., Keane, M. and Boal, F. (1998) 'Space for religion: a Belfast case study', *Political Geography*, 17(2): 145–170.

Platt, J. (1988) 'What can case studies do?', in R. Burgess (ed.), *Studies in Qualitative Methodology*. Stamford: JAI Press. pp. 1–23.

Salvato, C. (2003) 'The role of micro-strategies in the engineering of firm evolution', *Journal of Management Studies*, 40(1): 83–108.

Sharp, V. (1975) *Social Control in the Therapeutic Community*. Farnborough: Saxon House.

Simmons, H. (1996) 'The paradox of case study', *Cambridge Journal of Education*, 26(2): 225–240.

Stake, R. (1995) *The Art of Case Study Research*. Thousand Oaks: Sage.

*Yin, R. K. (1994) *Case Study Research: Designs and Methods* (2nd edn). London: Sage.

Citizens' Jury

Definition

A methodology for **public participation** in the policy-making process, using the principles of jury decision making found in the judicial system: a small number of representative citizens hear expert evidence on a formally defined topic and then deliberate to arrive at a consensual judgement.

Distinctive Features

Citizens' juries were originally developed in Denmark and Germany and were used particularly to resolve local government decision-making and health issues. An independent steering committee sets the matter to be deliberated, oversees the process and arranges for the attendance of witnesses (though the jury may ask for others to attend). The jury (which can be more than 12 persons) is selected randomly to be representative, meets over a period of several days, hears presentations and cross-examines the witnesses, and deliberates as a body or in small groups. A skilled moderator is normally appointed, rather than allowing the jury to nominate one of their number as a foreman. The recommendations are public and are normally binding on the commissioning body.

Examples

An ambitious example of the citizens' jury system was an All-Wales jury set up by the Welsh Institute for Health and Social Care to consider the issues relating to population testing for genetic susceptibility to common diseases and reporting to the Human Genetics Advisory Commission, which accepted the jury's report but was not bound by its recommendations. The All-Wales jury was assessed by Dunkerley and Glasner (Dunkerley and Glasner, 1998; Glasner and Dunkerley, 1999).

Evaluation

Coote and Lenaghan (1997) judge the jury model to be more effective than similar methods for extending public participation such as 'consensus conferences' or 'people's parliaments', but note that the running costs may be quite substantial and that juries are most effective in addressing a specific and narrow topic. The latter point is reiterated by Glasner and Dunkerley (1999) who, in addition, stress the difficulty of addressing the issue of representativeness (Wales is a heterogeneous late-modern society and jury selection inevitably involves a degree of self-selection) and argue that the dichotomous distinction between jury (laity) and witnesses (experts) is artificial and unhelpful. Nevertheless, different observers have noted the ability of the jury to absorb complex arguments and data, and jury members' willingness to participate and to take on a representative role rather than be self-directed.

Associated Concepts: Public Participation.

Key Readings

Coote, A. and Lenaghan, J. (1997) *Citizens' Juries: Theory into Practice.* London: Institute for Public Policy Research.

Dunkerley, D. and Glasner, P. (1998) 'Empowering the public? Citizens' juries and the new genetic technologies', *Critical Public Health,* 8: 181–192.

*Glasner, P. and Dunkerley, D. (1999) 'The new genetics, public involvement, and citizens' juries: a Welsh case study', *Health, Risk and Society,* 1: 313–324.

Cognitive Mapping

Definition

A technique used in operational research/management science to allow the schematic representation of the system of concepts used by a respondent to communicate the nature of an organizational problem.

Urban planners and geographers use the term cognitive mapping to describe a method which is completely different to that used by management scientists. For these disciplines, cognitive mapping is a mental abstraction that enables individuals to organize, store, recall and manipulate information about their spatial environment (Downs and Stea, 1977).

Distinctive features

Cognitive mapping has its intellectual antecedents in Kelly's (1955) theory of personal constructs, which focuses on the attempts of humankind to control their social worlds by continual sense-making activities. The map is a series of linked axiomatic statements about a problem or issue, the various statements being separately identified as an aid to the consensual resolution of the problem. The map is interactively produced by the researcher and respondent(s) (usually in workshop settings), respondent 'ownership' of the map being essential to successful problem resolution.

Maps may be elicited from individuals or from groups. Where individual maps are produced these may be contrasted, and eventually integrated, with the individual maps of other organization members. The group map short-circuits the laborious process of individual mapping but seeks the same integrated end; it has similarities with both **focus groups** and **group interviews**.

Systematic mapping undertaken by a skilled researcher/facilitator generates complex schemas. Eden and Ackermann (2001) claim that individual maps will typically contain from 40 to 120 'concepts' (axiomatic statements) and the aggregated maps of several respondents will therefore consist of several hundred concepts. It is therefore commonplace for specially designed software to be used to generate and project the maps in the workplace setting. Skilled facilitation is seen as essential to effective practice, with SODA (strategic options development and analysis) being reported as a popular systematic method of facilitation.

Alternatively, within the context of urban planning, one might use cognitive mapping to plan one's route to work or the most efficient route for a multipurpose shopping trip. A cognitive map (popularly referred to as a mental map) is therefore a person's organized representation of some part of the spatial environment whether it be a sketch map to show friends how to get to your house, a child's picture of their home and garden, or a subway map. Of course most cognitive maps are stored internally by the individual (like a taxi-driver's road map of London), but urban planners have encouraged individuals to recreate these maps in physical form by sketching freehand or on to a base map. Spatial cognitive maps are important to social scientists as they are representations of the world as some person believes it to be. Studying cognitive maps provides a basis for understanding everyday behaviour, can give access to a person's perspective of the world and also provide insights into their self-identity (Golledge, 1987).

Examples

Ackermann and Eden (2001) offer their own work with senior officials in the UK Government's National Audit Office as an extended demonstration of group cognitive mapping. The NAO is the external auditor of government bodies, producing public reports on those bodies' efficiency and effectiveness. The cognitive mapping exercise concerned establishing how the NAO could successfully undertake a 'value-for-money' evaluation of the HM Customs and Excise efforts to combat VAT (sales tax) avoidance.

33

An example of using spatial cognitive mapping in empirical research is provided by Kennedy and colleagues (1998) who asked police officers and gang-mediation outreach workers to provide mental maps of Boston's gang geography (to map their turf, their rivals and alliances, locations of fights etc.). The resulting sociogram of gang relationships provided city planners with a powerful addition to mapping crime which supported the design and implementation of strategies to address those problems.

Evaluation

Since cognitive mapping is primarily undertaken by commercial consultants in competitive relations with each other, it is unsurprising that practitioners should stress the need for skilled facilitation. However, the potential complexity of the maps that may be generated does indeed argue the need for skilled practitioners and also raises the question about the reproducibility of maps elicited by particular practitioners in particular settings. Nevertheless, it is a particularly valuable technique for the very detailed representation and close comparison of individual perceptions and beliefs which could be used by researchers outside of management research.

Associated Concepts: Focus Groups, Group Interviews.

Key Readings
Ackermann, F. and Eden, C. (2001) 'SODA – Journey making and mapping in practice', in J. Rosenhead and J. Mingers (eds), *Rational Analysis for a Problematic World Revisited* (2nd edn). New York: Wiley.

Downs, R.M. and Stea, D. (1977) *Maps in Minds: Reflections on Cognitive Mapping.* New York: Harper Row.

Eden, C. and Ackermann, F. (2001) 'SODA – the principles', in J. Rosenhead and J. Mingers (eds), *Rational Analysis for a Problematic World Revisited* (2nd edn). New York: Wiley.

Golledge, R.G. (1987) 'Environmental cognition', in D. Stokols and I. Altman (eds), *Handbook of Environmental Psychology.* New York: Wiley pp. 131–174 .

Kelly, G. (1955) *The Psychology of Personal Constructs.* New York: Norton.

Kennedy, D.M., Braga, A.A. and Piehl, A.M. (1998) 'The (un)known universe: mapping gangs and gang violence in Boston', in D. Weisburd and T. McEwen (eds), *Crime Mapping and Crime Prevention.* New York: Willow Tree Press. pp. 219–262.

Computer-Assisted Data Analysis

Definition
The analysis of textual data aided by computer software which has been designed to support the analyst with the storage, coding and systematic retrieval of qualitative data.

Distinctive Features
The social science disciplines have seen a growing interest in the use of computer-assisted qualitative data analysis (CAQDAS) since its introduction in the mid-1980s. A number of software programs have been developed: popular programs include NVivo, NUD*IST (now N6), ATLAS/ti and The Ethnograph.

In essence the principles of computer-assisted data analysis are similar to that of non-computerized analysis. Having obtained textual data by whatever method – interview or focus group transcripts, fieldnotes or documentary sources – the researcher examines the data for emerging themes. Sections of text are then marked or 'tagged' with particular codes with usually more than one code being assigned to a given piece of text. The researcher then scrutinizes data held within each code and re-codes the data by creating sub-categories of codes. This iterative process allows the **indexing**, modification and elaboration of data into a tree-like structure where the branches represent progressively more fine-grained analysis.

Although the process of data coding is similar whether performed by hand or computer assisted, CAQDAS really shows its true value in the context of data searching and retrieval. Qualitative data analysis packages can assist in a number of ways. For example the computer can perform a textual search for a particular string of characters and thus retrieve all data that contains the occurrence of words or phrases. Index searches are another common method of data retrieval and may be simple or can be made more elaborate with the use of Boolean search operators. Therefore a researcher can request the software to retrieve all data coded at code A and code B, but not at code C. By conducting index searches such as this the researcher is able to test the robustness of the coding tree and seek patterns or themes in the data. This process also supports the researcher as he or she begins to develop and test hypotheses from the data. Analytic memoranda may also be attached to codes. These may provide a description of the themes of the code or analytical hunches about the data held within it.

As mentioned previously, the basic principles of textual coding and searching are similar whether the researcher uses computer-based or manual

35

data analysis. However, computer analysis can offer a number of advantages over manual methods (Coffey, Holbrook and Atkinson, 1996; Seale, 2000). Perhaps the most significant benefit is that computer analysis has negated the need for the time-consuming task of cutting, pasting and sorting textual data. What the researcher once did by hand, equipped with piles of paper **transcripts**, coloured pens and a pair of scissors, can now be done by computer, therefore enabling the task to be conducted much more quickly. This is of clear benefit to researchers because the time saved can be invested in other facets of data collection and analysis or can enable researchers to include more data in their projects. A second perceived advantage of computer-assisted analysis is that the data searches will tend to be more rigorous, systematic and comprehensive. While a researcher conducting a manual search may be tempted to truncate the search once they have found enough data to provide evidence for their hypothesis, or have found a worthy quote or anecdote to illustrate their point, a computer search will execute the whole task until all occurrences of data have been found. A third advantage of computer-assisted analysis is that computers are able to process much more complicated tasks than the human brain. This has meant that increasingly more advanced Boolean search operators can be used, for example 'search for data assigned code A but not proximal to code B'. A final advantage of computer-assisted analysis is that it can assist with team analysis. Researchers working in large teams, perhaps even based at different sites, can analyse their data in isolation and then merge and share their data with other team members. Researchers may also code the same data independently thus corroborating each other's interpretations of the data.

More recent advances in the computer-assisted analysis programs have heralded the developmental use of hypertext linkages (Coffey, Holbrook and Atkinson, 1996). This technique allows the readers of the research to click a highlighted icon within the research report and be routed to a hyperlink that may either be a section of the original textual data, a picture or sound file, or perhaps a summary of the respondent's demographic characteristics. The hyperlinks to original data enable the reader to explore the concepts in as much detail as he or she wishes and can provide illustrations of the analyst's theories thus enabling a more transparent interpretation of the data.

Examples
Buston's (1997) paper offers a practical account of how CAQDAS may be applied. The paper, based on interview data from chronically ill young people, offers a step-by-step guide to how the data were introduced into and indexed within the NUD*IST programme. The paper also provides an overview of some of the main capabilities of the NUD*IST software including how base data (the

demographic characteristics of respondents) can be included and utilized in the analysis and how indexed data can be retrieved. The paper concludes with a discussion of the main methodological debate around CAQDAS software, that is, whether the software can influence how the analysis is conducted.

An example of the use of hypermedia within computer-assisted data analysis is provided by Dicks and Mason (1998) in their study of a coal-mining heritage park located in the South Wales valleys. The authors describe how they have constructed an ethnographic hypermedia environment that brings together the presentation of analysed data alongside the accumulated original data. In their paper the authors claim that the strength of the development is its ability to merge different forms of media (visual, verbal and pictorial) thus enabling a deeper ethnographic understanding for readers of their research. The hypermedia environment offers additional dimensions to their presentation of data and the analysis can be made more explicit for the reader to the extent that the reader becomes a co-author exploring and scrutinizing the original data which are presented through a range of media.

Evaluation

Many of the issues surrounding the evaluation of computer-assisted data analysis focus on questions such as 'will computers take over the analytical process?', 'can computers improve the validity of qualitative analysis?' and 'can computers make data analysis more transparent to the readers and users of research?'

Initially many qualitative researchers were suspicious of computer-assisted qualitative data analysis. The computer was considered to be an icon of the quantitative explanatory research paradigm that favoured distance rather than personal engagement with data. More recently computer-assisted data analysis has become more widely accepted due to its advantages in the management and retrieval of extensive amounts of textual data. There are, however, some remaining concerns about the use of computers to assist qualitative data analysis. Such criticisms include the sacrificing of depth for breadth of analysis and the application of quantitative principles such as frequency counting to qualitative data. Other researchers (see, for example, Coffey, Holbrook and Atkinson, 1996; Seale, 2000) have warned of the simplified association of computer-assisted qualitative data analysis with **grounded theory**. Their concern is that while CAQDAS facilitates the organization and retrieval of qualitative data, software packages are not a substitute for analysis itself. Researchers are still required to undertake the analytic process, to explore the meaning of the data and build theories in their own minds. The software is also considered unsuitable for certain types of qualitative analysis that use relatively short data extracts, such as discourse analysis or conversation analysis, as it has more use in the discovery of the thematic content of qualitative data than the form or structure of talk or text.

A discussion of the perceived merits and disadvantages of computer-assisted data analysis is a regular feature of many research articles which explore qualitative data analysis. It is also a pertinent question for many research students in deciding whether to invest the time to learn the intricacies of a new computer package in order to analyse their data. It is perhaps worth remembering that computer-assisted analysis is no substitute for the analytic mind nor can it offer a shortcut to data coding. Furthermore many of the features that researchers want from computer-assisted analysis, such as searching for strings of text, can be found in word-processing packages. There are, however, substantial benefits of CAQDAS particularly in terms of the speed and thoroughness of the data searches and the ability to link data with analysis through the use of analytic memos which can aid the transparency of the analytic process.

Associated Concepts: Grounded Theory, Indexing, Transcription.

Key Readings

Buston, K. (1997) 'NUD*IST in action: its use and its usefulness in a study of chronic illness in young people', *Sociological Research Online*, 2(3). http://www.socresonline.org.uk/socresonline/2/3/6.html

Coffey, A., Holbrook, B. and Atkinson, P. (1996) 'Qualitative data analysis: Technologies and representations', *Sociological Research Online*, 1(1). http://www.socresonline.org.uk/socresonline/1/1/4.html

Dicks, B. and Mason, B. (1998) 'Hypermedia and ethnography: reflections on the construction of a research approach', *Sociological Research Online*, 3(3). http://www.socresonlin.org.uk/socresonline/3/3/3.html

*Kelle, U., Prein, G. and Bird, K. (eds) (1995) *Computer-Aided Qualitative Data Analysis: Theories, Methods and Practice*. London: Sage.

Miles, M. and Weitzman, E.A. (1994) 'Choosing computer programs for qualitative data analysis', in M. Miles and M. Huberman (eds), *Qualitative Data Analysis: An Expanded Sourcebook*. Thousand Oaks: Sage. pp. 311–317.

Richards, L. and Richards, T. (1994) 'Using computers in qualitative analysis', in N.K. Denzin and Y.S. Lincoln (eds), *Handbook of Qualitative Research*. Thousand Oaks: Sage. pp. 445–462.

*Seale, C.F. (2000) 'Computer assisted analysis of qualitative data', in D. Silverman (ed.), *Doing Qualitative Research: A Practical Handbook*. London: Sage. pp. 154–174.

Conversation Analysis

Definition

Conversation analysis is a specific method of analysing qualitative data. Its main purpose is to characterize and explain the ways in which those engaged in conversation maintain an interactional social order by examining the 'technology of conversation' (Sacks, 1992: 339). Conversation analysis studies the various practices adopted by conversational participants during ordinary everyday talk. This may include how participants negotiate overlaps and interruptions, how various failures (such as hearing and understanding problems) are dealt with during the interaction and how conversations are opened and terminated. The technique is also sometimes referred to as 'talk-in-interaction'.

Distinctive Features

Conversation analysis was first established during the early 1960s within the University of California at Berkeley, and was influenced primarily by the disciplines of sociology, linguistics and anthropology. The prime movers of the technique were Harvey Sacks, Emanuel Schegloff and Gail Jefferson. However the technique was also influenced by the work of Erving Goffman, whose style of sociological analysis was based on observation of people as they interact, and Howard Garfinkel whose **ethnomethodological** methods focused on the study of common-sense everyday activities.

The growth of the technique since the 1960s can in part be explained by the adoption of progressively more accurate **audio-recording** devices within qualitative research. Such devices have enabled the analyst to make the data accessible to readers through the **transcription** process. Data transcripts made for the purposes of conversational analysis are different to those of other qualitative methods in that they contain significantly more details of the speech by capturing the minutiae of the ways in which words and utterances are produced. Consequently a detailed system of transcription was developed by Jefferson, which incorporates symbols into the transcript that provide insights into the subtleties of how utterances were produced. These include, for example, when speakers overlap, time intervals between utterances and variations in stress, pitch, amplitude, or in-breaths. A glossary of such symbols can be found in a number of texts, see for example Ten Have (1999).

Conversation analysis concentrates on naturally occurring data, that is, data that exist independent of the researcher's presence. As such, the technique shares characteristics of other qualitative techniques such as **ethnography** and

discourse analysis in that data are not co-produced with the researcher, as in the case of interviews and focus groups, but become data when they are observed, recorded and analysed by the researcher. Conversation analysis should therefore aim to capture natural interaction between participants as comprehensively as possible.

Typically conversation analysts have focused their attention on institutional settings where the technique has been applied to demonstrate how such institutions are 'talked into being' (Heritage, 1984: 290). A number of different institutions have been intensively studied by conversation analysts including courtrooms (Atkinson and Drew, 1979), news interviews (Heritage and Greatbatch, 1991) and classrooms (Mehan, 1979). It is perhaps in such large, formal and public settings, where there are a number of potential participants involved in producing the conversation and it is heard by an audience, that the talk is required to be ordered and rationed between participants depending on their institutional role. Analysis shows how participants within the setting are concerned with orientating themselves and others to their own specific goals which are linked to their own institutional identity – for example whether they are a judge or defendant, a doctor or patient, a teacher or pupil. Analysts have demonstrated that there are constraints on what is regarded as an allowable contribution depending on the participant's institutional identity and the business at hand. The overriding feature of most institutional conversation is the restriction of normal conversational possibilities for participants due to a required ordered nature of the conversation.

Two key analytical themes within conversation analysis are sequential organization and categorization. Sequential organization analysis examines how utterances can perform different actions depending on their sequential position within the conversation. Turn-taking is one fundamental aspect of sequential organization which is displayed through conversation. Thus it is suggested that conversation is organized in adjacency pairs such as question followed by answer; accusation followed by denial; compliment followed by acceptance. The sense of the second part of the adjacency pair is dependent on the first part. Breaches in such turn-taking (for example, when a question is followed by a further question in reply) are rare and suggest a breakdown in the order of the interaction. Breaches are useful to conversation analysts as it is usually when the rules have been subverted that the rules themselves become more explicit to the analysts.

Categorization is a further concern of conversation analysts and has its roots in the ethnomethodological tradition's ideas of membership category analysis (MCA). Membership category analysis rests on the principle that people are what they are as a result of their activities and thus it is by identifying activities that people may be defined as being one thing or another. For example 'the family' may be a membership categorization device in which 'baby' and 'mother' are categories and from which category-bounding activities may include 'living together' and 'caring'.

Examples

A classic study of conversation analysis is Harvey Sacks's analysis of phone calls to the Los Angeles Suicide Prevention Center. This early work from Sacks's PhD was initially presented as a lecture in 1964 and published many years later (Sacks, 1992). Sacks's aim was to compare the opening sequence of calls from an institutional context (a psychiatric service) and the different ways in which the conversational procedures were used. Sacks noted that professionals answering calls laid great importance on obtaining the caller's name. The study demonstrates a number of themes that have been taken up within conversation analysis. For example by providing their own name the call taker encourages the call maker to provide their own name in the next slot. The natural adjacency pair thus provides a means of obtaining the caller's name while managing to avoid asking a direct question.

Fitzgerald and Housley (2002) present a conversation analytic study of radio phone-ins to examine how both categorical and sequential identities are developed during the course of the short interaction. For example the radio host initiates the introduction by using 'call relevant identities' (including the name and location of the caller). This serves to introduce the caller and is also necessary to indicate to the caller that they are no longer the next caller but the caller on-air, for example, 'John Smith from Staffordshire do you agree with that?' Throughout the sequence both host and caller may occupy a number of membership categories. The host occupies membership categories of call recipient, introducer and questioner, and the caller occupies membership categories of call maker, introduced and then opinion giver. The data also illustrate how hosts negotiate topic-opinion categories. For example it is only after the caller has made his or her position clear as to whether he or she is 'for' or 'against' the issue under debate that the host then occupies the opposing argument. The radio host also uses sequential techniques of question and answer adjacency pairs that lead the caller to answer his or her questions and thus serve to re-focus the caller's arguments.

Evaluation

Conversation analysis has been employed within a number of academic disciplines including sociology, media studies, anthropology and linguistics due to its ability to offer a critique on the established conventions of social life. Initially it was conceived as a 'pure science', motivated by the desire to discover linguistic aspects of social interaction, but more recently analysts have used the technique in a more applied sense to learn more about the organization of institutions.

Conversation analysis differs from some of the more popular techniques of research in that it is not concerned with describing or explaining participants' actions and talk in terms of explanatory variables such as gender, age or social class. The conversation analysis approach also aims to treat context as 'locally produced' and 'incrementally developed' (Drew and Heritage, 1992: 21). However, it could be argued that no conversation is entirely locally produced as participants who are engaged in conversation will inevitably draw upon previous understandings during the course of their talk. For example a teacher's conversation with a pupil will in part be influenced by previous conversations and understandings that the pair have developed.

The differences between discourse analysis and conversation analysis can be illustrated in a study of medical consultations. Discourse analysis might analyse the talk in terms of medical discourse and the professional and lay social construction of the body or illness, while a conversation analysis approach might examine how the doctor and patient roles and diagnoses are interactionally achieved and accomplished by the participants' talk.

Many novice analysts appear to be discouraged by conversation analysis due to its apparent obsession with detail that can sometimes make the data appear impenetrable. However, more experienced analysts argue that it is the detail that is required in order to represent the data as fully and faithfully as possible, thus enabling the analyst to understand the talk-in-interaction that lies at the heart of conversation analysis. Therefore the minutiae of the talk such as pauses and overlapping do not serve to blur the main issues being discussed by the participants but rather to determine exactly what kind of action is being performed by the participants. Such analysis inevitably requires detailed transcription.

Associated Concepts: Audio-Recording, Discourse Analysis, Ethnography, Ethnomethodology, Transcription.

Key Readings

Atkinson, J.M. and Drew, P. (1979) *Order in Court: The Organisation of Verbal Interaction in Judicial Settings*. London: Macmillan.

Drew, P. and Heritage, J. (1992) *Talk at Work: Interaction in Institutional Settings*. Cambridge: Cambridge University Press.

Fitzgerald, R. and Housley, W. (2002) 'Identity, categorisation and sequential organisation: the sequential and categorical flow of identity in a radio phone-in', *Discourse and Society*, 13(5): 579–602.

Heritage, J. (1984) *Garfinkel and Ethnomethodology*. Cambridge: Polity Press.

*Heritage, J. (1997) 'Conversational analysis and institutional talk', in D. Silverman (ed.), *Qualitative Research: Theory, Method and Practice*. London: Sage. pp. 161–182.

Heritage, J. and Greatbatch, D. (1991) 'On the institutional character of institutional talk: the case of news interviews', in D. Boden and D.H. Zimmerman (eds), *Talk and Social Structure: Studies in Ethnomethodology and Conversation Analysis*. Cambridge: Polity Press. pp. 93–137.

Hutchby, I. and Wooffitt, R. (1998) *Conversation Analysis: Principles, Practices and Applications*. Oxford: Polity Press.

Mehan, H. (1979) *Learning Lessons: Social Organisation in the Classroom*. Cambridge, MA: Harvard University Press.

Sacks, H. (1992) *Lectures on Conversation* (vol. I). Ed. Gail Jefferson; Intro. by Emanuel A. Schegloff. Oxford: Blackwell.

*Ten Have, P. (1999) *Doing Conversation Analysis: A Practical Guide*. London: Sage.

Covert Research

Definition

The undertaking of research without the consent of research subjects, by the researcher posing as an ordinary member of the collectivity, or by the experimental manipulation of research subjects without their knowledge.

Distinctive Features and Evaluation

There is little point in trying to separate the evaluation of covert research methods from a discussion of its distinctive features, since the central preoccupation in all methodological writing on covert research is a concern with whether or not covert research is **ethical**. Although research ethics committees routinely require would-be researchers to obtain the informed consent of their research subjects, and informed consent is seen as a cornerstone of ethical research practice, not all guidelines on ethical research practice explicitly prohibit covert research. Thus, the Statement of Ethical Practice of the British Sociological Association states that the use of covert methods may be justified in certain circumstances, instancing the difficulties that arise when people change their behaviour because they know they are being studied and (more compellingly) the denial of open research access by powerful or secretive interests. However, the same guidelines state that covert research 'should be resorted to only where it is impossible to use other methods to obtain essential data'. In effect, two tests are being applied here: that other methods are impossible and that the data obtained by covert research are essential. These are stringent tests and it follows that, even where non-covert

43

research is prohibited, it will rarely be unambiguously justifiable: there are a number of instances on record of researchers receiving permission to undertake research on secretive organizations (for example, Fielding's 1982 research on the far-right political organization, the National Front); and comparatively few social scientists would be sufficiently megalomaniacal as to claim that their research was 'essential' for humankind.

It is sometimes argued that some data can only be obtained by participant observers who have withheld their true status from those in the study setting. For example, a number of early studies of mental hospitals in the 1950s and 60s (e.g. Caudill, 1958) involved the researcher simulating mental illness, and Buckingham (Buckingham et al., 1976) underwent severe weight loss in order to simulate a dying patient in both a hospice and a conventional hospital ward. These studies were important in their day and contributed to policies and practice, but the growth of **ethnographic** research in nursing studies has meant that access to 'backstage' hospital settings is now readily obtainable by trained nurse-ethnographers. The dissemination of qualitative research methods among different professional groups has transformed the conduct of ethnographies in institutional settings: the present case for the dissembling participant observer is less strong than in the past. Other arguments mobilized against covert research by its critics (for example, Dingwall, 1980) include the betrayal of **trust**, the pain suffered by research subjects who may subsequently discover that they have been the victims of fraud, the invasion of privacy, and the possible adverse effect on research **access** for future researchers. Sluka (1995) has argued that the deceptions of covert research may make fieldwork more **dangerous** for fieldworkers.

While the above seems to establish a strong case against *any* covert social science research as unethical, there nevertheless remains a contrary case to be made. In the first place, much **ethnographic** research in street settings begins as covert research: it is only when close relationships have been established with at least some research subjects that the researcher's purposes can be revealed and informed consent can be sought. In some cases, and for some sensitive research topics, the initial covert stage of street ethnography can last for a long period: Chambliss's (1975) study of organized crime in Seattle (which took place over a ten-year period), began with a three-month period of covert observation before he 'came clean' to a person he had come to know who ran an illegal backstreet gambling operation and whom Chambliss then asked for help. Relatedly, in any street ethnography, there will be collectivity members, who are only peripheral actors in the settings in which the researcher has a research interest, who will never receive any explanation of the research topic and will never have the opportunity to give or withhold their consent. Any ethnographer who stopped all and sundry on the streets to explain his or her purpose and seek their consent to his or her presence would quickly either empty the streets or get punched on the nose. So street ethnography depends on covert observation, at least for some research subjects and for part of the time.

Examples

Although covert qualitative research projects are still sometimes undertaken, the controversy surrounding covert methods has probably made such studies less common than they were previously. So it should be no surprise that our exemplar studies are drawn from the 1960s and 70s.

The experimental manipulation of research subjects without their knowledge occurs more frequently in quantitative studies, particularly in psychological laboratories (for example, the Milgram [1963] experiments on obedience, where the great majority of research subjects showed themselves perfectly willing to inflict pain on others when instructed to do so). But this manipulation can occur in qualitative studies also: in the course of Braginsky, Braginsky and Ring's (1969) mental hospital study, one group of patients were told that the purpose of their upcoming psychiatric assessment was to see whether they were fit for discharge, while another group of patients were told that the purpose was to see whether they were capable of remaining on their open ward (or must return to a locked ward). When the assessment results of the two groups were compared, new patients performed equally well no matter what they thought the purpose of the assessment was; but long-standing patients performed better in the assessments when they thought they might be banished back to the locked ward, than when they thought they might be discharged. This unethical experiment remains the best demonstration available of the ability of patients secretly to influence doctors' seemingly objective clinical judgements.

An example of covert research being used to penetrate a secretive and powerful group is Wallis's study of the Scientology cult. According to Wallis (1977), the Scientologists responded, not just by complaining to his research funders about his unethical behaviour and threatening legal action, but also by some covert activities of their own – espionage among his colleagues and students, attempted entrapment, and forged letters implicating him in homosexual acts and spying for the drug squad. The force of the Scientologists' alleged response to his research may perhaps be taken as a measure of the importance of his findings.

The most famous example of unethical covert research practice in qualitative social science is almost certainly Humphreys's (1970) *Tearoom Trade*. The book is an account of Humphreys's PhD research on anonymous sexual encounters in public lavatories ('tearooms' in American gay argot), which Humphreys observed while posing as a 'watchqueen' (one who gets his kicks by watching others have sex, while simultaneously keeping a look-out for intruders). At the suggestion of his Director of Research, Lee Rainwater, the distinguished Harvard sociologist, Humphreys went on to collect a sample of

45

tearoom users' car licence plates (most users drove to the tearooms). It is not clear whether the next step occurred at Rainwater's suggestion or on Humphreys's own initiative: 'friendly policemen' (without 'becoming too inquisitive' about the reason for Humphreys's interest – Humphreys, 1970: 38) then gave Humphreys access to the police licence registers to trace the tearoom users' names and addresses. (Quite apart from the misuse of police records, the known punitive attitude of the police to tearoom users made this method of sample tracing an exceedingly risky one for the unsuspecting sample members.) Having traced his sample, he was able to add their names to a university community health survey he was working on (with the permission of the director of the survey!), so that he could interview them and gain, by this deception, personal data on their employment, marital status and other matters. D.J. West, the Cambridge criminologist, wrote a foreword for the UK edition of *Tearoom Trade*, describing these research methods as 'enterprising'.

Associated Concepts: Access Negotiations, Dangerous Fieldwork Ethics, Ethnography, Trust.

Key Readings
Braginsky, B., Braginsky, D. and Ring, K. (1969) *Methods of Madness – The Mental Hospital as a Last Resort*. New York: Holt, Rinehart and Winston.

*British Sociological Association (not dated) *Statement of Ethical Practice*. www.britsoc.org.uk/about/ethic.htm

Buckingham, R., Lack, S., Mount, B., Maclean, I. and Collins, J. (1976) 'Living with the dying: use of the technique of participant observation', *Canadian Medical Association Journal*, 115: 1211–1215.

Caudill, W. (1958) *The Psychiatric Hospital as a Small Society*. Cambridge, MA: Harvard University Press.

Chambliss, W. (1975) 'On the paucity of original research on organized crime', *American Sociologist*, 10: 36–39.

Dingwall, R. (1980) 'Ethics and ethnography', *Sociological Review*, 28: 871–881.

Fielding, N. (1982) 'Observational research on the National Front', in M. Bulmer (ed.), *Social Research Ethics*. London: Macmillan. pp. 80–104.

Humphreys, L. (1970) *Tearoom Trade* (foreword by D.J. West). London: Duckworth.

Milgram, S. (1963) 'Behavioural study of obedience', *Journal of Abnormal and Social Psychology*, 67: 371–378.

Sluka, J. (1995) 'Reflections on managing danger in fieldwork: dangerous anthropology in Belfast', in C. Nordstrom and A. Robben (eds), *Fieldwork Under Fire: Contemporary Studies of Violence and Survival*. Berkeley: University of California Press. pp. 276–294.

Wallis, R. (1977) 'The moral career of a research project', in C. Bell and H. Newby (eds), *Doing Sociological Research*. London: Allen & Unwin. pp. 148–167.

Dangerous Fieldwork

Definition
Fieldwork which threatens the health and/or safety of the fieldworker.

Distinctive Features
Thanks in part to the demanding requirements of research **ethics** committees, research managers devote much time and effort to ensuring that social research has no harmful impacts on research subjects. Professional codes of practice have similar concerns. By contrast, the safeguarding of fieldworkers is typically little regarded and well-disseminated guidelines on safe fieldwork practice are absent. Thus, while the personnel departments of higher education institutions may expect research managers to undertake risk assessment exercises at the start of any major research project, few research managers in the social sciences are likely to be aware of such expectations and fewer still will comply with them. Again, institutions carry insurance policies covering staff and students against occupational injury, but many research managers appear to be unaware that insurers require prior notification of unusual risk of injury and may wish to impose an additional premium.

No census of dangerous incidents has been undertaken. It is thought that the prevalence of such incidents is small, but occasions have certainly been recorded where researchers have suffered death, rape, injury, robbery, infectious disease, mental illness, intimidation and harassment. Obviously, **ethnographic** fieldworkers in anthropology, criminology and sociology are most at risk, both because of the nature of the fieldwork settings in which they operate, and because of their prolonged periods of exposure in the field, Sluka (1995) suggested that **covert researchers** may face particular dangers. However, **interviewers**, particularly those making house-calls, are also at risk.

Lee (1995) makes a distinction between 'ambient' and 'situational' fieldwork risks: ambient risks are those encountered in inherently dangerous fieldwork settings, such as war zones, while situational risks are those deriving not from the setting itself but from the fieldworker's presence or actions (for example, the risks to female researchers in all-male environments). As Sampson and Thomas (2003) point out, certain ambient risks (such as remoteness) can amplify the situational risk to fieldworkers.

Examples

Personal reports of fieldwork in risky situations can be found in the collections by Lee-Treweek and Linkogle (2000) and by Nordstrom and Robben (1995). Lee (1995) provides an overview. Sampson and Thomas (2003) draw both on these earlier contributions and on the lessons of their own fieldwork experiences as isolated female researchers on cargo ships.

Evaluation

Sampson and Thomas discuss steps that researchers can take to minimize personal risk, but also draw attention to past failures by higher education institutions and research funding bodies to address researcher health and safety with sufficient seriousness. If we take as a model Rayner's (1986) application to occupational safety of Mary Douglas's grid-group work on the 'culture of risk', there seems no doubt that many social researchers could be characterized as 'individualists' who are prepared to accept dangerous fieldwork as a legitimate risk to be endured *en route* for the intrinsic and material rewards of an academic career. However, other researchers might best be characterized as 'fatalists', concerned about the risks they face, but lacking the knowledge and social solidarity to resist being placed in perilous situations. It is this latter group, often junior contract researchers, who are being betrayed by the current lack of institutional concern with their safety needs. This betrayal is all the worse because the procedures which would serve to reduce risk are straightforward and commonsensical. Such procedures include: 'doubling up' fieldworkers or interviewers in hazardous environments, requiring researchers to phone in an 'all-clear' at the end of an interview or fieldwork session, and providing a third party (supervisor or project secretary) with contact details in advance for all fieldwork or interview sessions.

Associated Concepts: Covert Research, Ethics, Ethnography, Interviews.

Key Readings

Lee, R. (1995) *Dangerous Fieldwork.* London: Sage.

Lee-Treweek, G. and Linkogle, S. (eds) (2000) *Danger in the Field: Risk and Ethics in Social Research.* London: Routledge.

Nordstrom, C. and Robben, A. (eds) (1995) *Fieldwork Under Fire: Contemporary Studies of Violence and Culture.* Berkeley: University of California Press.

Rayner, S. (1986) 'Management of radiation hazards in hospitals: plural rationalities in a single institution', *Social Studies of Science*, 16: 573–593.

*Sampson, H. and Thomas, M. (2003) 'Lone researchers at sea: gender, risk and responsibility', *Qualitative Research*, 3(2): 165–190.

Sluka, J. (1995) 'Reflections on managing danger in fieldwork: dangerous anthropology in Belfast', in C. Nordstrom and A. Robben (eds), *Fieldwork Under Fire: Contemporary Studies of Violence and Survival*. Berkeley: University of California Press. pp. 276–294.

Delphi Groups

Definition
A method for achieving consensual agreement among expert panellists, through repeated iterations (usually by email) of anonymized opinions and of proposed compromise statements from the group moderator.

Distinctive Features
Delphi groups are simply the most popular of several methods (others are nominal group techniques and **citizens' juries**) aimed at providing informed consensus statements on matters of policy importance or services provision. Participating experts are encouraged to gravitate towards a common position by representing (anonymously) to those with minority views that they are out of step with their colleagues, and by proposals of successively modified statements which may command progressively more support. The process may go through several rounds of communication (often done through emailing) before consensus is achieved. Although the conduct of a Delphi group is very similar to that of a 'virtual' **focus group**, the Delphi group practitioner or moderator is interested solely in the outcome of the communications involved.

Examples
Although Delphi groups can be found in range of settings (see the review by Rowe et al., 1991), they have been used most extensively in health services research, particularly to derive practice guidelines where systematic review evidence is lacking. Jones and Hunter (1995) discuss applications of the technique and give the extended example of a Delphi group of 20 UK hospital consultants asking to deliberate on the implications for patient care of reducing the levels of staffing by junior doctors.

Evaluation

Bias is the most serious difficulty with which Delphi groups must contend. Although careful group selection can ensure all shades of expert opinion are represented, attrition rates in the repeated rounds of email communication can be considerable and those with minority views may simply drop out rather than actively seek a moderated consensus. Further, although Delphi groups may include 'lay' representatives, they are essentially expert groups, and (unlike citizens' juries) might be characterized as undemocratic bodies for that reason.

Another distinct difficulty relates to the generation of consensus statements. If these consensus statements are framed in relatively abstract terms, simply with a view to concealing disagreement over specific applications, then the consensus achieved by the group will be illusory with no subsequent impact on variations in expert practice.

Associated Concepts: Bias, Citizens' Jury, Focus Groups.

Key Readings

*Jones, J. and Hunter, D. (1995) 'Qualitative research: consensus methods for medical and health services research', *British Medical Journal*, 311: 376–380.

Rowe, G., Wright, G. and Bolger, F. (1991) 'Delphi: a re-evaluation of research and theory', *Technological Forecasting and Social Change*, 39: 235–251.

Diary Methods

Definition

The recording of activities and experiences, usually in written format, within specific episodes of time. The diary is created specifically for the purpose of research and focuses on a particular topic of interest to the researcher.

Distinctive Features

Plummer (1983) has reviewed the use of diaries in social research and identifies three broad strategies. These approaches differ primarily in relation to the amount of structure imposed within the diary: unstructured written accounts, semi-structured diaries comprising reports of key activities or emotions, and finally a structured log of activities which essentially lists events with relatively little commentary.

Zimmerman and Wieder (1977) argue that diary methods can be a good alternative to research **fieldnotes** in **ethnographic** research. Diaries can provide access to naturally occurring sequences of activity which might otherwise be inaccessible to participant observation. Subjects themselves are able to record events but with the additional benefits of being able to do this on a continuous basis, whereas fieldworkers might only be present at restricted times. Thus the subjects themselves become adjunct ethnographers of their own circumstances.

Diary methods are particularly popular within the sub-discipline of medical sociology as they provide the means for respondents to record their symptoms and the actions they take to manage the condition. Although diaries are usually written documents, some researchers have experimented with the use of **video** diaries to record respondents' activities (Holliday, 2004).

Diaries as a research method are frequently used alongside qualitative interviews with the same respondent. The diary then becomes an *aide-mémoire* for both the respondent and researcher, with the interview serving to amplify and clarify events recorded in the subject's diary (Plummer, 1983).

Personal diaries have been used by researchers to study social life, for example the diaries of Samuel Pepys or Anne Frank, but this method is discussed under the entry on **documentary methods**. The experiences in these diaries only become data in retrospect. Diaries are also used in research to record the researcher's activities throughout the study. This use is described under its own entry on **research diaries**.

Examples

Johnson and Bytheway (2001) provide a detailed example of the merits and problems of diary research in their study of medicine management among people aged over 75 years old. Participants were asked to complete a two-week diary recording when they took prescribed and over-the-counter medicines. The diaries also prompted respondents to record the timing of other activities known to be associated with taking medicines such as experiencing symptoms, consumption of meals, contact with visitors and/or relatives, and trips outside the house. In addition to the diary, the respondents were visited by fieldworkers who interviewed respondents about their recent activities using the data recorded in the diary as a basis for discussion. Following pilots, changes were made to the methodology as some of the older people were struggling to complete the diary, partly due to problems of vision, manual dexterity and comprehension. Consequently on their first visit fieldworkers demonstrated how to complete the diary based on the previous and current day's activities. The fieldworker also made a subsequent visit a few days later and, together with the respondent, recorded additional activities which the respondent had omitted. The authors report additional problems with using diary methods in this study. There was a decline in the amount of detail recorded in the diary after the first week, some respondents dropped out of the study feeling that the task was too onerous or complicated, and it was felt that some respondents reported expected rather than actual events.

Evaluation

Lee (1993) extols the merits of diaries in research, but warns that their application is constrained by problems of sample **bias** and sample attrition due to the sometimes rather burdensome and prolonged commitment required of the respondent. Furthermore respondents may change their behaviour because of the act of reporting it in a diary. For example, keeping a record of how much money one spends, as was required in the UK Family Expenditure Survey (Office of National Statistics, 1999), will inevitably prompt reflection on, and potential curtailment of, spending. While diaries might change behaviour, Elliot (1997) argues that the ability of diaries to encourage reflection on the part of the respondent is a methodological advantage as it provides opportunity for the respondents to prepare for the subsequent interview. Diarists therefore become more equal collaborators with the researcher, retain more control over the research process, and raise the level of **public participation.** Video diaries have also become increasingly popular in recent years.

Despite the problems identified, diary methods can, particularly if complemented by interviews, provide insight into social life that would not be possible by other means. Perhaps their most obvious advantages are their ability to aid recall of activities and that they can provide data on actions and experiences over extended periods of time. As with observational methods, they can also help to distinguish what people actually do from what they say they do. Johnson and Bytheway (2001) also argue that data recorded in a diary should be regarded as particularly powerful as what is said in the written word often holds more significance and relevance to the subject than what is spoken.

Associated Concepts: Bias, Documentary Methods, Ethnography, Fieldnotes, Public Participation, Research Diary, Video-Recording.

Key Readings

*Elliot, H. (1997) 'The use of diaries in social research', *Sociological Research Online*, 2(2). http://www.socresonline. org.uk/socresonline/2/2/4.html

Holliday, R. (2004) 'Filming "the closet": the role of video diaries in researching sexuality', *American Behavioral Scientist*, 47(12): 1597–1616.

*Johnson, J. and Bytheway, B. (2001) 'An evaluation of the use of diaries in a study of medication in later life', *International Journal of Social Research* *Methodology: Theory & Practice*, 4(3): 183–204.

Lee, R.M. (1993) *Doing Research on Sensitive Topics*. London: Sage.

Office of National Statistics (1999) *Family Spending: A Report on the 1998–1999 Family Expenditure Survey*. London: The Stationary Office.

Plummer, K. (1983) *Documents of Life*. London: Allen & Unwin.

Zimmerman, D.H. and Wieder, D.L. (1977) 'The diary-interview method', *Urban Life*, 5(4): 479–497.

Discourse Analysis

Definition

Discourse analysis is the study of language in context. It is an approach that emphasizes how versions of the social world are produced within naturally occurring spoken or written discourse. The discourse analytic view is that all features of talk or texts perform some kind of action (for example exercizing power and control over others) and it is possible to analyse how language is used to achieve that action. It is therefore concerned with how participants construct themselves and others through their discourse and how these selves may be undermined.

Distinctive Features

There are a number of different approaches to discourse analysis (see Phillips and Jørgensen, 2002 for a full review) due in part to the developing nature of the field and to the number of disciplines in which it has its roots, including linguistics, sociology, psychology, philosophy and literary theory. However, all approaches share the same postmodern perspective that talk does not neutrally reflect our world and our social relationships but rather actively constructs and alters them. Discourse theory views discourse as a constantly changing entity and explores the struggle between competing forms of discourses each representing a particular way of understanding the world. Critical

53

discourse analysis accepts that discourse is just one among many aspects of social practice and that intertextuality (that is, how texts draw on elements of other texts) is a central concern. Discursive psychology sees individual actors as both the products and the producers of discourse and is more concerned with small-scale 'talk-in-interaction' rather than large-scale societal discourse.

Discourse analysis is not just a method of data analysis but an approach that combines philosophy, theory and method. Discourse analysts start with the acceptance that discourse is a form of social action that plays a part in producing the social world (including social relations and knowledge). Physical objects and events exist independently of people's thoughts and speech, but they have meaning only through discourse. For instance, most people would view cancer as an illness, but they would not necessarily describe it in the same way. Some would draw on discourses of behavioural risk, while others may see it as a result of medical mismanagement and others still might attribute it to God's will. Importantly, each of these discourses of explanation will suggest a different course of action to tackle the illness.

Discourse analysis can be applied in a number of data collection settings primarily to examine naturally occurring talk. For example discourse analysts might be interested in talk within institutions (schools, hospitals, prisons) or interested in written texts such as newspapers. Discourse analysis might be applied to examine a number of subjects such as gender inequalities, national identity or the construction of knowledge claims. Questions are not just asked about the content of the discourse but also about the author, its authority and its audience. Consequently discourse analysis is often applied in conjunction with **documentary methods**.

Discourse analysis also has similarities with **conversation analysis**, not least because of its use of naturally occurring speech. However, it differs from conversation analysis in that it deals with wider social science concerns such as gender relations and social control. Whereas conversation analysts exclude the context in which participants speak, discourse analysts argue that one cannot understand what is going on in a particular interactional episode unless one knows how to locate it within the macro societal context. Discourse analysis takes meaning above the utterance level to focus on the participants' roles and their institutional or ideological motives. Therefore, although **audio-recordings** and **transcription** are required to be of good quality, discourse analysis does not require the same attention to detail as the units of analysis are broader.

Examples

Sarangi et al. (2003) present a discourse analysis of data derived from genetic counselling clinics. Focusing on the discourse of risk assessment and risk communication they identify six strategies – abstraction, reformulation, externalization, localization, temporalization and agentivization – by which both patients and counsellors seek to relativize risk status. For example the strategy of abstraction involves statements of the risks of other individuals: 'about one in three people get a cancer somewhere in their body in their life'. In contrast the strategy of reformulation places risk in the very personal context of the individual's life. It is often coded in figures of speech and metaphors in order to be made relevant to the patient's lived experiences: '... it's like betting on a horse, and so it's important for you not to say oh well it's only one in seven, couldn't happen to me. It's important to think through the issues.' The authors conclude that it is through the use of these strategies that counsellors are able to present the same risk information in either more reassuring or more alarming terms, thereby balancing the needs of accurate transmission of facts with promoting appropriate behaviour and avoidance of unnecessary anxiety.

An example of a discourse analysis of textual material is Torck's (2001) cross-cultural study of the voices of homeless people in street newspapers. Torck's analysis challenges the claim that the purpose of street newspapers is to raise the profile of homelessness issues and to be a platform for homeless people to regain independence. The article shows how papers' topics and genres are framed to reinforce the negative social ethos of the homeless. For example where homeless people are given a platform for their voice they are usually limited to personal narratives and poetry. The emphasis on feelings and pathos in the voices of the homeless was found to be less prevalent in the American compared to the European papers.

The idea that discourse constructs the world rather than representing it has also been popular within the sociology of science. Research has focused on the importance of scientific discourse and texts particularly in relation to scientific persuasion and practical reasoning. For example Mulkay and Gilbert (1982) show how scientists use two distinct interpretative repertoires, or linguistic registers, when discussing their work. The empiricist repertoire is used by scientists when discussing work in a formal context, and is characterized by a conventionally impersonal style, where references to human actors are minimized and the natural world appears to speak for itself. In contrast the contingent repertoire is characterized by references to the personal and social contingencies in scientific action and belief. Mulkay and Gilbert (1982) describe how scientists apply these two repertoires asymmetrically to account for correct and incorrect beliefs. Thus they present correct belief, which is invariably identical to their current views, as arising unproblematically from the experimental evidence, and incorrect belief is explained by reference to the distorting effects of personal and social factors.

55

Evaluation

Discourse analysis has been described as a craft skill (Potter, 1997). Researchers are required to develop an analytic mentality to their data that comes with experience, although familiarity with other discourse analytic studies will aid the grasp of general principles and methodological strategies. Wood and Kroger (2000) provide a number of suggestions and analytical concepts for novice discourse analysts in order to develop their analytic resources and assist with generating interpretations of the data. These suggestions include considering what is missing from the discourse (for example, an apology or a greeting) and considering how the discourse makes the reader feel (for example, amused or angry), and trying to identify the features of the text that produced such feelings.

There are concerns that discourse might be affected by the act of **audio-recording**, in which case the data cannot be said to be naturally occurring. There are occasions when recording would not result in **bias**, for example when recording from a radio broadcast. Even if speakers are aware that their speech is being recorded, the discourse might not be affected if, for example, they are highly involved with the task at hand or if recording takes place over periods of time (Wood and Kroger, 2000).

Discourse analysis has been criticized for not attending to the non-verbal aspects of interaction. Such concerns emerge from a belief that non-verbal interaction is more trustworthy than verbal because it is less controllable and hence more likely to disclose true meaning. This position fails to recognize that language is an action and indeed that most people seem to have difficulty controlling the details of their speech. In fact discourse analysts do attend to the non-verbal. Potter's (1997) analysis of the BBC interview with Princess Diana explicitly draws attention to the significance of the Princess's non-verbal actions (head shaking and distant gazes) within the exchange.

Discourse analysis is a generic term covering a range of approaches and perhaps would not be considered by some as a method at all. However, discourse analysis has been influential in enabling researchers to expose the inconsistencies and inequities within social relationships.

Associated Concepts: Audio-Recording, Bias, Conversation Analysis, Documentary Methods, Transcription.

Key Readings

Cameron, D. (2001) *Working with Spoken Discourse*. London: Sage.

Mulkay, M. and Gilbert, G.N. (1982) 'Accounting for error: how scientists construct their social world and how they account for correct and incorrect belief', *Sociology*, 16(2): 165–183.

Phillips, L. and Jørgensen, M. (2002) *Discourse Analysis as Theory and Method*. London: Sage.

Potter, J. (1997) 'Discourse analysis as a way of analysing naturally-occurring talk', in D. Silverman (ed.), *Qualitative Research: Theory, Method and Practice.* London: Sage. pp. 144–160.

Sarangi, S., Bennert, K., Howell, L. and Clarke, A. (2003) ' "Relatively speaking": relativisation of genetic risk in counselling for predictive testing', *Health, Risk and Society,* 5(2): 155–171.

Sarangi, S. and Coulthard, M. (2000) *Discourse and Social Life.* London: Pearson.

Schiffrin, D. (1994) *Approaches to Discourse.* Oxford: Blackwell.

Torck, D. (2001) 'Voices of homeless people in street newspapers: a cross-cultural exploration', *Discourse and Society,* 12(3): 371–392.

*van Dijk, T. A. (ed.) (1985) *Handbook of Discourse Analysis* (vol. 4). London: Academic Press.

Wetherell, M., Taylor, S. and Yates, S. (2001) *Discourse Theory and Practice: A Reader.* London: Sage.

*Wood, L. and Kroger, R.O. (2000) *Doing Discourse Analysis: Methods for Studying Action in Talk and Text.* London: Sage.

Documentary Methods

Definition
The careful examination of documents and their content in order to draw conclusions about the social circumstances in which the documents are produced and read. Documentary analysis does not display a clear-cut methodology but rather encompasses a variety of approaches to documentary sources. A document may be defined as an artefact that has a written text regardless of its physical embodiment. Researchers may use a wide variety of documents including letters, official reports, administrative records, web pages, diaries and newspaper articles.

Distinctive Features
Writing is an important activity within society and accordingly documents should be important resources to social researchers. However, documents are often considered to be the preserve of historical researchers and consequently contemporary documentary materials are rarely given the attention they deserve (Platt, 1981; Prior, 2003; Scott, 1990). Documents are social products (Prior, 2003) constructed according to specific conventions, reflecting specific discourses and are dependent on collective production and consumption.

Although documentary analysis can be a research method used in isolation, it is often used in conjunction with other research methods, for example

57

as a component within an **ethnographic** study of a professional group or to supplement **interview** data.

A number of typologies of documents have been developed. For example Scott (1990) reviews documents according to authorship (personal or official) and **access** (closed, restricted or open). Documents can also be distinguished by whether they are primary or secondary sources (a primary source being material that came into existence during the study period and a secondary source being interpretations of material that came into existence during the study period). Primary sources can also be divided into deliberate sources (produced for the attention of researchers) and inadvertent sources (produced for purposes other than research).

Newspaper reports have been a key source of data for researchers working within journalism and media studies. Research in this field might, for instance, examine how categories of people (doctors, teachers, criminals) are constructed and amplified. Researchers may analyse official documents and reports produced by national governments or official documents produced at the local or institutional level, such as minutes of schools' parent and teacher meetings. Administrative records can also be a rich source of data for the researcher who is lucky enough to negotiate access to them. Such records are regularly compiled by a variety of institutions (hospitals, schools, prisons) and are used by these organizations to record factual information about their populations as well as the activities and decisions made by the institution. Documents such as these are crucial to the study of organizations as they are produced and used in social settings and are often loaded with the organization's cultural values or concerned with the organization's self-image (Atkinson and Coffey, 2004).

Jupp and Norris (1993) have reviewed three different approaches to documentary analysis. The first of these, content analysis, is really an interloper to a text on qualitative methods as it is primarily a quantitative technique using a positivistic approach. The purpose of content analysis is to describe the characteristics of the document's content by examining who says what, to whom and with what effect. The method is performed by counting occurrences of themes, words or phrases within one or more documents. The approach is objective, systematic and concerned with the surface meaning of the document rather than hidden agendas. The purpose of the second, interpretative approach to documentary data is to explore the meaning within the content. Unlike the positivist approach, the interpretative approach takes the stance that social phenomena are not objective but are actively constructed by individuals. The purpose is therefore to examine the way meaning is assigned by authors and consumers of the document, perhaps through rhetorical devices. Finally, the critical approach focuses on the relationship between the document and aspects of social structure (class, social control, power). Thus the researcher is less interested in what the text says about the biography of the author but rather in how the text exerts social control. Researchers who use this approach may use **discourse analysis** to examine the role of official documents and how they regulate social order.

Examples

There are many examples of research studies that have analysed newspaper media to explore public understanding of science and medicine. For example Conrad (2001) examined a sample of 110 stories from major US newspapers arguing that newspapers reflect an overly optimistic stance of the capabilities of genetic developments for psychiatric health. Within the articles he found three major themes, namely: that a gene for psychiatric illness exists, that it will be found and that the outcome will be good. Conrad concludes that the overly optimistic reporting stance is likely to contribute to the perpetuation of public confidence in genetic science leaving little opportunity for critical evaluation of the potential impacts. Seale (2001) explored the media portrayal of people with cancer. His article shows how media cancer stories portray a dominant struggle narrative whereby individuals demonstrate self-willed victory over the cancer. However Seale argues that the articles also reflected gender-specific behaviour which emphasized women's skills in emotional labour and self-transformation, and men's testing of pre-existing character.

Ethnographies of science, such as those by Latour and Woolgar (1986), demonstrate how scientists (like academics and policy makers) conduct much of their work through the written form. By analysing scientific documents the authors show how scientists transform opinions into facts through the selective use of vocabulary, as the scientific claim progresses from laboratory bench notebook to peer-reviewed publication.

Cicourel's (1968) classic study of the social organization of youth justice is a good example of an interpretative approach to documentary data. Cicourel examined the working practices of a range of professionals involved in youth justice (police, probation officers and court officials) and the documents produced by these agencies. In doing so he argued that the documents were vital to the process of labelling and confirming young people as 'delinquents'.

Evaluation

As with other social science methods, researchers engaged in documentary methods need to be concerned with the quality of data that are available for analysis. Scott (1990) suggests four criteria on which the validity of any document is dependent: authenticity (is the document original and genuine?), credibility (is it accurate?), representativeness (is it typical of its kind?), and meaning (is its intention clear?).

In addition to these problems of validity, researchers are also faced with problems of access. One cannot assume that just because a document exists it will be available for research purposes. Where access is restricted researchers may be left with a shortage of data or poor quality data. Conversely, if multiple documents exist of the same type, then the researcher may need to develop a **sampling** strategy in order to examine a number of typical documents.

Different types of document may possess their own conventions, specialized vocabulary and style that are often associated with professional groups. These conventions define who produced the document and who can read and share it (Atkinson and Coffey, 1997). Platt (1981) also makes the point that in order to understand a document's meaning one needs to be familiar with the 'genre' of document types (contracts, letters, adverts) so that one can understand what interpretation is implied.

Atkinson and Coffey (1997) have raised the issue of 'intertextuality', that is, documents are dependent on their relationship with other documents. For example minutes of a committee meeting will typically refer to previous minutes or a legal letter may refer to a previous letter. If taken out of context, researchers may run the risk of misinterpreting the intention of the document.

Associated Concepts: Access Negotiations, Discourse Analysis, Ethnography, Interviews, Sampling.

Key Readings

*Atkinson, P. and Coffey, A. (2004) 'Analyzing documentary realities' in D. Silverman (ed.), *Qualitative Research: Theory, Method and Practice* (2nd edn). London: Sage. pp. 56–75.

Cicourel, A.V. (1968) *The Social Organization of Juvenile Justice.* New York: Wiley.

Conrad, P. (2001) 'Genetic optimism: framing genes and mental illness in the news', *Culture, Medicine and Psychiatry,* 25(2): 225–247.

*Jupp, V. and Norris, C. (1993) 'Traditions in documentary analysis', in M. Hammersley (ed.), *Social Research: Philosophy, Politics and Practice.* London: Sage. pp. 37–51.

Latour, B. and Woolgar, S. (1986) *Laboratory Life: The Social Construction of Scientific Facts.* London: Sage.

Platt, J. (1981) 'Evidence and proof in documentary research. Some shared problems of documentary research', *Sociological Review,* 29(1): 31–52.

*Prior, L. (2003) *Using Documents in Social Research.* London: Sage.

Scott, J. (1990) *A Matter of Record: Documentary Sources in Social Research.* Cambridge: Polity Press.

Seale, C. (2001) 'Cancer heroics: a study of news reports with particular reference to gender', *Sociology,* 36(1): 107–126.

E

Electronic Data Collection

Definition
Data collection through the medium of the internet or the telephone.

Distinctive Features
As with face-to-face or depth **interviews**, researchers who conduct telephone interviews will have a general plan of enquiry and will usually have a written list of the topics they wish to cover (known as an interview schedule). An unstructured interview is similar to a guided conversation in which the interviewer introduces the general purpose and the main topics but may also pursue topics raised by the respondent.

Telephone interviews can be easily **audio-recorded** using an adapter that is available relatively cheaply. The type of equipment varies, but the adapter usually connects the telephone and the recording device (minidisc, digital or tape recorder). The voices of both the interviewee and interviewer can then be recorded and later can be **transcribed**.

Growing in popularity is computer-mediated interviewing through the use of world-wide web based interviewing software (see Chen and Hinton, 1999 for a review). The internet facilitates the communication by recording the interviews directly to a file (thereby avoiding transcription costs). The method requires the interviewer to have access to technical equipment such as frame-capable browser software and space on an internet web server that supports the technology, and the interviewee to have access to a similar browser. The web page then becomes a screen between the interviewer and interviewee. The questioning and response occurs in 'rounds' so that one participant types and sends a message and the second participant responds. Consequently the resulting transcript is more ordered than it would be from a traditional face-to-face interview. The authors draw an analogy with a telephone conversation in which one participant rings to ask a question then hangs up the phone. The respondent then rings back with their answer and again hangs up. The world-wide web also offers a graphical medium in which to conduct interviews. The interviewer may wish to tailor the pages used during the interview to the interests of his or her respondents by the creative use of animated graphics, images, fonts and colours. Although, as Chen and Hinton (1999) point out, the more complex the pages with video and audio clips, the more likely the sample will be limited because of software incompatibility.

This form of 'real-time' computer-mediated communication is different from the use of standard electronic mail for research purposes. Email interviewing (Selwyn and Robson, 1998) is an electronic version of postal interviewing using written questions and answers. Although electronic mail can be delivered at high speeds, email interviewing differs from on-line interviewing in that it is not conducted in real-time, thus limiting the immediacy and spontaneity of email communication.

Examples

Lewis, Elwyn and Wood (2003) utilized telephone interviews (alongside surveys and documentary analysis) in an evaluation study of appraisal for family doctors. The telephone interviews aimed to explore in more depth those aspects of appraisal that were important to both the appraisees and appraisers. Telephone interviews lasted approximately 15 minutes and were conducted with 50 family doctors across Wales. The telephone interviews allowed the researchers to conduct a sizeable number of interviews with individuals who were geographically dispersed. It is also likely that the respondents felt confident talking about their work on the telephone because, as with other professional groups, they were familiar with telephone discussions as an essential part of their work. Telephone interviews have been successfully conducted with other professional groups such as senior social services personnel (Wright, 2003) and school governors (Jones, 1998).

Smith (1998) accessed internet 'chat rooms' to conduct ethnographic research on members of a virtual community known as the WELL (Whole Earth 'Lectronic Link). In addition to reading selected postings, a series of on-line interviews were carried out with members of the community. By using this resource the author obtained a research sample who were, by nature, technically literate.

Evaluation

It is now rare that respondents within developed societies cannot access a telephone, but many social researchers seem to dislike conducting telephone interviews possibly because the method smacks of consumer surveys and sales campaigns. Telephone interviewing also appears to hinder the relationship between interviewer and respondent thereby inhibiting necessary **trust** and making it more difficult to elicit real feelings and experiences. Although some writers argue that respondents may be more likely to respond to sensitive questions on the phone due to a perception of increased anonymity (Babbie, 1992; Oppenheim, 1992), many people find it difficult to talk in depth about their feelings or experiences on the phone. Indeed there is perhaps a perception that telephone calls belong to the sphere of work communications and catching up with friends and family, whereas real discussions need to take place face-to-face. Perhaps because of their association with business communication, telephone interviews also tend to concentrate on the research topic in hand and respondents are less likely to take the interview into new and interesting directions.

Telephone interviews do have some key advantages over face-to-face interviews. They can significantly keep research costs down in terms of time and travel expenses. This benefit also encourages researchers to select respondents from a wider geographical area thereby possibly increasing the **generalizability** of their findings. Telephone interviews are often more suitable for short interviews, perhaps only lasting ten minutes or a quarter of an hour. They may also be a means of encouraging busy professionals to participate in the research as they might feel they have more control over terminating a short telephone interview than a face-to-face interview. Telephone interviews also have benefits in terms of increased personal safety for the researcher as they circumvent the need for a lone researcher to be interviewing in a respondent's home.

Telephone interviews can be used if probability samples are required. Researchers can easily generate a random **sample** of respondents through some form of random-digit dialing.

Interviews conducted via the world-wide web share many of the benefits of telephone interviews: namely that they enable interviews to be conducted over geographical distance and consequently reduce costs associated with travel and time. However, there are concerns about lost aspects of communication and interpretation in the absence of paralinguistic cues. The method is also dependent on written language rather than spoken language and consequently is more likely to be in a more formal register. Computer-mediated interviewing also requires that the interviewees are able to access the technology, that they are amenable to it, and that the interviewer has the skills to use the technology.

Associated Concepts: Audio-Recording, Generalization, Interviews, Sampling, Transcription, Trust.

Key Readings

Babbie, E. (1992) *The Practice of Social Research*. Belmont, CA: Wandsworth.

*Chen, P. and Hinton, S.M. (1999) 'Real-time interviewing using the world wide web', *Sociological Research Online*, 4(3). http://www.socresonline.org.uk/socresonline/4/3/1.html

Fielding, N. and Thomas, H. (2001) 'Qualitative interviewing', in N. Gilbert (ed.), *Researching Social Life*. London: Sage. pp. 123–145.

Jones, J.L. (1998) 'Managing the induction of newly appointed governors', *Educational Research*, 40(3): 329–352.

Lewis, M., Elwyn, G. and Wood, F. (2003) 'Appraisal of family doctors: an evaluation study', *British Journal of General Practice*, 53: 454–461.

Oppenheim, A.N. (1992) *Questionnaire Design, Interviewing and Attitude Measurement*. New York: Basic Books.

Selwyn, N. and Robson, K. (1998) 'Using email as a research tool', *Social Research Update*, 21, Summer.

Smith, M.A. (1998) 'Voices from the WELL: the logic of the virtual commons'. http://www.sscnet.ucla.edu/soc/csoc/papers/voices/Voices.htm

Wright, F. (2003) 'Discrimination against self-funding residents in long term residential care in England', *Ageing and Society*, 23(5): 603–624.

Ethics

Definition

Ethics are guidelines or sets of principles for good professional practice, which serve to advise and steer researchers as they conduct their work. The word ethics is derived from the Greek word *ethos* meaning a person's character, nature or disposition. Ethics is a branch of philosophy which is concerned with thinking about morality, integrity and the distinction between right and wrong.

Distinctive Features

Social scientists typically engage in researching controversial and sensitive subjects and consequently it is inevitable that ethical problems will emerge from their research. This does not mean that researchers should avoid sensitive topics, but rather the methods by which the research is conducted should be ethically justifiable.

Professional ethics relate to the willingness of a profession to self-regulate the actions of its members so as to protect the interests of the public. Codes of good practice define the rights and responsibilities of researchers and their relationships with their research subjects, employers and funding bodies.

However, conducting ethical research is sometimes not a simple matter of applying prescribed rules that provide solutions for major methodological decisions. Ethical dilemmas may arise if researchers are faced with competing values and a choice between different methodological strategies, where none of those strategies can realise all those values in practice. Indeed, in research involving human subjects, there can often be conflicts between various parties: the subject, the researcher, the researcher's discipline, the funding body and society itself. Furthermore ethics do not present themselves just at the crucial junctures when we take significant decisions and actions, but rather pervade our everyday actions and decisions that we make almost imperceptibly during the course of our research.

The initial impetus for written guidelines for ethical research came in the field of biomedicine. These guidelines included the Nuremberg Code of 1947 (established to prevent further atrocities such as those conducted under the guise of medical science under the Nazi regime) and the World Medical Association's Declaration of Helsinki (1964), revised in 1975, 1983, 1989 and again in 2000. From the 1960s social scientists and professional bodies in individual disciplines have developed their own ethical guidelines based upon these early codes. For example, guidelines have been produced by the British Psychological Society, the British Sociological Association, the British Educational Research Association, the British Society of Criminology and the American Anthropological Association. Rather than serve as a set of inflexible rules, the guidelines are intended to provide advice to researchers and encourage them to take responsibility for their own ethical conduct. In doing so they recognize that researchers often face ethical dilemmas and that digressions from the guidelines should be the result of careful deliberation rather than ignorance. The guidance from each discipline varies in detail but the principles are common to all. These principles can be summarized into three main categories: professional integrity (including recognizing professional boundaries, the need to disseminate research results and protecting research from misuse); responsibilities to research participants (including informed consent, protection of identity and the principle of 'no harm'); and responsibilities to funders and sponsors (including clarifying obligations, guarding privileged information and not accepting restrictions on research outcomes).

Within the UK one of the obligations on researchers is that they process research data according to the requirements of the Data Protection Act (1998). The Act provides guidance for individuals and organizations working within the public and private sector to ensure that data (written data, **electronic data** and **audio recordings**) are handled appropriately. Stipulations include that data are processed for limited purposes, are accurate, secure and not kept for longer than is necessary. Countries other than the UK may have different data protection laws.

65

Due to the abundance of research in the field of medical science, patients are one sector of the public who are frequently subjected to research. Research Ethics Committees are convened to provide independent advice to participants, researchers, funders/sponsors and health-care organizations on the extent to which research proposals comply with recognized ethical standards. Their objectives are to ensure ethical standards in medical research are maintained and to protect research subjects' mental and physical well-being. Their remit covers research involving NHS patients, foetal material, the recently deceased, access to medical records, and NHS staff, premises and facilities. Local Research Ethics Committees (LRECs) cover the geographical boundaries of Health Authority Areas, but for large-scale studies conducted on a number of sites researchers may also submit their research to Multi-Centre Research Ethics Committees (MRECs). The committees comprise both professional membership (including representation from medical specialities and professions allied to medicine such as pharmacy and nursing) and lay members who are unconnected professionally with health care. The Central Office for Research Ethics Committees (COREC; http://www.corec.org.uk) offers guidance to researchers on when and how to apply to committees as well as guidance on the content and style of patient information sheets and patient consent forms. Typically the ethical committee submission forms are designed for quantitative, experimentally based research such as is characteristic of pharmaceutical trials. However ethical approval is also a prerequisite for qualitative research conducted within the NHS and the COREC guidance is of considerable use.

Many universities also require that proposed research should obtain ethical approval from the University Ethics Committee. The purpose of these committees is to assess the ethical propriety of all research on human beings undertaken in or under the auspices of the institution irrespective of whether or not the research is being conducted by staff or students. Submitting an application for ethical approval should not just be considered an unnecessary administrative hurdle, as researchers who fail to obtain ethical approval may not be protected by the university should a grievance claim arise from the research. Individual institutions should be contacted for guidance on whether a research project requires ethical approval.

Examples

Perhaps the most infamous research in terms of disputed ethical violation is Humphrey's 1970 study of homosexual behaviour (see **covert research** in this volume for a full discussion). Other examples of covert research are perhaps less notorious but nevertheless lead to problematic situations for the researcher. Simon Holdaway's (1982) account of covert participant observation during his employment as a police officer provides a good example. Holdaway argues that covert research was necessary as, due to the protective occupational culture of the police, senior officers would have refused him permission to conduct the research. Furthermore, as Holdaway's observations often focused on situations when police officers broke rules of conduct (for example unwarranted levels of physical force when handling suspects), it is likely that police officers would alter their behaviour if aware they were being observed for research purposes. In the account Holdaway reflects both on the advantages of being a participant observer due to his understanding of the occupational culture, but also of the stress of conducting the research. Stress arose from his fear of exposure, needing to remain on the fringes of unacceptable behaviour and ultimately from his concerns about harming his subjects during publication and dissemination.

Other authors have demonstrated that ethical dilemmas also present themselves in more subtle ways and permeate almost every aspect of social research work from **access negotiation**, throughout fieldwork to dissemination. For example, Burgess's (1989) **ethnographic** study of a comprehensive school demonstrated that there are many 'grey areas' when trying to reconcile ethical codes with the reality of daily fieldwork. Although Burgess had secured access to staff appointment interviews through the school governors and the headteacher, he reflects that candidates were probably unlikely to object to his presence knowing that access had been granted by the very people who were conducting the interview. Burgess also demonstrates that, particularly in ethnographic research, it is not always possible to inform one's subjects at the beginning of the study exactly what data will be collected and how they will be used. Thus even when research activities are overt rather than covert it can be problematic to claim that consent has really been given.

Evaluation

It is perhaps worth evaluating some of the ethical codes relating to researchers' responsibilities towards research subjects in more detail, as it is these principles that receive most attention, concern and criticism. The principle of informed consent requires that, as far as practically possible, it is the responsibility of the researcher to brief participants in appropriate detail and in terms which are meaningful to the lay public about the following: the nature of the research, what would be required from their participation, who is undertaking and financing it, why it is being undertaken and how it will be disseminated and used. There are, however, situations when the principle of informed consent may be vulnerable to contravention. For example, as discussed in this volume under 'covert research', the decision to withhold informed consent may be defended and justified in some circumstances, such as when it may alter the behaviour of research subjects. However, as Burgess (1989) demonstrates, even when the methodology is not covert, there may be situations where research subjects feel an obligation to participate despite the best efforts of the researcher to advise them of their rights to refuse. Such obligations may stem from a fear of being thought to be obstructive or where they are fearful of certain services or privileges being removed from them. The resulting 'assent' rather than 'consent' may be particularly prevalent when researching vulnerable or powerless groups such as elderly persons, the young and those with a physical or mental disability.

The principle of protection of participants' identities also poses its own challenges to qualitative researchers. There are, of course, effective ways of protecting identities through secure data storage, removal of identifiers, amendments to biographical details and the use of pseudonyms (applicable to names of individuals, places and organizations). However, there may be circumstances, for example in ethnographic research on scientific communities, when it is possible for other scientists working within the field, and possibly others outside of the core community, to attribute views or even verbatim extracts to individuals – a situation known as 'deductive disclosure'. In such circumstances it is prudent for the researcher to anticipate threats to confidentiality and to inform participants of the difficulties in disguising their identities.

The principle of 'no harm' to participants reminds researchers of their duty to be aware of the possible research consequences to their subjects. Even having given informed consent, participants may feel the research experience a negative one, particularly if there have been intrusions into their personal worlds. A respondent could feel deceived and cheated by the **trusted** researcher, or may fear for their reputation if they are recognized in the researcher's account. There are further consequences as harmful research brings social science as a discipline into disrepute and could limit access for other social researchers wishing to conduct future research. While there are always potential risks for subjects, research participation is not devoid of gains. Respondents may benefit from expressing their views and sharing their story with a sympathetic listener. The research experience may therefore help respondents to make sense of their own experiences and feel they have participated in something that they believe to be important. Social scientists often justify incursions into private lives on the basis that an understanding of social issues is the starting point towards lessening social problems. There is an obvious conflict here between the right to know (defended on the basis of benefits to society) and the right to privacy (defended on the rights of the individual). However, social scientists themselves disagree about in which circumstances a violation of ethical principles are justified.

Associated Concepts: Access Negotiations, Audio-Recording, Covert Research, Electronic Data Collection, Ethnography, Fieldwork Relationships, Trust.

Key Readings

Burgess, R.G. (1989) 'Grey areas: ethical dilemmas in educational ethnography', in R.G. Burgess (ed.), *The Ethics of Educational Research*. Basingstoke: Taylor and Falmer. pp. 60–76.

Dingwall, R. (1980) 'Ethics and ethnography', *Sociological Review*, 28: 871–881.

Holdaway, S. (1982) ' "An inside job": a case study of covert research on the police', in M. Bulmer (ed.), *Social Research Ethics: An Examination of the Merits of Covert Participant Observation*. London: Macmillan. pp. 59–80.

*Homan, R. (1991) *The Ethics of Social Research*. New York: Longman.

Humphreys, L. (1970) *Tearoom Trade*. London: Duckworth.

Kimmel, A. (1988) *Ethics and Values in Applied Social Research*. London: Sage.

Laine, M. de (2000) *Fieldwork Participation and Practice: Ethics and Dilemmas in Qualitative Research*. London: Sage.

Lee-Treweek, G. and Linkogle, S. (2000) *Danger in the Field: Risk and Ethics in Social Research*. London: Routledge.

Rowe, H. (2000) *Data Protection Act 1988: A Practical Guide*. London: Tolley.

Useful Websites for Ethical Guidance

American Anthropological Association – www.aaanet.org/committees/ethics/ethcode.htm

British Educational Research Association – www.bera.ac.uk/publications/guides

British Psychology Society – www.bps.org.uk/about/rules5.cfm

British Society of Criminology – www.britsoccrim.org/ethics.htm

British Sociological Association – www.britsoc.org.uk/about/ethic.htm

Central Office for Research Ethics Committees (COREC) – www.corec.org.uk

Declaration of Helsinki – www.holybrook.co.uk/Pdfs/helsinki.pdf

Ethnography

Definition

The description and interpretation of a culture or social group. Literally the word means the description (graphy) of cultures (ethno). The purpose is to provide an in-depth study of a culture that includes behaviour, interactions, language and artefacts. The aim is to understand another way of life from the native point of view by focusing on ordinary, everyday behaviour.

Distinctive Features

Ethnography has its roots within the social anthropology of pre-industrial exotic societies (among the most notable studies are those by Boas, Mead, Malinowski and Evans-Pritchard). During the early twentieth century the Chicago School extended the range of social anthropology, making detailed examinations of social problems within urban settings. These produced clear portraits of real life in the city with studies on boys' gangs, professional thieves and such like. Later the Chicago School turned its attention to observational studies among professional groups and organizations, such as studies of TB wards (Roth, 1963) and medical schools (Becker et al., 1961).

There are a number of methodological commitments associated with ethnography. First, ethnographic research emphasizes the need to think oneself into the perspective of the members of the social group that one is studying. This involves an empathic process that Weber termed *verstehen*. One of the best ways for the ethnographer to achieve this is to become immersed within the natural setting, transcending objectivity and distance or, as Geertz (1988: 6) recommends, 'close in contact with far out lives'. Ethnography requires prolonged periods of fieldwork in order for the researcher to infiltrate and be accepted within the setting.

Second, ethnography has a commitment to naturalistic enquiry. This means that people are studied in everyday settings interacting as they would normally and naturally do. A consequence of this commitment is that ethnography may arguably sometimes require **covert** research so that the ethnographer does not influence the social group and the setting.

Thirdly, the ethnographic tradition recognizes the relativistic status of knowledge in which there is no one objective reality but rather a number of realities. Ethnography is an active process during which a particular aspect of the world has been produced through selective observations and interpretations.

There is not one single ethnographic method, rather it comprises a number of different data collection methods including unstructured **interviews** (including **life histories** and **narrative** interviews), observations and **documentary methods**. The ethnographic tradition tends to reject formal data collection protocols, preferring to adopt whatever is considered suitable and useful: 'the ethnographic researcher participates, overtly or covertly, in people's daily lives for an extended period of time, watching what happens, listening to what is said, asking questions; in fact collecting whatever data are available to throw light on the issues with which he or she is concerned' (Hammersley and Atkinson, 1995: 2).

Spradley (1979) provides guidance on the conduct of ethnographic interviews, stating that while they display features of a friendly conversation they also contain striking differences. For example turn-taking is less balanced, the ethnographer regularly repeats what the informant has said, the ethnographer expresses interest and ignorance more often and finally the ethnographer encourages the informant to expand on what he or she is saying.

Observation is perhaps the key instrument in acquiring ethnographic knowledge (Spradley, 1980). Researchers may observe actions/interactions, behaviour and listen to conversations while simultaneously observing the context (particularly the time and location) in which these actions are undertaken. One of the main debates surrounding observational research is the extent to which the fieldworker should become a part of the social world that he or she is studying. There is a spectrum of involvement from complete participant, through participant observer and observer as participant, to complete observer. Some authors (for example, Hammersley and Atkinson, 1995) warn against the problems of over-rapport or 'going native', as the purpose is to study the culture not to provide the group with a new member. Consequently researchers often adopt a middle ground, balancing involvement with detachment, familiarity with strangeness. Observation is generally aided by observational schedules and research diaries. Observational schedules may include grids or charts in which the fieldworker notes what was said and done and with what frequency along with a description of the physical setting. **Research diaries** record **fieldnotes** and the researcher's analytic and methodological memoranda, including the documentation of working hypotheses and reflections about the implications of his or her own role within the research process.

Different methods of data collection may throw light on different aspects of the research. For example interviews enable researchers to access their respondents' descriptions, rationalizations and reflections about their behaviour, but observational data enable the researcher to tap into the more chaotic, non-rational behaviour that may be less likely to be disclosed in an interview (McKeganey et al., 1988). Observation therefore enables researchers to access what their subjects actually do, rather than what they say they do.

Good **fieldwork relationships** are essential in ethnographic research as establishing a good rapport with one's research subjects has an effect on what one is told and allowed to observe. Gaining support from the 'gatekeepers' of the social group is generally the key to successful **access**. Gatekeepers can assist in providing informal sponsorship, vouching for the researcher's credibility, introducing the researcher to others within the field and steering the researcher towards interesting insights.

Ethnographic research can raise certain **ethical** problems particularly if the research focuses on deviant sub-cultures such as drug users. Ferrell and Hamm (1998) have developed a typology of ethnographic research **dangers for fieldworkers** including danger from physical violence, emotional strain, and legal danger arising from 'guilty knowledge' of clandestine activities.

Ethnographic **writing** usually incorporates the description of the social group alongside the interpretations of the social life. Usually starting with a description of the setting, ethnographic writing then identifies themes and patterns in the data before extending the analysis to interpretation and the generation of theory (Wolcott, 1990). Ethnographic writing also tends to recognize the personal and emotional aspects of fieldwork as it reflects the intimate relations between the setting, participants and the self (Coffey, 1999). The close involvement of the researcher within the culture requires that the researcher remains **reflexive** about his or her role and its effects on the field.

Examples

Ethnographic studies of science typically employ careful and detailed observations about the small and seemingly insignificant actions of scientists. Science ethnographies have attempted to demystify the scientific process by studying how scientific groups fabricate a world for themselves and how they live within that world. Perhaps the most celebrated science ethnography was that conducted by Latour and Woolgar (1986) of endocrinologists working within the Salk Institute. By turning their attention to scientific work undertaken by relatively junior but technically competent benchworkers, they attempted to reveal the 'soft underbelly of science'. Thus they examined how scientists negotiate by means of 'inscriptions' (tables of data, graphs, papers) and the process of reification that involves the transformation of everyday uncertainties into facts.

Ethnography has also been an essential method for uncovering the situated meaning of crime and deviance and identifying the social and cultural forces that draw people into criminal or risk behaviour. For example, Taylor (1993) used ethnographic methods to study a female drug-injecting community and Monaghan (2001) used ethnographic methods to explore a bodybuilding subculture, focusing on how bodybuilders try to maintain competent social identities while managing the risks of using steroids and other physique-enhancing drugs. Such studies therefore explore activities that, to a large degree, are constructed collectively out of the common experiences of participants and out of shared cultural codes.

Ethnographies have also been conducted within organizations and professional groups. For example Atkinson (1995) explored the construction of medical opinion among haematologists by examining the ways in which professional interaction and language served to mediate medical knowledge. In particular Atkinson studied the ritualized occasions of medical work such as case presentations and student teaching, both at the microscope and at the bedside, to illustrate how practical medical knowledge is produced and reproduced.

An example of an ethnographic community study is Wight's (1993) exploration of material lifestyle in an industrial village in central Scotland. The study emphasized the importance of appropriate consumption (in particular alcohol consumption) in maintaining one's respectability and the interconnectedness of drinking, masculinity and employment. Wight and his co-worker spent three years living within the village and describe how, while initially their participation in the culture was often self-conscious and contrived, it became increasingly spontaneous and eventually they became accepted by most of their informants as unthreatening.

Evaluation

Some ethnographers argue that researchers should belong to the same group as those they study, or at least should have some degree of insider knowledge in order to speak from a position of authority on the subject. Research subjects' responses to the research will be partly based on their assumptions about who the investigators are and what social categories they belong to (age, gender and social background). Social distance between the researcher and the respondent can result in lack of trust, a lack of understanding, or not knowing enough about the phenomena under study to ask the right questions. Other sociologists argue that there is no need for the ethnographer to acquire an expert knowledge of drug use, science or whatever. The anthropological position of strangeness can thus be maximized so as not to take for granted what an insider would consider to be routine.

It is very difficult to determine the exact direction of an ethnographic study during the planning stages, and consequently researchers are required to adopt a flexible approach to research design that will operate throughout the project (Hammersley and Atkinson, 1995). During the pre-fieldwork and early fieldwork stages the ethnographer might develop a set of theoretical questions or issues (foreshadowed problems) to be explored and might specify the range and types of settings in which research might be usefully carried out. However changes to the original theoretical question are frequent and may be due to realization of early erroneous assumptions or because they are not able to answer the question within the given context.

Ethnography has sometimes been dismissed as subjective and lacking scientific rigour. Furthermore, as research sites for ethnographic studies are chosen more for the insights that they generate rather than for their typicality, ethnographies (as with **case studies**) are sometimes criticized for lack of **generalizability**. However, advocates of the method claim that only ethnographic research can capture the true meaning of social processes and human activity which would remain hidden by other methods such as questionnaire surveys.

There have also been appeals that ethnography should be made more relevant to social and political practice. This may be achieved either by making ethnography more generalizable to other populations or by ensuring that it has more theoretical relevance. But, as Hammersley (1992) points out, judgements of relevance are themselves contestable and any relationship between ethnographic research and practice is likely to be general and indirect rather than offering practical solutions.

Postmodernist writers (for example Denzin, 1994) argue that the modernist attitude that the empirical world can be studied objectively by qualitative methods is no longer sustainable. Thus the postmodern critique of ethnography has encouraged a scepticism about the realist claims of an author to represent the truth about the social world. The suppression of authorial authority allows multiple interpretations none of which lay claim to a privileged status, and has encouraged intense levels of **reflexivity**. Realist commitments (the idea that there is a reality independent of the researcher, and the researcher's aim is to come to know and produce accounts that reflect that one reality) have therefore been challenged by relativism (the idea that people construct their social world). However if ethnographic research is in itself a social activity, and therefore socially constructed, ethnographers create social worlds rather than representing some independent reality. The ethnographer's commitment to relativism is therefore in conflict with his or her commitment to realism. Hammersley (1992) has suggested a solution to this conflict is to find some middle ground between the two extremes and adopt a position of 'subtle realism'. Subtle realism requires that knowledge claims must be assessed on the plausibility and credibility of competing claims. If ethnographic accounts are required to represent reality not to reproduce it, there can be multiple and non-contradictory descriptions of the same phenomena.

Associated Concepts: Access Negotiations, Case Study, Covert Research, Dangerous Fieldwork, Documentary Methods, Ethics, Fieldnotes, Fieldwork Relationships, Generalization, Interviews, Life History (*see* Oral History), Narratives, Reflexivity, Research Diary, Writing.

Key Readings

Atkinson, P. (1995) *Medical Talk and Medical Work: A Liturgy of the Clinic.* London: Sage.

*Atkinson, P., Coffey, A. and Delamont, S. (2001) *Handbook of Ethnography.* London: Sage.

Becker, H.S., Geer, B., Hughes, E.C. and Strauss, A.L. (1961) *Boys in White: Student Culture in Medical School.* Chicago: University of Chicago Press.

Charlsworth, M., Farrall, L., Stokes, T. and Turnball, D. (1989) *Life Among the Scientists: An Anthropological Study of* an *Australian Scientific Community*. Oxford: Oxford University Press.

Coffey, A. (1999) *The Ethnographic Self*. London: Sage.

Denzin, N.K. (1994) 'Postmodernism and deconstructionism', in D.R. Dickens and A. Fontana (eds), *Postmodernism and Social Inquiry*. London: UCL Press. pp. 182–202.

Ellen, R.G. (ed.) (1984) *Ethnographic Research: A Guide to General Conduct*. London: Academic Press.

Ferrell, J. and Hamm, M. (1998) *Ethnography at the Edge: Crime, Deviance and Field Research*. Boston: Northeastern University Press.

Geertz, C. (1988) *Works and Lives: The Anthropologist as Author*. Cambridge: Polity.

Hammersely, M. (1992) *What's Wrong with Ethnography?* London: Routledge.

*Hammersley, M. and Atkinson, P. (1995) *Ethnography: Principles in Practice* (2nd edn). London: Routledge.

Latour, B. and Woolgar, S. (1986) *Laboratory Life: The Social Construction of Scientific Facts*. (2nd edn). London: Sage.

McKeganey, N., McPherson, I. and Hunter, D.J. (1988) 'How they decide: exploring professional decision making', *Research Policy and Planning*, 6: 15–19.

Monaghan, L.F. (2001) *Bodybuilding, Drugs and Risk*. London: Routledge.

Roth, J. (1963) *Timetables*. New York: Bobbs-Merrill.

Spradley, J.P. (1979) *The Ethnographic Interview*. Orlando: Holt, Rinehart and Winston.

Spradley, J.P. (1980) *Participant Observation*. New York: Holt, Rinehart and Winston.

Taylor, A. (1993) *Women Drug Users: An Ethnography of a Female Injecting Community*. Oxford: Clarendon Press.

Wight, D. (1993) *Workers Not Wasters: Masculine Respectability, Consumption and Employment in Central Scotland*. Edinburgh: Edinburgh University Press.

Wolcott, H.F. (1990) *Writing up Qualitative Research*. London: Sage.

Ethnomethodology

Definition

Ethnomethodology literally means 'people's methods' but may be more fully translated as 'the study of people's methods for making sense of the world'. The central aim for ethnomethodologists is to describe and analyse the practical procedures that members use to make sense of the social world. The intention is therefore to focus upon identifying and understanding the methods which people employ to decide whether or not something is real.

Distinctive Features

Ethnomethodology is a branch of sociology usually associated with Harold Garfinkel, although the starting point is in the **phenomenological** writings of Alfred Schutz, since ethnomethodology might be deemed to be an exploration of the implications of Schutz's arguments about the nature of social knowledge.

Ethnomethodology also has similarities with **symbolic interactionism** which is concerned with the ways in which people define and share meanings of the social world through interaction. Like symbolic interactionism, ethnomethodology is also concerned with interactions, but ethnomethodology focuses on the *methods* by which people make sense of social worlds.

Ethnomethodologists therefore examine the ways in which people go about their daily lives (at work, at home, at leisure etc.). Ethnomethodologists argue that in order to organize action, people need to make frequent decisions as to what is 'unquestionably true' for them. Popular examples are that if people switch their computer on it is unquestionably true that poisonous gas will not emit from the hard disc, or if they make a cup of coffee it is unquestionably true that they will find it bitter without sugar. These decisions (to switch the computer on, to put sugar in one's coffee and so on), and taken-for-granted assumptions, pervade everyday activities.

A key feature of ethnomethodology is that it is concerned with people's practical actions in situated contexts. Using one of the previous examples of coffee making, the situated context may change if the coffee bean is a different brand to one's usual coffee or the coffee is made in a different kitchen. Therefore the practical situatedness of actions still provides for the possibility of improvisation in even the most routine activities. Ethnomethodologists are then able to study how people work out a course of action while they are engaged in the activity.

There have been two main ways in which ethnomethodology has been applied. The first relates to the order (and disruption) of daily life. It is a favoured technique among ethnomethodologists to temporarily disrupt the world which people take for granted and see how they react. For example, Garfinkel asked his students to behave at home as if they were lodgers and note the reaction of family members. The consequent response of surprise followed by hostility was an illustration of the fragility of daily social order.

The second type of ethnomethodological investigation is **conversation analysis** which is the study of the social organization of talk. Conversation analysis originated as a sub-set of ethnomethodological studies and is now best treated as a separate but related area of research.

Examples

One of the most famous examples of ethnomethodology is Garfinkel's study of jurors' work (Garfinkel, 1967). Garfinkel demonstrated how jurors are engaged in a number of decisions: deciding between what is fact and fiction, what is credible and what is calculated, what is personal opinion and what is publicly agreed. In short they decide 'facts' among alternative claims. Garfinkel argued that jurors achieve this by comparing the consistency of alternative claims with their own common-sense models and in doing so become practical reasoners. Garfinkel did this by describing the rules of decision making that were used by jurors in their daily lives and the rules of decision making within their official lives which they had learnt from instructions from the court, literature and other media. Garfinkel observed slight modifications that jurors made from the former type of decision rules to the latter and consequently described the process that people go through to 'become a juror'.

Evaluation

One of the key criticisms of ethnomethodology is that in focusing on face-to-face interactions it ignores, and arguably denies, the existence and importance of wider complex social systems such as class structure and social norms. As Cuff, Sharrock and Francis (2003) explain, ethnomethodology cannot explain the prolific development of software engineering in the western world. Therefore, it is argued, rather than being a comprehensive sociology, ethnomethodology can only aspire to be a sociological specialism which focuses on the details of face-to-face interactions. Ethnomethodologists have responded to this charge by arguing that their neglect of the wider social context is the result of their decision to treat as important that which their subjects are orientated to (everyday action). And it is undeniable that the constitutive practices of everyday life were under-researched before the development of ethnomethodological studies. It should be noted that one early methodological technique – the disruption of everyday reality in order to lay bare how it is constituted – would not be sanctioned by twenty-first century ethics committees: 'Children, do not try this at home!'

Associated Concepts: Conversation Analysis, Phenomenological Methods, Symbolic Interactionism.

Key Readings

Boden, D. and Zimmerman, D.H. (1991) *Talk and Structure: Studies in Ethnomethodology and Conversational Analysis.* Cambridge: Polity Press.

Cuff, E.C., Sharrock, W.W. and Francis, D.W. (2003) *Perspectives in Sociology.* London: Routledge.

*Francis, D. and Hester, S. (2004) *An Invitation to Ethnomethodology:*

Language, Society and Interaction. London: Sage.

Garfinkel, H. (1967) *Studies in Ethnomethodology.* Englewood Cliffs, NJ: Prentice Hall.

Livingston, E. (1987) *Making Sense of Ethnomethodology.* London: Routledge and Kegan Paul.

Lynch, M. (1993) *Scientific Practice and Ordinary Action: Ethnomethodology and Social Studies of Science.* Cambridge: Cambridge University Press.

Feminist Methods

Definition
Research methods which are specific to promoting feminist principles. A feminist research framework would be concerned with more than just how data are collected, but also what research questions are studied, which methods are used, how the data are analysed, how the results are written and for what audience.

Distinctive Features
Delamont (2003) reviews the history of feminist research methods, stating that the debates surrounding this area have been 'angry, far-reaching and long-lasting' (p. 60). In brief, feminist researchers began to publish their concerns about the implications of the sexist choice of research questions, methods and analysis during the 1980s (Clegg, 1985; Harding, 1986; Oakley, 1981; and Roberts, 1981). The authors were promoting their ideas following a time when sexist assumptions were rife within research. For example, researchers were focusing on research questions which were purported to be universal to the sexes but which actually only related to men, were building gender assumptions into their research instruments, and were even leaving data on women unanalysed, unpublished or dismissed as claims rather than facts. Since the 1990s calls for feminist research have reduced somewhat, probably reflecting the fact that there is much less sexism generally within society and consequently there is less of an issue within contemporary non-feminist studies.

Feminist researchers have argued that, as knowledge is power, research should have a political goal in addition to purely providing new knowledge for knowledge's sake. Consequently feminist methodologists question the value-free approach of positivist research, arguing instead that research should be concerned with values, morality and the improvement of society. Social researchers would therefore have a duty to reflect upon the question of **'whose side are we on?'** Such a standpoint has obvious links with other radical emancipatory methods and social movements with roots in the ideals of justice and a commitment to social change, such as gay and lesbian studies and critical race studies.

The traditional male approach to research is said to be characterized by detachment, objectivity and a hierarchical relationship between the researcher and the researched. This has led to calls for an explicitly feminist science in which, to quote an oft-repeated mantra, 'feminist research is by women, on women, for women'. Feminist methods are consequently characterized by subjectivity, personal involvement and mutual benefit. For example, Oakley (1981) discusses the traditional advice given to interviewers that they should avoid answering respondents' questions for fear of revealing their own beliefs and values and consequently biasing the data. For Oakley, having developed **trust** and even lasting friendships with her respondents, the traditional objective approach is morally indefensible. Furthermore, Oakley argues that it is only by investing one's own identity in the fieldwork relationship that a researcher can gain access to the richness of data afforded in a mutual relationship of trust.

Examples

Probably the most famous example of feminist research is provided by Oakley (1980) in her powerful study of transition to motherhood. This study is discussed in this volume under the entry for **fieldwork relationships**. An alternative example is provided by Finch (1984) who discusses two studies of interviewing: first, 95 wives of clergymen and their relationship with their husbands' work; and second, her research on 48 women using and working in a pre-school playgroup. Both studies focused on the women's identity and their experience of marriage and motherhood. Drawing on Oakley's (1979) previous advocacy of feminist research methods, Finch (1984) also discusses the special character of the research relationship in which women are able to talk to other women in an informal way and that the only morally defensible way for a feminist to interview women is in a relationship of non-hierarchy in which the researcher reveals some of her identity. Similarly to Oakley, Finch was surprised at the readiness with which these women would talk to her about their private lives (although she reflects that her own declaration of being a clergy-wife enhanced the trust between researcher and respondent), and also at the hospitality that was offered to her (cakes and home-grown cabbages). Finch also reflects that the social isolation of many of her respondents was also partly instrumental in their willingness to share their stories with a friendly face. However, Finch goes on to discuss the ethical issues and potential exploitation that may arise from such research, in particular how her data could be used against the collective interest of women. Finch was concerned that her data seemed to be reflecting the idea that women were content with a supportive role to their husband's work, or that her pre-school study reinforced a view that working-class women were inadequate and incompetent childcarers. For Finch, as with other feminist researchers, there is an emotional as well as an intellectual commitment to promoting the interests of women.

Evaluation

Because of its commitment to subjectivity, feminist methods are almost always associated with qualitative methods, although Maynard (1994) has questioned whether qualitative methods must be used for the research to be true to the experiences of women. Other feminists, such as MacDonald (1994), have also been opposed to the idea of an anti-positivist feminist method due to their belief that political goals are best achieved on the basis of objective data.

In a review article of Anne Oakley's work on childbirth and motherhood, Reid (1983) makes the claim that Oakley's feminist approach, while being received enthusiastically both within and outside of academia, is actually poor science. Reid's main criticisms are that the outwardly feminist stance makes the research vulnerable to **bias** and indeed, as Reid demonstrates, Oakley makes her biases plain. The resulting research therefore becomes more of a political state-ment than a piece of scientific reporting. More specifically, Reid is sceptical that Oakley's cosy relationships with her respondents, in which friendships were maintained over years, were developed purely on the basis of gender. She muses that if Oakley had included a broader sample in which working-class women were more fully represented, then the bonds of friendship might not have been so sustainable. Developing her argument, Reid is also critical of Oakley's claims (Oakley, 1981) that there is a specific methodology which can be identified as fem-inist. On this point Reid challenges the view that women have exclusive rights to be sensitive researchers capable of feelings of equality and non-exploitation, as well as challenging the claim that the principles of the women's movement can be directly translated into a research methodology.

Associated Concepts: Bias, Fieldwork Relationships, Trust, Uses of Qualitative Research, 'Whose Side Are We On?'

Key Readings

Clegg, S. (1985) 'Feminist methodology', *Quality and Quantity*, 19(1): 83–97.

Delamont, S. (2003) *Feminist Sociology.* London: Sage.

Finch, J. (1984) 'It's great to have someone to talk to: the ethics and politics of interviewing women', in C. Bell and H. Roberts (eds), *Social Researching: Politics, Problems and Practice.* London: Routledge and Kegan Paul. pp. 70–87.

Harding, S. (1986) *The Science Question in Feminism.* Milton Keynes: Open University Press.

MacDonald, L. (1994) *The Women Founders of the Social Sciences*. Ottawa: Carleton University Press.

*Maynard, M. (1994) 'Methods, practice and epistemology', in M. Maynard and J. Purvis (eds), *Researching Women's Lives from a Feminist Perspective*. London: Taylor and Francis. pp. 10–26.

Oakley, A. (1980) *Women Confined: Towards a Sociology of Childbirth*. London: Martin Robertson.

Oakley, A. (1981) 'Interviewing women: a contradiction in terms', in H. Roberts (ed.), *Doing Feminist Research*. London: Routledge and Kegan Paul. pp. 30–61.

Oakley, A. (2000) *Experiments in Knowing: Gender and Method in the Social Sciences*. Cambridge: Polity Press.

Reid, M.E. (1983) 'A feminist sociological imagination? Reading Anne Oakley', *Sociology of Health and Illness*, 5(1): 83–94.

Roberts, H. (1981) *Doing Feminist Research*. London: Routledge and Kegan Paul.

Fieldnotes

Definition
Fieldnotes are used by researchers to record observations and fragments of remembered speech. Although researchers may use other means of recording (such as video) and of other forms of data (such as interview transcripts), fieldnotes remain one of the primary analytic materials used in **ethnography**.

Distinctive Features
Fieldnotes were first used as a primary analytic material within the discipline of anthropology. The pioneers of modern anthropology did not make their fieldnotes public. Indeed, the private nature of fieldnotes led to a frisson of scandal when the fieldnotes of Anthropological Founding Fathers were subsequently published revealing a backstage at odds with the anthropologists' public personae. The private status of fieldnotes has also meant that there was, until recently, a shortage of models for novice ethnographers to follow and some mystery about the kind of coverage that should be aimed at.

Spradley has suggested a checklist of eight items that the researcher should bear in mind in writing fieldnotes: the space or location observed, the objects that are co-present at the location, the actors, the activity observed, the component actions, the wider event in which the activities occur, the sequencing of activities over time, the goal that the actor is striving for, and the feelings expressed (Spradley, 1980: 78). Such a checklist should not be followed slavishly, but it does serve as a useful reminder that fieldnotes should aim for detail and for the kind of multi-layered, richly contextualized description termed **thick description**. Too often the ethnographer stares at his or her laptop after the rigours of fieldwork, tired by the past emotional labour of maintaining good fieldwork relations, seduced by the siren voices of family and friends offering company and good cheer, or intimidated by the felt need to put the child to bed or paint the bathroom. And in consequence, meaningful events go unrecorded or are only 'thinly' described, conversations and utterances are lost, and the insider understanding experienced during fieldwork is not captured on the page.

It follows that fieldnotes should be written up as soon as possible after the events to which they refer. Where possible, short *aides-mémoire* or pocket dictaphones may be used in fieldwork settings themselves, for fleshing out into proper fieldnotes later on. These 'notes made in the field setting', as opposed to fieldnotes, may be particularly useful for noting research subjects' verbatim speech: utterances recalled only hours afterwards are bound to be recalled inaccurately and are therefore better reported as indirect speech. In a minority of fieldwork settings, for example educational institutions, note-taking is a natural activity to be engaged in openly, but in most others blatant note-taking is apt to make research subjects self-conscious (or worse). So it is best for ethnographers to repair to the privacy of the lavatory.

Fieldnotes in the first days of fieldwork should have a different character from those recorded in the last days of fieldwork. At the outset, the researcher should aim for broad-brush descriptions of settings and events, conversations and local argot, constrained only by the foreshadowed problems framed at the outset of the research. In later days, fieldnotes will typically be shorter – since the ethnographer has now become habituated to much that was once fresh and strange – and will also be narrower in focus, shaped by emergent analytic concerns. These early analytic thoughts may also be recorded as part of the fieldnotes, or as part of a separate **research diary**-keeping activity.

Although the bones of fieldnote-recording can be set down, it remains – like most writing – a craft skill which has to be worked at and developed. Too often, fieldnote-recording feels like a mere addendum to a hard day's fieldwork. At the risk of sententiousness, it needs to be stated that ethnographers should be prepared to put as much effort into their fieldnotes as they put into their fieldwork.

Examples

Hammersley and Atkinson give an example of good and bad practice in fieldnote-recording with two fieldnote extracts describing the same staffroom interaction in a secondary school: the first fieldnote is much more compressed than the second and mingles reportage with speculation; the second fieldnote is three times the length of the first, preserves fragments of direct speech, and makes the contrast between report and opinion clear (Hammersley and Atkinson, 1995: 181–182).

Evaluation

Ethnographic texts frequently use quotations from fieldnotes to illustrate – like a photograph – a textual argument, as if the quoted fieldnote was a slice of everyday reality captured in prose. But this simple 'realist' approach is under attack, not least from distinguished ethnographers like Clifford Geertz (1988). Since fieldnotes are self-evidently written and authored products, they cannot be treated as straight-forward objective representations of the reality of the fieldwork setting: they are selective in what they choose to describe, and the descriptions themselves convince the reader partly through their authorial style, rhetorical devices and artful use of local 'colour'.

This postmodern critique of ethnography has led some researchers to retreat from fieldwork altogether into analyses of texts, including analyses of forms of ethnographic **writing**. Meanwhile others have continued to report data, typically single interview transcripts reproduced at length, but modestly present their analyses as one of many competing inferences which the reader may assent to or oppose (see Seale, 1999 for a critical overview of such studies). A third possible escape route for ethnographers from the relativist coils of post-modernism is to accept (and be reflexively aware) that authorial style and rhetorical device play their part in establishing the authority of an ethno-graphic text, but to defend the view that sound argument, appropriate use of evidence and methodological rigour also play their part in making a convinc-ing case. This awareness of the complex relation between rhetoric and science and the *pragmatic* use of scientific method in ethnography has been termed 'subtle realism' (Hammersley, 1992) – cf. the discussion on **naturalism**.

Associated Concepts: Ethnography, Naturalism, Research Diary, Thick Description (*see* Theoretical Saturation), Writing.

Key Readings

Geertz, C. (1988) *Works and Lives; The Anthro-pologist as Author.* Cambridge: Polity.

Hammersley, M. (1992) *What's Wrong with Ethnography?* London: Routledge.

*Hammersley, M. and Atkinson, P. (1995) *Ethnography: Principles in Practice* (2nd edn). London: Routledge.

Seale, C. (1999) *The Quality of Qualitative Research.* London: Sage.

Spradley, J.P. (1980) *Participant Obser-vation.* New York: Holt, Rinehart and Winston.

Fieldwork Relationships

Definition
The nature of the interaction that a researcher has with his or her research subjects.

Distinctive Features
Good fieldwork relations are very often crucial for the conduct of valid research as the relationship with respondents inevitably affects what the researcher is allowed to observe or be told. A good fieldwork relationship is characterized by **trust**, openness, and commitment but the depth of the interaction will vary depending on the methods of data collection used. For example if data collection is by **focus group, telephone interview** or a one-off face-to-face **interview** the researcher will not be able to invest too much time into developing the relationship. In such situations the researcher should be concerned to present him or herself in a manner that puts the respondent at ease and encourages him or her to talk openly about his or her views. Typically this would mean presenting oneself as friendly, interested and open to the subject's opinions. Field relations may be damaged if the researcher presents him or herself as too radical, with a particular axe to grind or point to make.

By contrast other data collection methods involve the researcher engaging in more intense field relationships. In **ethnography** the researcher engages in close contact with members of a social group for extended periods of time. Furthermore, ethnography often requires the researcher to engage with members of the culture across a range of activities, such as social events, leisure activities or times when the researcher is simply just spending time 'hanging out' with members of the group. Inevitably in such situations friendships will develop, particularly between the researcher and **key informants**. Similarly researchers, particularly those writing from a **feminist** perspective who have conducted repeated face-to-face interviews with respondents (for example Cornwell, 1984; Oakley, 1981), describe how their fieldwork relationships change over time as friendships and mutual trust develop, thereby enabling them to access **private accounts** where more personal thoughts are revealed.

A number of sociologists have commented on the influence of gender on field relations. These accounts maintain that social knowledge is realized within a pre-existing framework of understanding. If the researcher's experiences and biography reflect the same circumstances as the respondent then the two are more likely to have shared understandings. In ethnographic research gender also influences the types of activities that the ethnographer might

85

easily have **access** to co-participate in, with activities in many social groups being gendered (for example playing football, childcare). The majority of accounts of the influence of gender on fieldwork relationships have been written by female researchers studying women (see for example Oakley, 1981), although researchers have described cross-gender fieldwork relationships of women studying men (see for example Cunningham-Burley, 1984), and there have been a few accounts from male researchers of their gendered fieldwork relationships (see for example McKeganey and Bloor, 1991). The issue of symmetry of perspective is not limited to gender. There are the more obvious social classifications such as the researcher's age, ethnicity and educational and professional background, but also more subtle influences such as the use of vocabulary or regional accents.

Examples

Emerson and Pollner (1988) provide an example of how field relationships may be undermined by circumstances outside of the researcher's control. The authors describe how their fieldwork relationships with members of a Psychiatric Emergency Team (PET) deteriorated sharply when funding for the teams was being threatened. In these circumstances the respondents, understandably concerned for the welfare of their clients and their own jobs, became reluctant to tolerate research findings that might in any way be construed to justify service cuts.

Oakley (1981) discusses the limitations of traditional textbook recommendations that fieldwork should be a one-way eliciting of information conducted with objectivity and detachment. In her fieldwork relationships with women for research on their transition to motherhood she argues that, in order for her repeated interviews to be successful, her fieldwork relationships were characterized by friendship, trust and emotional involvement that took the relationship far beyond a question-answer session: she was frequently offered refreshments, answered questions that the women asked her and was often phoned by the women who kept her informed of their important experiences. Indeed four years after the data collection had taken place Oakley was still in contact with more than a third of the women, several of them having become close friends.

Evaluation

Although the lack of a shared socialization may impair the researcher's ability to understand the perspective of the respondent, accounts of fieldwork relationships may overstate the importance of obvious social categories (gender, ethnicity, etc.). Perhaps of more importance, for the research subjects at least, is the researcher's personality and performance in the setting.

Researchers should avoid the pitfall of thinking that respondents have a hidden authentic self that they will reveal to the researcher only in the context of an empathic fieldwork relationship: the belief that truth lies beneath the surface waiting for the skilled researcher to access it is characterized by Silverman (1989) as romanticism.

Research accounts of field relationships typically describe how rapport between the researcher and subjects improves over time, however there are situations in which the relationship can deteriorate. When operating in illicit or quasi-illicit settings, or sensitive settings where gatekeepers are eager to protect the interests of more vulnerable subjects (for example in schools or hospitals), the relationship might be particularly fragile to perceived threats to confidentiality or betrayal. Consequently researchers will need to closely monitor and delicately manage their relationships with their informants as well as the wider context in which the study is conducted.

Associated Concepts: Access, Ethnography, Feminist Methods, Focus Group, Interviews, Key Informants, Public/Private Accounts, Telephone Interviewing (*see* Electronic Data Collection), Trust.

Key Readings

Cornwell, J. (1984) *Hard Earned Lives: Accounts of Health and Illness from East London.* London: Tavistock.

Cunningham-Burley, S. (1984) 'We don't talk about it: issues of gender and method in the portrayal of grandfatherhood', *Sociology*, 18(3): 325–338.

Emerson, R. and Pollner, E. (1988) 'On the uses of members' responses to researchers' accounts', *Human Organization*, 47: 189–198.

McKeganey, N. and Bloor, M. (1991) 'Spotting the invisible man: the influence of male gender on fieldwork relations', *British Journal of Sociology*, 42(2): 195–210.

Oakley, A. (1981) 'Interviewing women: a contradiction in terms', in H. Roberts (ed.), *Doing Feminist Research.* London: Routledge. pp. 30–61.

*Roberts, H. (ed.) (1981) *Doing Feminist Research.* London: Routledge and Kegan Paul.

Scott, S. (1984) 'The personal and the powerful: gender and status in sociological research', in C. Bell and H. Roberts (eds), *Social Researching: Politics, Problems and Practice.* London: Routledge and Kegan Paul. pp. 165–178.

Silverman, D. (1989) 'The impossible dreams of reformism and romanticism', in J.F. Gubrium and D. Silverman (eds), *The Politics of Field Research: Sociology Beyond Enlightenment.* London: Sage. pp. 30–48.

Focus Groups

Definition
A series of audio-recorded group discussions held with differently composed groups of individuals and facilitated by a researcher, where the aim is to provide data (via the capture of intra-group interaction) on group beliefs and group norms in respect of a particular topic or set of issues.

Distinctive Features
Although it is possible to trace the origins of focus group work to academic research on the persuasiveness of US government propaganda in the Second World War (Merton and Kendall, 1946), focus group research was until quite recently a technique of commercial market research, rather than academic social research. It has been estimated that more than a thousand Americans earn their living conducting focus groups in market research and the average facilitator conducts over a hundred groups a year. But in recent years academics have sought to adapt market research focus group techniques for their own social research purposes and there is now considerable divergence between the two approaches. There is a large literature covering focus groups in commercial market research (for example, Greenbaum, 1998), but our concern here is rather with academic social research.

A focus group should likewise be distinguished from a **Delphi group** and a **group interview**. The former is a panel of experts which may be repeatedly consulted or reconvened to derive authoritative consensus statements of group belief or policy. The latter is a question-and-answer session between the facilitator and the group, used to gain rapid and economical data on group behaviour. Focus groups, in contrast, should not be used to collect data on behaviour, since minority voices will be muted or silenced by the perceived need to conform to the majority practice of the group. Rather than attempt to collect data on the behaviour of individual group members, a focus group should be used to collect data on the *norms* of behaviour current within that social group – that is, on what kinds of behaviour are approved and disapproved of by that group. And, rather than proceed by question-and-answer, the facilitator should seek to generate a general discussion within the group on the selected topic. The facilitator can achieve this in a self-effacing way by asking the group to perform a set task, or 'focusing exercise'. A common type of task used in these circumstances is a ranking exercise, where the group will be asked to look at a series of statements and then rank them in order of correctness or importance – for example, a series of statements about the different reasons that people may have for visiting a pharmacy. In the course of the intra-group discussion about which are the most important reasons and why, the norms within that group on appropriate pharmacy use will begin to emerge.

It follows that groups should be so composed that, while different groups may contrast with each other, each individual group should be relatively homogeneous: it is better to have doctors in one group and nurses in another, even though some of the nurses and doctors work on the same hospital ward. From this example it will be clear that there is no necessary bar on focus group members being known to one another, and some authorities (for example, Kitzinger, 1994) have argued that, by recruiting from pre-existing friendship groups, work groups, neighbourhood groups and the like, focus group researchers may be able to tap into group interaction that approximates to naturally occurring data that might otherwise be only slowly and painfully accumulated by an ethnographer. Whether focus groups are pre-existing or purpose-constructed may depend on the sensitivity of the topic: the dangers of over-disclosure – the reporting by participants, in the heat of the moment, of information which they subsequently feel uncomfortable about having revealed – are greater in pre-existing social groups (Morgan and Krueger, 1993). Smaller groups are said to provide more depth exploration of issues than larger groups (Kerr et al., 1998), but recruitment problems are arguably the greatest source of failure in focus group research and obviously smaller groups are more likely to be vitiated by the non-arrival of participants. Accordingly, it is prudent to compensate for possible non-arrival by a degree of over-recruitment. The payment of an attendance allowance and the selection of a convenient and welcoming venue are also important. As a rough guide, groups of six to eight individuals appear to operate quite well, without being so vulnerable to disruption by non-attendance (Bloor et al., 2001).

Analysis of focus groups in academic social research is normally based on the study of transcripts of **audio-recordings** and, where more than half a dozen groups have been recorded, it may be advisable to make use of one of the **computer-assisted data analysis** packages (such as NVivo) to assist in the ordering of the data. Bearing in mind that a single focus group will typically generate more than 100 pages of transcript, the number of focus groups being conducted should be the absolute minimum consistent with covering the range of the study population.

While the uses of focus groups as a stand-alone research method are rather restricted (limited to the exploration of group meanings or beliefs and of group norms), their value as an ancillary method is considerable. Focus groups are often used in the initial **pilot** stage of a larger study to collect data on group norms, on everyday language use by the group and on group narratives, all in the service of planning the next phase of the study – for example in the formulation of survey questions in terms with which respondents will be familiar. Additionally, focus groups may simply be employed as one component in a **multi-method** design, where focus groups are used to extend or qualify findings produced by different methods.

The growth of **electronic data collection** has created new opportunities for focus group research (Stewart and Williams, 2005). A 'virtual' focus group, where the facilitator operates a closed email distribution list, has a number of advantages, not least the elimination of attendance and **transcription** costs. They can take place over a period of weeks and months, but it is usual for the moderator to specify at the outset a time limit on contributions, in order to encourage contributions by deadline setting. Clearly, virtual focus groups are best used among study populations where email communication would not be unusual, but they can also be used alongside conventional focus groups.

Examples

An example of a study which used focus groups as a stand-alone method is the project reported by Waterton and Wynne (1999) to examine the meanings and beliefs of people in West Cumbria concerning the risks associated with the local nuclear power and reprocessing plants at Sellafield. Their analysis was explicitly designed to contrast with local opinion polling on the same topic. In contrast to the cut-and-dried judgements expressed in the polls, the group attenders expressed themselves in more fluid and ambiguous ways, aware of a range of cross-cutting factors: the ability of experts to identify levels of risk, the importance of the plants to the local economy, but also their powerlessness to influence political decision making, and the stigma of being a 'dumping ground' for nuclear waste. Attenders frequently shifted and developed their views interactively in the course of the discussions.

An example of a study which used focus groups as part of a multi-method research strategy is the project conducted by Middleton et al. (1994) for the Child Poverty Action Group examining patterns of consumption, budgeting and welfare benefits among UK families. Twenty four groups of mothers and 16 groups of children were run, composed to represent differences in children's ages, differences in family affluence and differences of locality. Forty groups are a large number to analyse, but comparisons were eased because different groups undertook different tasks: some groups were convened primarily to check on the acceptability and comprehensibility of research instruments; some were convened primarily to provide analogous qualitative data from both mothers and children to set alongside the quantitative findings; and some were convened to undertake the group task of drawing up minimum weekly budget standards for different household expenditure items (food, children's clothes, children's activities, etc.), after the manner of expert Delphi groups.

An example of a virtual focus group project is Robson's study on the employment experiences of inflammatory bowel disease sufferers (reported in Bloor et al., 2001), where 57 participants in an on-line patient support network were recruited on to a closed subscription private distribution list which ran for two months. 'Threading' was permitted, the simultaneous conduct of multiple topics of conversation, and large amounts of very rich data were generated. One obvious advantage of the method in this instance was the fact that a number of the virtual group participants would have been prevented by their disability from attending a 'real time' focus group.

Evaluation

Focus groups have been a fashionable research method in the recent past, but the popularity of conventional focus groups (as opposed to virtual focus groups) may now be on the wane with the realization that difficulties with recruitment and analysis mean that focus groups are not necessarily a cheap and quick alternative to individual interviews. They do, however, have some advantages over ethnographic methods, particularly in the investigation of topics where conventions of domestic privacy would rule out observational work. And the continuing spread of internet access will allow increasing recourse by researchers to virtual focus groups.

Associated Concepts: Audio-Recording, Computer-Assisted Data Analysis, Delphi Groups, Electronic Data Collection, Group Interviews, Multiple Methods, Piloting, Transcription.

Key Readings

*Bloor, M., Frankland, J., Thomas, M. and Robson, K. (2001) *Focus Groups in Social Research*. London: Sage.

Greenbaum, T. (1998) *The Handbook of Focus Group Research* (2nd edn). Thousand Oaks: Sage.

Kerr, A., Cunningham-Burley, S. and Amos, A. (1998) 'Drawing the line: an analysis of lay people's discussion about the new genetics', *Public Understanding of Science*, 7: 113–133.

Kitzinger, J. (1994) 'The methodology of focus groups: the importance of interaction between research participants', *Sociology of Health & Illness*, 16: 103–121.

Merton, R. and Kendall, P. (1946) 'The focused interview', *American Journal of Sociology*, 51: 541–557.

Middleton, S., Ashworth, K. and Walker, R. (1994) *Family Fortunes: Pressures on Parents and Children in the 1990s*. London: CPAG.

Morgan, D. and Krueger, R. (1993) 'When to use focus groups and why', in D. Morgan (ed.), *Successful Focus Groups: Advancing the State of the Art.* Thousand Oaks: Sage. pp. 3–19.

Stewart, K. and Williams, M. (2005) 'Researching online populations; the use of focus groups for social research', *Qualitative Research*, 5: 395–416.

Waterton, C. and Wynne, B. (1999) 'Can focus groups access community views?, in R. Barbour and J. Kitzinger (eds), *Developing Focus Group Research: Politics, Theory and Practice.* London: Sage. pp. 127–143.

Generalization

Definition
The extent to which the findings of a study can apply to a wider population. Research which is generalizable enables the results and implications of a study to be brought into more general use.

Distinctive Features
Generalizability is often referred to as external **validity**. Again this refers to the extent to which the researcher's conclusions still hold true when applied to other cases outside of the study sample.

Research which uses **sampling** based on probability theory, such as random sampling or systematic sampling, improves the generalizability of research findings on the basis that the sample is more likely to be representative of the population from which it is drawn. Qualitative research rarely utilizes probability samples and, furthermore, typically uses small samples. There is a danger that qualitative researchers might know a lot about the subjects of their research but not much about the wider population. As a consequence, qualitative research is often criticized for its lack of generalizability and, following from this, the use of qualitative research for policy purposes is seen as being limited.

Rather than aiming for statistical or empirical generalization, qualitative research often seeks to produce concepts which are theoretically generalizable. Mitchell (1983), an advocate of the case study method, argues that cases should be chosen on the basis of their power to explain rather than their typicality. Sampling on the basis that such critical cases will be of particular interest to the researcher in terms of being able to confirm or contrast emergent theory is termed theoretical sampling.

The extent to which concepts are generalizable will vary over space and time. For example research that is conducted in Welsh schools on pupils' attitudes to school uniforms may be generalizable to English school pupils, but the findings could not be said to be generalizable to school pupils in other parts of the world due to the hugely varying cultural context. In practice, the research audience must make a common-sense judgement about the transferability and relevance of the findings for their own situation.

Case studies are particularly criticized for their lack of generalizability. In many accounts researchers will take care to describe the context and particulars of the case and highlight for the reader the similarities and differences between the case studied and other cases of the same type. Case studies which involve evaluation of a programme or intervention are typically worth investigating for their own sake and consequently generalization is not an important consideration.

The generalizabilty of qualitative research may be improved by using **multiple methods** or combining qualitative and quantitative methods. This could be done through early survey work to establish the distribution of the variable of interest, thereby enabling the researcher to deliberately select representative schools, hospitals, streets or whatever. This technique can be extended to sampling within the case to find typical teachers, doctors or homes.

Examples

An example of theoretical generalization can be provided by Southerton et al. (2001) who borrow Goffman's concept of 'a script' (that is, a device which configures its users) to explore the nature of caravans and caravanners. The authors argue that the material characteristics of the activity of caravanning underpins the social ordering of caravanning communities. Or, in other words, caravans serve to set caravanners apart from other tourists. The authors make no claims for the empirical generalizability of their work by stressing the universal nature of caravanning and its impact on the tourism industry. Rather they make claims for theoretical generalizability by informed discussion of the ways in which objects (in this case caravans) are implicated in the delineation of social boundaries.

Seale (1999) provides a useful overview of how educational research has combined qualitative and quantitative research in order to aid the generalizability of findings. Seale reviews a number of studies exploring topics such as equal opportunities within schools and parental involvement. In these studies the researchers conducted preliminary surveys in order to select representative samples from which to conduct further in-depth qualitative research.

Evaluation

Qualitative methods have been criticized for their lack of generalizability (Babbie, 2001). The disapproval stems from the view that no matter how interesting or insightful the research is, if it is not generalizable then it is not considered to be research evidence that can be put to use.

While some researchers have responded to this criticism by considering how far the research findings might be extrapolated to other contexts, others have questioned the need for generalizability in qualitative research (Lyotard, 1993). It is argued that the aim of qualitative research is not to provide typical accounts but rather to explore particularities through **thick description**. Qualitative studies are said to be strong on **naturalism** or 'ecological validity', producing research which is theoretically (or conceptually) generalizable. Qualitative research is therefore able to produce concepts which are a useful aid to thinking outside of the immediate research setting in which they were conceived. Green and Thorogood (2004) have taken up this point, arguing that the issue of generalizability may have less relevance than the ability to sensitize readers to new concepts. Qualitative research generates concepts that are 'good to think with' and consequently are of use to other settings beyond the immediate context in which they were produced.

Associated Concepts: Case Study, Multiple Methods, Naturalism, Sampling, Thick Description (*see* Theoretical Saturation), Uses of Qualitative Research, Validity (*see* Reliability).

Key Readings

Babbie, E. (2001) *The Practice of Social Research.* Belmont, CA: Wadsworth Thomas Learning.

Green, J. and Thorogood, N. (2004) *Qualitative Methods for Health Researchers.* London: Sage.

Lyotard, J.F. (1993) 'Answering the question: what is postmodernism?', in T. Docherty (ed.), *Postmodernism: A Reader.* London: Harvester Wheatsheaf. pp. 38–46.

Mitchell, J.C. (1983) 'Case and situational analysis', *Sociological Review,* 31(2): 187–211.

*Seale, C. (1999) *The Quality of Qualitative Research.* London: Sage. pp. 106–118.

Southerton, D., Shove, E., Warde, A. and Deem, R. (2001) 'The social worlds of caravanning: objects, scripts and practices', *Sociological Research Online* 6(2). http://www.socresonline.org.uk/6/2/southerton.html

Grounded Theory

Definition

Grounded theory is commonly written about as if it were a *technique* of analysis, but it is probably more accurately described as an *approach* to analysis, which may use a bundle of specific techniques in flexible and different ways, with the aim of generating theoretical insights from qualitative data. The important point is that the theory comes from the data: the approach is therefore *inductive*, rather than *deductive* – moving from specific instances to general conclusions.

Distinctive Features

The term 'grounded theory' comes from Glaser and Strauss's (1967) book, *The Discovery of Grounded Theory*, which grew out of their study of the social world of dying hospital patients, their relatives and the nursing staff. Glaser and Strauss wanted, first, to contest that approach to social science research which viewed the task of empirical researchers as the testing of pre-formulated theory, and second, to argue against the (rather inadequate) attempts of researchers to relate their research findings to grand and abstract social science theories. Instead, they wished to advocate the generation of new and useful 'middle range' theories of situated social behaviour, deriving those theories from careful and systematic analysis of qualitative data. In their own study, for example, they generated the concept of 'awareness contexts' to depict the different degrees of knowledge and mutual understanding about the patient's imminent death found among different patients, relatives and hospital staff (Glaser and Strauss, 1965). The concept of awareness contexts owes nothing to grand theories, such as structural-functionalism, but is sufficiently developed from everyday common-sense thinking to have been of durable value to subsequent generations of researchers.

Grounded theory is generated, according to Glaser and Strauss, by a number of different processes, operating in concert. One such process is the multiple 'coding' (more accurately, **indexing**) of data according to a number of different analytical categories. Another is the constant comparison of data to elaborate and extend those categories, assisted and recorded by the periodic writing of analytical memos. And another is 'theoretical **sampling**', the extension of data collection by the search for particular sub-populations of cases which appear to be of particular interest as confirming or contrasting the emergent theorizing in the analytical memos, sampling continuing until **theoretical saturation** occurs.

The need for grounded theorizing to march hand in hand with data collection should seemingly make it a difficult approach to apply in qualitative interview or focus group studies where detailed indexing and analysis must await the (long-winded) transcription of the audio-recorded interviews; nevertheless, grounded theory has proved popular with researchers using a range of qualitative techniques. It has proved straightforward to combine grounded theory with **computer-assisted data analysis**. Indeed, Coffey and Atkinson (1996) have criticized the way that some qualitative software packages presuppose a grounded theory approach to analysis.

Examples

As previously mentioned, Glaser and Strauss's own joint research on dying patients (Glaser and Strauss, 1965; 1967; 1968) provides extended examples of the technique. Charmaz is an author whose work is often cited as a more recent application of grounded theory (and who has also published overviews of the approach): she has shown how persons with chronic illness may come to lose their previous sense of self and adopt another as they intentionally 'surrender' to their sick body (Charmaz, 1995). Silverman (2000) reviews several examples of studies where grounded theorizing appears to have been less successfully applied.

Evaluation

Grounded theory filled a near-vacuum in the reporting of processes of data analysis. Prior to Glaser and Strauss's work, descriptions of qualitative research methods had concentrated on the reportage of data collection, access negotiation and fieldwork relationships: it was as if the tasks of qualitative analysis were a craft skill which could only be transmitted through apprenticeship and practice, rather than be communicated on the printed page. The term 'grounded theory' rapidly became very popular: to propose in a grant application to undertake the analysis of one's data according to the principles of grounded theory became a public demonstration of commitment to methodological rigour. Indeed, among the cynical it was muttered that some researchers had conveniently adopted the term 'grounded theory' rather than the approach.

The rise of grounded theory to talismanic status perhaps made it inevitable that an adverse reaction should eventually set in. Since Glaser and Strauss's description of their approach was that of a set of guidelines, rather than a set of prescriptive procedures, it was inevitably the case that some of these grounded theory analyses were better than others. Silverman's (2000) critical overview of deficiencies in some grounded theory studies draws particular attention to the need to search out 'deviant cases' (cases that do not accord with the researcher's preliminary analytical thinking) and to broaden the analysis so as to account for those deviant cases. The search for, and incorporation of, deviant cases is implicit in the principles of 'theoretical sampling' and the 'constant comparative method', but that which is only implicit is sometimes missed. In the kindred analytical method of **analytic induction** (aka deviant case analysis), this implicit search and elaboration/incorporation is made an explicit requirement and this alternative may therefore be preferred by some research practitioners.

Glaser and Strauss themselves disagreed in their later (separate) methodological writings, with Glaser (1992) taking Strauss to task for what he saw as a return to mere theory verification in Strauss's later writings on grounded theory (Strauss and Corbin, 1990). More serious than these collegial spats are the suggestions, influenced by **postmodernism**, that grounded theory is simply outdated in its commitment to a modernist social science – a world capable of improvement and susceptible to skilled expert enquiry, where those experts followed suitable scientific research techniques, such as those of grounded theory. In this reading, grounded theory is not erroneous, merely old-fashioned: those who wish to embrace a postmodernist approach will opt for very different approaches, concerning themselves with, for example, textual deconstruction or collaborative writing with research subjects. Seale (1999) considers postmodernist responses to grounded theory at some length and concludes that the grounded theory approach need not necessarily be tied to a modernist sensibility: rather, the inductive approach with its openness to new ideas and critical self-awareness may also be a fitting procedure for postmodern enquiry.

Associated Concepts: Analytic Induction, Computer-Assisted Data Analysis, Indexing, Postmodernism, Sampling, Theoretical Saturation.

Key Readings

Charmaz, K. (1995) 'Body, identity and self: adapting to impairment', *The Sociological Quarterly*, 36: 657–680.

Coffey, A. and Atkinson, P. (1996) *Making Sense of Qualitative Data Analysis: Complementary Strategies.* London: Sage.

Glaser, B. (1992) *Emergence versus Forcing: Basics of Grounded Theory Analysis.* Mill Valley, CA: Sociology Press.

Glaser, B. and Strauss, A. (1965) *Awareness of Dying.* Chicago: Aldine.

Glaser, B. and Strauss, A. (1967) *The Discovery of Grounded Theory.* Chicago: Aldine.

Glaser, B. and Strauss, A. (1968) *Time for Dying.* Chicago: Aldine.

*Seale, C. (1999) *The Quality of Qualitative Research* [see Chapter 7]. London: Sage.

Silverman, D. (2000) *Doing Qualitative Research, A Practical Handbook.* [see Chapter 26]. London: Sage.

Strauss, A. and Corbin, J. (1990) *Basics of Qualitative Research: Grounded Theory Procedures and Techniques.* Newbury Park: Sage.

Group Interviews

Definition
An interview in which several respondents are simultaneously questioned by the researcher.

Distinctive Features
Group interviews are often considered synonymous with **focus groups** although Morgan (1997) makes the point that group interviews are a generic term of which focus groups, nominal groups and **Delphi groups** are examples. Bryman (2001) suggests that group interviews may be distinguished from focus groups in three ways. First, focus groups discuss one topic in depth whereas group interviews may cover a variety of topics; second, the purpose of group interviews is to collect data from more than one person at the same time thereby saving time and money; and thirdly, focus groups are concerned with how individuals as members of a group discuss certain issues while group interviews are interested in their opinions simply as individuals. Consequently group interviews tend to proceed as a question-and-answer session with the researcher posing the questions, whereas focus groups will be characterized by more debate among the participants themselves perhaps facilitated by focusing exercises.

Group interviews have been associated with market and political research where the intent is to assess either consumer or voter reaction. However, group interviews have also been used in academic research, often in conjunction with other research methods.

Examples
Phoenix, Frosh and Pattman (2003) studied constructs of masculinity among 11 to 14-year-old schoolboys using both group and individual **interviews**. The authors report that the boys were more likely to talk freely in individual interviews about mixing with and identifying with the girls. In contrast during group interviews the boys were more likely to engage in stereotypically boyish discussions. Despite the contradiction between the different versions of self that the boys constructed within the two types of interviews, the researchers concluded that both constructs were valid and thus both group and individual interviews are important to research on identities.

99

Evaluation

The primary advantages of group interviews are that they are quicker and cheaper to conduct than individual interviews with the same number of respondents. They can also spark off lively discussion and can be rewarding and enjoyable for participants. However, they may be harder to organize and they require the researcher to possess skills in managing group dynamics. For example the interviewer may need to manage individuals who dominate the group and encourage those voices which are more silent in order to ensure that responses from the entire group have been heard (Frey and Fontana, 1991). Furthermore, as demonstrated by the paper by Phoenix et al. (2003), respondents may only produce accounts of their beliefs or behaviours which they feel comfortable disclosing to other individuals. Consequently research on sensitive topics may be difficult using this technique.

Associated Concepts: Delphi Groups, Focus Groups, Interviews.

Key Readings

Bryman, A. (2001) *Social Research Methods*. Oxford: Oxford University Press.

*Frey, J.H. and Fontana, A. (1991) 'The group interview in social research', *Social Science Journal*, 28: 175–187.

Morgan, D.L. (1997) *Focus Groups as Qualitative Research*. London: Sage.

Phoenix, A., Frosh, S. and Pattman, R. (2003) 'Producing contradictory masculine subject positions: narrative of threat, homophobia and bullying in 11–14 year old boys', *Journal of Social Issues*, 59(1): 179–195.

Indexing

Definition

Indexing (or coding) is the activity where a researcher applies meaning to raw data by assigning key words or phrases. These key words then act as signposts to themes within the data. Indexing is an activity by which data is broken down, conceptualized and then re-formulated. The term indexing is distinctly different from the use of the term index within quantitative research which refers to the combining of a number of variables into a single composite measure or index. Although the terms 'coding' and 'indexing' are often used interchangeably, strictly speaking coding refers to the allocation of an exclusive code to a particular section of **fieldnotes** or interview transcript, while indexing allows the same piece of text to be allocated multiple codes, just as in a book index where a single page can be indexed to refer to a number of different and overlapping index items.

Distinctive Features

A number of qualitative methods textbooks have discussed the process of indexing (see for example Dey, 1993; Lofland and Lofland, 1995; Miles and Huberman, 1994). The first stage of data analysis typically involves familiarization with the data through a series of re-readings in order to obtain a general sense of their meaning. The familiarization (or data immersion) is usually carried out on a small section of the full data set, for example maybe a handful of interview transcripts. At this point the analyst may be writing notes on the types of topics contained within the data. A thematic framework is then developed according to the key research objectives and emergent themes, with similar topics clustered together. Sections of data are then indexed according to the framework, with coding categories refined appropriately in response to the data. Essentially the process relies on the researcher's common-sense interpretations of the meaning of different segments of data. The process may be conducted by hand (in which case abbreviated codes may be written in the margins or coloured pens may indicate the allocation of different codes) or through the use of computer-assisted analysis. Either way, the aim is to have sections of data with multiple codes and for the process to be as inclusive as possible, codes being added to reflect all kinds of nuances in the data rather than trying to fit the data into a few core codes.

Although qualitative researchers are encouraged to index their data on the basis of what the data themselves are able to yield, some writers (see for example Bogdan and Biklen, 1982) have provided novice researchers with suggestions for possible types of codes, such as 'perspectives held by respondents', 'activity' codes, and 'relationship and social structure' codes. Contextual codes are also often used to indicate the basic socio-demographic characteristics of the respondent(s), such as their gender, age group and so on. Index headings are essentially labels which serve to summarize the meaning of a topic into a key word or phrase. These headings may be formed on the basis of the actual language of the respondent. The index headings can then be supplemented by a longer description (or memo) of the meaning of the index term.

Strauss and Corbin (1990) have suggested an approach to data analysis which is associated with **grounded theory**. The first stage is open coding (or indexing) whereby the researcher scrutinizes data and breaks them down into thematic categories. This may be followed by axial and selective coding which involves the researcher examining each code in turn to explore its nature through a process of constant comparison of data held within each code and comparing it to other categories. The process of coding therefore involves multiple waves of coding whereby each cycle of coding represents a more satisfactory synthesis of earlier codes.

Examples

Frankland and Bloor (1999) demonstrate the process of indexing for a section of data derived from a focus group with schoolchildren on quitting smoking. Initially they develop broad themes that arise in the data, for example 'peer pressure', into which large amounts of text are indexed. The process is then refined with narrower sub-themes identified such as 'bullying' and 'exclusion from groups'. The authors illustrate how sections of text can be multiply indexed.

Evaluation

The **reliability** with which indexing is consistently applied both by the same researcher and between researchers is often raised as a concern. Reliability of indexing can be improved through the rigorous comparison of the same data indexed separately by multiple researchers (LeCompte and Goetz, 1982). This strategy requires analysts to demonstrate consistency in their coding and allows them to resolve inter-coder ambiguities through discussion.

The steps of data coding outlined by Strauss and Corbin (1990) have appeal to those researchers and research funders who desire scientific rigour. If research reports contain accounts of indexing and coding schemes with illustrative examples for each code, some readers may be more willing to believe that a logical and systematic approach to analysis has been taken.

However, Coffey et al. (1996) are critical of the narrow, reductionist analytic strategy that is imposed when coding is used as a first step to theory generation. Their concerns are heightened if analysis is conducted with **computer-assisted qualitative data analysis** as, it is argued, this encourages standardized, mechanistic procedures which fragment and decontextualise data into discrete sections. This objection to coding has far less force if the data analysis is an indexing process, allowing the same piece of data to represent a range of index items. They also argue that, if done badly, researchers often merely index according to the respondent's common-sense categories and neglect to develop their own insights and theories.

Seale (1999) argues that indexing is an attempt to fix meaning on to the world, and that while this process excludes other viewpoints, this exclusivity is required in order to persuade audiences of the validity of the research. An issue remains, however, if coding fixes meanings too prematurely during the process of analysis thereby preventing the analyst from seeing beyond his or her initial ideas. Seale therefore argues that indexing should be seen as an early stage within the process of coding and represents an initial signposting of data to aid developmental thinking rather than representing final theories.

Associated Concepts: Computer-Assisted Data Analysis, Fieldnotes, Grounded Theory, Reliability.

Key Readings

Bogdan, R.C. and Biklen, S.K. (1982) *Qualitative Research for Education: An Introduction to Theory and Methods.* Boston: Allyn and Bacon.

Coffey, A., Holbrook, B. and Atkinson, P. (1996) 'Qualitative data analysis: technologies and representations', *Sociological Research On-line*, 1(1). http: www.socreonline.org.uk/socreonline/ 1/1/3.html

Dey, I. (1993) *Qualitative Data Analysis: A User Friendly Guide for the Social Sciences.* London: Routledge.

*Frankland, J. and Bloor, M. (1999) 'Some issues arising in the systematic analysis of focus group materials', in R. Barbour and J. Kitzinger (eds), *Developing Focus Group Research*. London: Sage. pp. 144–155.

LeCompte, M. and Goetz, J. (1982) 'Problems of reliability and validity in ethnographic research', *Review of Educational Research*, 52(1): 31–60.

Lofland, J. and Lofland, L. (1995) *Analyzing Social Settings: A Guide to Qualitative Observation and Analysis.* London: Wadsworth.

*Miles, M.B. and Huberman, A.M. (1994) *Qualitative Data Analysis: An Expanded Source Book* (2nd edn). London: Sage.

Seale, C. (1999) *The Quality of Qualitative Research.* London: Sage.

Strauss, A.L. and Corbin, J. (1990) *Basics of Qualitative Research: Grounded Theory Procedures and Techniques.* Newbury Park, CA: Sage.

Interviews

Definition

The elicitation of research data through the questioning of respondents. While quantitative (or 'structured') interviews have a semi-formal character and are conducted in surveys using a standardized interview schedule, by contrast qualitative (or 'semi-structured', or 'depth', or 'ethnographic') interviews have a more informal, conversational character, being shaped partly by the interviewer's pre-existing topic guide and partly by concerns that are emergent in the interview.

Distinctive Features

Forty years ago Cicourel (1964: 76–81) summed up the central impulse of depth interviewing as the sacrifice of reliability in pursuit of validity: the interviewer sacrifices standardization and repeatability between interviews in order to grasp more fully the social meanings of the respondent's world. Deriving their philosophical justification from the works of G.H. Mead and Alfred Schutz, depth interviewers seek an inter-subjective bridge between themselves and their respondent to allow them to imaginatively share (and subsequently describe) their respondent's world.

This inter-subjective bridge may be found and crossed, allegedly, with the help of particular interview techniques – expressing empathy, asking open-ended questions, pausing to allow respondents to elaborate, and so on. Spradley's (1979) text, *The Ethnographic Interview,* is particularly detailed in its depiction of interviewing techniques. Spradley emphasizes the need for the researcher to state his or her explicit purpose and assume direction of the interview. He also specifies the various kinds of explanations that the interviewer should offer – explanations of the project, explanations for the recording of the interview, explanations for why the interviewer is seeking native language terms or argot, and explanations for particular questions or a particular line of questioning. Further, Spradley lists particular classes of questions – descriptive questions ('Can you tell me how you go about writing a dictionary entry?'), structural questions ('What are the different components of a dictionary entry') and contrast questions ('What's the difference between the *distinctive features* component and the *evaluation* component in an entry?').

Depth interviewing grew in popularity alongside a developing dissatisfaction with the positivist assumptions of survey research. But depth interviewing in turn drew critical commentary, from both constructivist and postmodernist camps. Silverman (1989) has described the search for intersubjectivity as the same quest as the nineteenth century Romantic Movement's doomed search for authenticity of experience. Postmodern writers like Denzin (1991) have argued the futility of an enterprise that seeks to capture authoritatively the essential features of the social world, advocating instead a multitude of partial perspectives. Constructivists and postmodernists alike have pointed to the context-bound character of all interviews, that the interview is a setting in which interviewer and interviewee collaborate to produce a context-bound description of a social world: the interviewer does not elicit a description of the interviewee's social world, rather the interviewer actively contrives to produce that description with the interviewee.

These criticisms have led to a number of different approaches to interviewing studies. The ethnomethodological, or **conversation analytic**, approach to analysing interviews seeks to address not issues of content, but those of form – the conversational methods by which interview participants create narratives and convey meanings. **Postmodernist** approaches to interviewing will be various by definition, experimenting with different forms of representation (including poetry), but have frequently sought to collaborate with respondents in allowing them a platform to tell their stories in a manner which is oddly consonant with **oral historians**. Finally, there are those researchers who recognize that interviews are context-bound social occasions and not a neutral conduit for social facts, but nevertheless see them as 'a site of, and occasion for, producing reportable knowledge' (Holstein and Gubrium, 2004: 141), for producing analyses of how meanings are generated within the interview situation itself.

Depth interviewing, compared to survey research, involved a shift of skill from the interview schedule to the interviewer. But skills in data collection need to be matched by skills in analysis. Approaches to analysis, such as **grounded theory** and **analytic induction**, and new methods of **computer-assisted data analysis** storage and retrieval, developed alongside qualitative interviewing studies. These analyses have depended on the **transcription** of **audio-recordings** of the interviews. In all cases the requirement is for comprehensive recording of the interaction, for it to be rigorously **indexed**, and for systematic rather than impressionistic analysis. Analytic induction, for example, requires the analyst to search systematically for 'deviant cases' that would falsify a preliminary analytic hypothesis and modify the hypothesis so as to accommodate the previously deviant case.

Examples

Spradley (1979: 61–66) has bravely reproduced one of the transcripts from his cocktail waitress study to illustrate different types of questions and explanations and the interactional work that must be done to maintain rapport. The chintzy cheeriness of this exchange is, however, foreign to many interviews on more sombre topics. Some of the most famous interview studies have sought to reproduce the social worlds of the disadvantaged – prisoners, drug-users, prostitutes and itinerants – but interview studies have also been used to convey a sense of the living worlds of whole communities. One good example of such a study is Thompson et al.'s (1983) analysis of how the fishing villages of northeast Scotland and Shetland survived and prospered in late twentieth-century Britain in an economic climate that killed off the supposedly more efficient industrial trawler fleets in Grimsby, Hull and Aberdeen – a study all the more impressive for having been conducted without the aid of single research grant!

Most conversation analysts are of course concerned with the analysis of conversations in natural settings, rather than with the analysis of research interviews. However, Baker's analysis of how adolescents construct in their everyday talk their adolescent identities is based on her own interviews with Australian and Canadian adolescents (Baker, 2004). Both Hammersley (1995) and Seale (1999) provide extended critical discussions of a number of postmodernist interview studies. Analyses of the generation of meaning in interview situations are perhaps most illuminating when the interview context causes the interviewee to reflect for the first time on what was previously an unconsidered activity. In the extract below, a junior doctor is being asked about his practice in completing death certificates on a busy hospital ward where deaths were a frequent occurrence. He is being asked about which clinical conditions he believed should be entered on the more important Section I of the certificate (conditions – Ia, Ib, Ic – leading directly to death) and which conditions should more properly be assigned to Section II (other significant conditions not related to the cause of death):

> *Bloor:* Would you actually have dementia on the certificate as well as, say, bronchopneumonia? And if you did have it, would you have it in Section I or Section II?

Dr: [...] Em, difficult to say. I would have put it in 'II' if I was going to put it in at all. Perhaps I wouldn't have put it in at all, thinking about it [...]. But thinking about it, probably should go into 'II' if its going to go in. I can't think of any specific reason to put it into 'I' if they'd died of broncho-pneumonia, but then it's a very woolly thing [...]. No right answer to that is there? Because I mean you could effectively – phew! – you know? I'm sure people could put arguments for it going into 'Ib', as being an ongoing dementing process. (Bloor, 1991: 282)

The interview provided an occasion for the interviewee to reflect on previous certification practice and depict it as a routinized, rather than a calculative, activity, reconstituting as problematic that which was previously taken for granted.

Evaluation

Silverman (2000), in an influential text, although careful to state that he is not against the use of open-ended interview methods as such, is critical of inadequate rigour in analysis and particularly critical of interview methods in pursuit of inappropriate topics. A longstanding attack has been mounted on the aspiration of many qualitative interviewers to reproduce the social worlds of their respondents, but the claim that such an aspiration is unrealistic could be sharply contested. As Schutz (1967) has pointed out, all social life depends on the assumption that inter-subjectivity can be achieved, that the reciprocity of perspectives is a practical possibility. So it may be unreasonable to repudiate inter-subjectivity as a scientific objective when it is the entire basis of everyday social interaction. Relatedly, hermeneutic philosophical writings have long sought to conceptualize the processes of empathic understanding that may be said to underlie the aspiration to inter-subjectivity.

However, if current criticisms of interview studies found in constructionist writings (see above) are accepted, then the long dominance of interview methods in qualitative research may be on the wane, since interviews will only be accepted as an appropriate methodology for a narrower range of research topics. One undoubted enduring legacy of both constructionist and postmodernist criticisms will be the emergence of the interviewer and analyst as a **reflexive** subject in the research process.

Associated Concepts: Analytic Induction, Audio-Recording, Computer-Assisted Data Analysis, Conversation Analysis, Grounded Theory, Indexing, Oral History, Postmodernism, Reflexivity, Transcription.

107

Key Readings

Baker, C. (2004) 'Membership categorization and interview accounts', in D. Silverman (ed.), *Qualitative Research: Theory, Method and Practice* (2nd edn). London: Sage.

Bloor, M. (1991) 'A minor office: the variable and socially constructed character of death certification in a Scottish city', *Journal of Health and Social Behavior*, 32: 273–287. Reprinted in M. Bloor (1997) *Selected Writings in Medical Sociological Research*, Aldershot: Ashgate.

Cicourel, A. (1964) *Method and Measurement in Sociology*. New York: Free Press.

Denzin, N. (1991) 'Representing lived experiences in ethnographic texts', *Studies in Symbolic Interaction*, 12: 59–70.

*Gubrium, J. and Holstein, J. (eds) (2002) *The Handbook of Interview Research*. Thousand Oaks, CA: Sage.

Hammersley, M. (1995) *The Politics of Social Research*. London: Sage.

Holstein, J. and Gubrium, J. (2004) 'The active interview', in D. Silverman (ed.), *Qualitative Research: Theory, Method and Practice* (2nd edn). London: Sage.

Schutz, A. (1967) 'Common-sense and scientific interpretations of human action', in M. Natanson (ed.), *Alfred Schutz Collected Papers Volume I*. The Hague: Martinus Nijhoff.

Seale, C. (1999) *The Quality of Qualitative Research*. London: Sage.

Silverman, D. (1989) 'The impossible dreams of reformism and romanticism', in J. Gubrium and D. Silverman (eds), *The Politics of Field Research: Sociology Beyond Enlightenment*. London: Sage.

Silverman, D. (2000) *Doing Qualitative Research: A Practical Handbook*. London: Sage.

Silverman, D. (2001) *Interpreting Qualitative Data: Methods for Analysing Talk, Text and Interaction* (2nd edn). London: Sage.

Spradley, J. (1979) *The Ethnographic Interview*. New York: Holt, Rinehart and Winston.

Thompson, P., Wailey, T. and Lummis, T. (1983) *Living the Fishing*. London: Routledge.

Key informants

Definition
Key informants are those research subjects in ethnographic studies who have a disproportionate weight and role in the conduct and outcome of the research.

Distinctive Features
These informants may be 'key' in that they facilitate **access** through sponsorship or through the extensiveness of their social networks, that is, they act as gate-keepers, particularly in the early stages of the research. Alternatively or additionally, they may be 'key' in that they may provide particularly important understandings to the researcher on aspects of their collectivity, perhaps because they have a particularly rich knowledge of the collectivity through their seniority or through their specialist roles in the setting. Key informants may also be asked to respond to early analyses (see **triangulation**), in some instances informally taking on the role of a co-researcher (see **public participation**).

Examples
The key informant role is one that is familiar from historical examples. Thus, the extraordinary success of Cortez and his tiny band of Conquistadores in the overthrow of the Aztec kingdom is said to owe an enormous amount to Marina, the Mexican Indian princess, presented to the Spaniards as a slave, who became Cortez's translator, secretary and mistress. Prescott, in his classic 1843 history of the conquest, wrote that 'her knowledge of the language and customs of the Mexicans, and often of their designs, enabled her to extricate the Spaniards, more than once, from the most embarrassing and perilous situations' (Prescott, 1925: 141), including uncovering a plot by Montezuma to massacre Cortez and his band in the city of Cholula.

The best known sociological example of a key informant is 'Doc', the Italian-American who facilitated Whyte's access to the inner-city slum society described in Whyte's (1955) *Street Corner Society*, and who Whyte credited (in retrospect) as an informal co-researcher. More influential an informant still was Tally Jackson, who Liebow met on his second day of **fieldwork** in the ghetto, causing Liebow to abandon his previous fieldwork plans and instead focus his Tally's Corner **ethnography** exclusively on the doings of Tally and his friends (Liebow, 1967).

Evaluation

Key informants do not operate like the State Intourist Guides of the old Soviet Union, with detailed rational explanations of every local social phenomenon available in response to casual enquiry. They have their own concerns and pre-occupations, duly reflected in their talk and advice (see Emerson, 1981). Moreover, the relationship between key informants and researchers may be a fluctuating one, even a rocky ride. The example of Marina, who ingratiated herself into intimacy with the Cholula nobility in order to betray the designs of her fellow Mexicans to her lover Cortez, seemed splendid to the readers of Prescott's day. But late-modern readers will find her a more ambiguous figure. Edgerton (1965) in a classic paper has charted how the relationship between the anthropologist and his or her native 'friend' has a typical career path, ending in mutual disillusionment. Where the researcher has much higher status than the key informant, then the respondent is unlikely to take the researcher's protestations of friendship at face value and instead will 'test' the researcher by demanding increasingly high-cost proofs of that friendship (such as smuggling liquor on to the reservation), until the threshold of tolerance is crossed and the researcher is proven, to the respondent's satisfaction, to be just like all the other white men. Not all key informants last the course.

Associated Concepts: Access Negotiations, Ethnography, Fieldwork Relationships, Public Participation, Triangulation, Trust.

Key Readings
Edgerton, R. (1965) 'Some dimensions of disillusionment in culture contact', *Southwestern Journal of Anthropology*, 21: 231–243.
Emerson, R. (1981) 'Observational fieldwork', *Annual Review of Sociology*, 7: 351–378.
Liebow, E. (1967) *Tally's Corner*. London: Routledge.

Prescott, W. (1925; first published 1843) *The History of the Conquest of Mexico*. London: Allen and Unwin.
*Whyte, W.J. (1955) *Street Corner Society: The Social Structure of an Italian Slum* (2nd enlarged edn). Chicago: University of Chicago Press.

Leaving the Field

Definition

'Leaving the field' is the social process of withdrawal from fieldwork. It is a further aspect of the construction of **fieldwork relationships** that began with **access negotiations**. While it is a process of primary concern in **ethnography**, it may also be an issue in **interview** studies conducted in community or organizational settings.

Distinctive Features

The timing of an ethnographer's departure from the field is usually determined by external constraints – limits of funding, the exhortations of a Ph.D. supervisor, even the closure of the fieldwork setting itself (as in the closure of schools for the summer holidays). But the manner of the ethnographer's departure needs to be carefully managed.

The First Law of Research is 'Do no harm' and the ethnographer must take care that the disruption of close fieldwork relationships that occurs on the ethnographer's departure does no harm to the research subjects left behind. When the time came for McKeganey to end his fieldwork in a residential therapeutic community for children with learning disabilities, there was concern that his departure might be disturbing to some of the children with whom he had developed close relationships. Accordingly, McKeganey phased his withdrawal from fieldwork, continuing to drop in at the community for social visits for months after the end of fieldwork. However, the pains of parting are not just felt by research subjects: often the regrets, discomforts and guilt of disengagement are also acutely felt by the ethnographer, as McKeganey recorded (Bloor et al., 1988: 226–227).

Orderly withdrawal should occur in a manner consonant with the norms of departure current at the fieldwork site. At one site, a farewell party might be held with a presentation; at another site, formal individual goodbyes might occur with handshakings and exchanges of addresses.

Some ethnographers make a practice of feeding early findings back to research subjects, thus generating valuable further data on research subjects' reactions to the researcher's analysis. Arrangements for this procedure (known as **member validation**) may also be made at the point of departure from the field, and may have the incidental value of making departure seem less final.

Of course, responsibilities to one's research subjects do not end at the point of departure from the field. In the 'colonial' era of anthropology, when indigenous peoples' own leaders had little legitimacy in the eyes of colonial administrations, it was commonplace for anthropologists to take on a continuing advocacy role in the corridors of power on behalf of 'their tribe'. Likewise, some anthropologists take on certain responsibilities in the course of their fieldwork (for example, agreeing to act as a godparent), responsibilities which will continue long after fieldwork is finished. The continuing, or recurrent, contacts associated with those responsibilities of course have the incidental advantage of easing the ethnographer's access, should he or she ever wish to return for a further period of fieldwork.

Examples
Hammersley and Atkinson (1995: 120–123) summarize the contrasting experiences of a number of ethnographers attempting to leave the field, including those of Snow (1980) whose attempt to leave a Buddhist group actually served to stimulate the leadership of the group into redoubled efforts to strengthen Snow's adherence to the group and its beliefs.

Evaluation
Where the researcher leaves the field in a manner consonant with the norms of the group being studied, this is unlikely to cause any problems for research subjects, although particular attention has to be given to the needs of vulnerable groups such as children or patients. By and large, it is the ethnographer, with his or her heightened sensitivity to fieldwork relationships, who is more likely to feel distress on separation.

Associated Concepts: Access Negotiations, Ethnography, Fieldwork Relationships, Interviews, Member Validation (*see* Triangulation).

Key Readings
Bloor, M., McKeganey, N. and Fonkert, D. (1988) *One Foot in Eden: A Sociological Study of the Range of Therapeutic Community Practice.* London: Routledge.
*Hammersley, M. and Atkinson, P. (1995) *Ethnography: Principles in Practice* (2nd edn). London: Routledge.

Snow, D. (1980) 'The disengagement process: a neglected problem in participant observation research', *Qualitative Sociology*, 3: 100–122.

Logical Analysis

Definition

A systematic procedure for the analysis of respondents' belief systems which seeks to identify logically connected statements or premises within a respondent's talk and then to group associated statements so identified into a particular set of beliefs. Like **analytic induction**, logical analysis offers a rigorous procedure for qualitative analysis, rather than the less precise guidelines found in **grounded theory**.

Distinctive Features

Logical analysis was developed by Williams (1981; 1990) as an analytic procedure for describing and comparing the health beliefs in his interview data of a sample of elderly Aberdonians. The requirement to identify logical premises in respondents' speech should not be thought of as a reductive exercise, stripping transcripts down to some bedrock of an ideologically pure and consistent set of propositions. In fact, the logical premises are simple 'if X, then Y' sets of paired statements that frequently have an axiomatic quality, such as 'if I retire early, then I am more likely to be ill'. Moreover, few of us are ideologues and, as Williams shows, logical analysis is perfectly capable of identifying more than one group of premises (one perhaps inconsistent with another) within the speech of a single individual. Indeed, inconsistency in belief systems is thought by Williams to be more common than consistency among humankind.

Since transcripts must be indexed to identify relevant logical premises, logical analysis is best attempted in association with **computer-assisted data analysis**.

Examples

Williams's own work remains the most extensive application of the method. He begins by teasing out the logical premises in Herzlich's analysis of the health beliefs of her Parisien interviewees (Herzlich, 1973), beliefs which she variously categorizes as 'illness as an occupation', 'illness as a destroyer' and 'illness as a liberator'. Williams then shows how, using respondents' own language terms, a set of premises can be derived from 'Mrs Stone's' interview to correspond to the group of premises associated with 'illness as a destroyer' and from 'Mrs Hannay' to correspond to 'illness as an occupation', while 'Mr Grant' incorporates premises from both of these categories.

113

Evaluation

The technique has the advantages of procedural clarity and methodological rigour. In principle, it appears that it would be possible to apply the technique to the analysis of focus group data, as well as interview data. But it is probable that the technique is only well fitted for the analysis of beliefs and attitudes; it is difficult to see how it could be used for the analysis of descriptions of behaviour.

Associated Concepts: Analytic Induction, Computer-Assisted Data Analysis, Grounded Theory.

Key Readings

Herzlich, C. (1973) *Health and Illness: A Social Psychological Analysis*. London: Academic Press.

*Williams, R.G.A. (1981) 'Logical analysis as a qualitative method', *Sociology of Health and Illness*, 3: 141–187.

Williams, R.G.A. (1990) *A Protestant Legacy: Attitudes to Death and Illness Among Older Aberdonians*. Oxford: Clarendon Press [cf. Appendices 1 and 2, pp. 331–345].

Meta Ethnography

Definition
Meta ethnography is an attempt to increase the **generalizability** and analytic potential of qualitative research findings by means of systematic synthesis.

Distinctive Features
Meta analyses are an established feature of quantitative research, particularly evaluative research in health and social services, where the results from several randomized controlled trials on the same topic may be combined and re-analysed to produce more elaborate and authoritative results with greater statistical power. Meta ethnography is analogous in aim but not in method, since it relies not on the aggregation of findings, but on inductive further interpretation, often of a deliberately restricted sub-set of relevant studies (Noblit and Hare, 1988). The analytic task is to seek to establish how far the different conceptual schemes used in different studies can be translated from the particular studies in which they were first developed to apply to other data sets, with the hope that the task of translation will lead to further conceptual development and integration across the different studies.

Examples
The term meta ethnography is rather misleading, since the same techniques have been used to attempt to synthesize qualitative **interview** studies, especially in educational and nursing research. Britten et al. (2002) have attempted to synthesize four *interview* studies on patient compliance with the taking of prescribed medicines, producing a more elaborate analysis of patients' attempts to cope with their illnesses through 'self-regulation', the use of coping strategies as alternatives to full compliance with the prescribed regime of medication, combined with concealment of their non-compliance from health professionals.

Evaluation
Meta ethnography has an intuitive appeal to social scientists who see their work disvalued as anecdotal by practitioners and policy-makers accustomed to

the scientific authority of the synthetic tools of meta analyses and systematic reviews. However, it will remain a controversial technique because of uncertainty about whether the selected studies are commensurate. Commensurability is problematic, not just because every study setting is to some extent unique, but also because no straightforward quality threshold can be applied to the candidate studies (some studies may simply be less analytically developed than others), and because synthesis may lead to an under-emphasis on either the (celebrated) poly-vocalism of **postmodern** scholarship, or the reflexive awareness of unique authorship found in late-modern **ethnography**.

Associated Concepts: Ethnography, Generalization, Interviews, Postmodernism.

Key Readings

Britten, N., Campbell, R., Pope, C., Donovan, J., Morgan, M. and Pill, R. (2002) 'Using meta ethnography to synthesise qualitative research: a worked example', *Journal of Health Services Research & Policy*, 7: 209–215.

*Noblit, G. and Hare, R. (1988) *Meta-ethnography: Synthesising Qualitative Studies*. London: Sage.

Multiple Methods

Definition

The combining of different methods within the same study design. The purpose of such a combination may be additive, with different methods addressing different sub-topics (often sequentially), or interactive, with the same sub-topic being approached from different angles.

Distinctive Features

Additive multiple methods are frequently used at different stages of the research process. Thus, a large-scale quantitative survey may begin with some focus groups to familiarize researchers with lay terminology and concepts, to be followed by depth **interview piloting** to check on the comprehensibility and acceptability of possible survey questions. Similarly, **focus groups** can be used at the end of a project to feed back early findings to research subjects or **key informants**. However, additive multiple methods can also run in parallel, most notably in the case of qualitative **process evaluations** (Parry Langdon et al., 2003) conducted alongside survey evaluations in controlled trial designs, in order to try and answer the question of why the trial intervention has succeeded or failed. The main premise of additive multiple methods is that there is always one best method for any given particular research task, so that addressing a particular research question hinges on breaking the answering of that question down into particular specific tasks and then selecting a method best suited to completing that specific task.

Interactive multiple methods (discussed at length under 'triangulation') serve to extend and deepen an analysis. Thus, the most useful interactive multiple methods are not qualitative and quantitative methods (since the findings from such methods are rarely straightforwardly commensurate), but rather combinations of different qualitative methods, focused on the same topic or research task. Thus, while additive multiple methods aim for comprehensive coverage, interactive multiple methods aim for depth of analysis of a narrower topic.

The use of multiple methods in **rapid assessment** forms a special case, in that different methods are chosen in an attempt to both extend coverage and deepen the fragmentary and superficial picture yielded by any one method.

Examples
Barbour (1999) has reviewed, with examples, the case for combining qualitative and quantitative methods in health services research.

Evaluation
The use of multiple methods has been associated with overblown claims that interactive multiple methods can validate the subsequent analysis. This is not the case (see **triangulation**), but a commitment to multiple methods (both additive and interactive) has become the hallmark of a rigorous research design.

Associated Concepts: Focus Groups, Interviews, Key Informants, Piloting, Process Evaluation, Rapid Assessment, Triangulation.

Key Readings

*Barbour, R. (1999) 'The case for combining qualitative and quantitative approaches in health services research', *Journal of Health Services Research and Policy*, 4: 39–43.

Parry Langdon, N., Bloor, M., Audrey, S. and Holliday, J. (2003) 'Process evaluation of health promotion interventions', *Policy and Politics*, 31: 207–216.

Narratives

Definition

Narratives are continuous stories or accounts of people's experiences. A narrative account could relate to a complete life story, but equally it may refer to the account of a discrete event, such as an experience of pregnancy, which has a clear beginning and ending.

Distinctive Features

Narrative analysis has been popular among many disciplines within the social sciences. For example, linguists might examine the internal structure of narratives, psychologists might focus on the process of recalling and summarizing stories, and anthropologists might look at the function of stories cross-culturally. The increasing popularity of narrative analysis is reflected in the publication of a dedicated journal on the method (*The Journal of Narrative and Life History*). While narratives are traditionally associated with face-to-face-interviews, narratives can also be collected through documents such as **diaries**, **biographies** or ethnographic **fieldnotes** (Lieblich et al., 1998).

One of the strengths of narrative analysis is that humans are natural story-tellers. It is argued that through such stories we reveal not only our experiences but also our identity (Lieblich et al., 1998). We know and reveal ourselves to others by the stories that we tell.

One of the principles of the narrative method is minimal interviewing. Researchers are required to concede control of the interview to the narrative-teller, suppress any desire to interrupt and become a passive audience to the story being told. Often biographic narrative techniques use a single initial narrative-inducing question at the beginning of the interview such as 'tell me about your experiences at school' or even as broad as 'tell me the story of your life'. Like depth **interviews**, narrative researchers use a broad topic guide. If uninterrupted, respondents are likely to continue in an extensive narrative. These rich and lengthy data mean that narrative researchers tend to use small respondent samples in their research.

A key (and arguably essential) feature of a narrative account is that it should have a sequence with a clear beginning and end. The narrator should tell the story in the same sequence of events as they happened so that the cause and effect of the events are clear. In addition to the importance of the story trajectory, Labov (1972) has argued that fully formed oral narratives have six properties:

- Abstract (a summary of the story)
- Orientation (time, place and people)
- Complicating action (what happened)
- Evaluation (why this is important)
- Resolution (what finally happened)
- Coda (bridging the audience back to the present)

Toolan (1988) has described other characteristics of narratives. These include a degree of artificial fabrication, that is, narratives are constructed in a different way to spontaneous conversation. Aspects of the talk such as pace and emphasis have usually been planned and sometimes even performed to other audiences. Narrative tellers also tend to use 'displacement', that is, speakers refer to events and people that are removed in space and time. Narratives also tend to have a rhetorical function. Accounts are expected to have some kind of effect on the audience with the narrator typically making a moral point.

Analysis of narrative accounts is concerned with the examination of how respondents impose order on to their story, the linguistic and cultural resources that it draws upon and how the narrator seeks to persuade the listener of the story's authenticity (Reissman, 1993). Narrative analysts have argued that traditional qualitative analysis tends to dissect stories during the analysis process thereby using data out of context and suppressing the narrative. In contrast, narrative analysis is concerned with how the story is told, what is told, what is omitted and what is emphasized. Thus, the key analytical question for narrative researchers is: 'why did that respondent tell their story in that way?'

Examples

Williams (1984) interviewed 30 patients with arthritis to explore their understandings of the cause of their illness. In his paper he describes three cases in detail in which the patient used narrative reconstruction to explain their illness in terms of the world in which they lived. 'Bill' reconstructed his illness as a public or political issue, 'Gill' explained her illness in terms of the conflicts she experienced in her social roles, and 'Betty' narrated how her illness lay within God's will. These three respondents, who faced the biographic disruption of a chronic illness, therefore reconstructed a coherent self within their narratives. The paper demonstrates how people often use narratives when there has been a breach between their ideal and real selves or between the self and society.

Cortazzi (1993) took an unusual approach to narrative analysis in that he collected nearly a thousand 'narrative anecdotes' from interviews with teachers working within UK primary schools, supplemented by naturally occurring data collected in staff rooms and school corridors. Using narrative-inducing questions such as 'have you had any children in your class who have had a breakthrough recently?' he discovered dominant metaphors emerging in their stories. These led him to develop a linear model of learning that encompassed learning as a struggle, a light dawning (which happens suddenly or was noticed suddenly), joy, and finally the reward of teaching. At the end of his chapter he reflects that while some may dismiss the accounts as mere anecdotes, when collected together these stories show evidence of common experience, perception and thinking among teachers.

Evaluation

Narratives are representations of people's lives and therefore essentially fictitious. However, as researchers rarely have direct access to people's experiences it is necessary to use people's own representations of their lives. Most narrative researchers take a middle view that narratives should neither be treated as fiction, nor should they be taken at face value as complete and accurate versions of reality (Lieblich et al., 1998; Reissman, 1993). Their point is that truth becomes a secondary concern to the narrative researcher's primary interest in how his or her respondent sees him or herself when asked to recall his or her experiences.

In addition to **validity**, the **reliability** of narrative accounts has also been a potential source of concern. It is unlikely that a narrative told on one occasion to one researcher will mirror the same story told on a different occasion to a different researcher. However, as Reissman (1993) points out, telling complex and often emotionally charged stories should vary because stories are told within a context. While constructed around a core, the story will vary according to the expressed aim of the interview, the mood of the narrator and his or her relationship with his or her audience.

Associated Concepts: Biographies, Diary Methods, Fieldnotes, Interviews, Oral History, Reliability, Validity (*see* Reliability).

Key Readings

Cortazzi, M. (1993) *Narrative Analysis.* London: Falmer Press.

Josselson, R. and Lieblich, A. (eds) (1993) *The Narrative Study of Lives.* Newbury Park, CA: Sage.

Josselson, R., Lieblich, A. and McAdams, D. (2003) *Up Close and Personal: The Teaching and Learning of Narrative Research.* Washington: American Psychological Association.

Labov, W. (1972) 'The transformation of experience in narrative syntax', in W. Labov (ed.), *Language in the Inner City.* Philadelphia: Pennsylvania University Press. pp. 27–44.

*Lieblich, A., Tuval-Mashiach, R. and Zilber, T. (1998) *Narrative Research: Reading, Analysis and Interpretation.* London: Sage.

*Reissman, C. (1993) *Narrative Analysis.* Newbury Park, CA: Sage.

Toolan, M. (1988) *Narratives: A Critical Linguistic Introduction.* London: Routledge.

Williams, G. (1984) 'The genesis of chronic illness: narrative reconstruction', *Sociology of Health and Illness,* 6(2): 175–200.

Naturalism

Definition

Naturalism is the philosophical (properly epistemological) position, associated particularly with qualitative research in the **symbolic interactionist** and Goffmanian traditions, which requires that social life should be studied, as far as possible, in its naturally occurring state, and not through the artificial prisms of postal surveys, formal interviews, or psychological laboratory experiments.

Distinctive Features

Naturalism developed as an epistemology in contradistinction to the positivist position dominant in the social sciences in the 1950s, which sought to establish objective facts via research exploring and replicating testable (falsifiable) hypotheses conducted by neutral scientific observers. As Hammersley and Atkinson (1995: 6) put it, while positivist social science drew its inspiration from twentieth-century physics, naturalism drew on nineteenth-century biology: Goffman, in a letter, (disarmingly?) described his work as that of a 'one-armed botanist' (quoted in Bloor, 1996). Naturalist research aspires simply to a descriptive realism, rather than seeking to derive universal explanatory laws of human conduct.

Naturalism is also concerned fundamentally with capturing the cultural meanings attributed to social phenomena, a preoccupation that had its warrant both in the symbolic interactionism of the Chicago School (with its dictum that 'If men define situations as real, then they are real in their consequences' – Thomas, 1923) and the **phenomenology** of Husserl and his follower Alfred Schutz, who described the interpretation of the social world in terms of an individual's 'stock of knowledge', and the response to that interpretation in terms of an individual's 'recipes for action' (Schutz, 1970). The qualitative researcher must seek to capture these meanings through an immersive understanding in the culture under study. This immersive understanding is the *verstehen* of Max Weber and has earlier roots in the nineteenth-century hermeneutic writers. Thus, the researcher is no neutral observer but is his or her own research instrument, seeking empathetic appreciation of a culture through the experience of co-participation.

Examples

Carey's (1975) history of the Chicago School contains many short accounts of individual pieces of naturalistic research. An appropriate exemplar of the naturalistic approach is Becker's (1953) study *Becoming a Marihuana User*, on how novice users must learn from more experienced users on how to interpret the physical experiences of drug use as pleasurable – a very widely cited study that has laid the foundation for subsequent studies of 'deviant' activity, but which never had any discernable impact at all on government drug policies.

Evaluation

The lack of policy impact of Becker's study is typical of naturalistic studies, a consequence partly of their descriptive focus and partly of their uncertain **generalizability**. However, naturalistic studies have been subject to more fundamental criticisms than their lack of policy pay-off. Naturalistic studies (with their claim to be able to represent an apprehensible social reality) suffered under the same fate as positivist social science, undermined by the new Kuhnian philosophy of science (Kuhn, 1970) which pointed to the relative and provisional nature of all scientific claims. But naturalistic studies' claims to grasp social reality through direct immersive experience of a culture have also been derided as romanticism, kindred to the nineteenth-century romantic poets' attempts to directly apprehend 'Nature' (Silverman, 1989). Relatedly, **postmodernism** has attacked the idea that social worlds are coherent (and describable) wholes and has also pointed out that the descriptions of social worlds furnished by naturalistic researchers are not transparent, but rather are persuasive texts with rhetorical devices designed to influence readers and confound critics.

Qualitative researchers have responded to these criticisms of naturalism. Naïve realism has given way to the 'subtle realism' of Hammersley (1992) and postmodernism has spawned the 'reflexive turn' in ethnography. It may be argued that, while the postulate of intersubjectivity (that one human being can imaginatively place him or herself in the position of another) remains the basis for all human interaction, there thus remains a qualified warrant for reporting social reality on the basis of immersive understanding.

Associated Concepts: Ethnography, Generalization, Phenomenological Methods, Postmodernism, Reflexivity, Symbolic Interactionism.

Key Readings

Becker, H. (1953) 'Becoming a marihuana user', *American Journal of Sociology*, 59: 41–58.

Bloor, M. (1996) 'Review essay: Philip Strong (1945–1995), an appreciation of an essayist', *Sociology of Health & Illness*, 18: 551–564.

Carey, J. (1975) *Sociology and Public Affairs: The Chicago School*. London: Sage.

Hammersley, M. (1992) *What's Wrong with Ethnography*. London: Routledge.

*Hammersley, M. and Atkinson, P. (1995) *Ethnography: Principles in Practice* (2nd edn). London: Routledge.

Kuhn, T. (1970) *The Structure of Scientific Revolutions*. Chicago: University of Chicago Press.

Schutz, A. (1970) *Reflections on the Problem of Relevance* (ed. R.M. Zaner). New Haven, CT: Yale University Press.

Silverman, D. (1989) 'The impossible dreams of reformism and romanticism', in J. Gubrium and D. Silverman (eds), *The Politics of Field Research*. London: Sage.

Thomas, W.I. (1923) *The Unadjusted Girl*. Boston: Little, Brown & Co.

Oral History

Definition

The collection and analysis of accounts of past events from eyewitness participants for the purposes of historical reconstruction. Oral history is spoken history and, as well as **interviews** with participants, it includes the collection of stories and ballads concerned with historical events that have been handed down from generation to generation in a continuing oral tradition.

Distinctive Features

The collection of oral history materials from social and political elites can be a valuable supplement to documentary evidence in historical research. But the main thrust of oral history work has been to interview persons whose perspectives on events would otherwise be lost to posterity, those who have been 'hidden from history' (Rowbotham, 1973) – women and workers, indigenous peoples and oppressed minorities. In some cases, oral history materials have been able to document clandestine events that were otherwise unrecorded, for example, this reminiscence of the days when coalminers could only receive compensation from the courts for 'Miners Lung' (pneumoconiosis) if they could prove contact with silica dust as well as coaldust – South Wales miners would therefore sometimes 'doctor the evidence' of silica dust before a mine was visited by an expert witness: 'The boys got very artful about this. Knowing that the geologist would be coming about next week, some of the boys would be in there spreading about silica' (Harold Finch, South Wales Miners Library, Aud 336 – quoted in Bloor, 2000: 133).

But for the most part, it is not the event itself that is rescued for posterity, but the particular partisan perspectives of those who lived through events. Reed has summarized well the nature of these partisan perspectives in his analysis of the Border Ballads, songs that were handed down through the oral tradition for hundreds of years in the English–Scottish Border region until they were collected in the 1800s: 'They [the ballads] are a commemoration, emotionally generated, of family and regional loyalties *within* the events the narratives portray. They look upon joy and disaster alike with the eye and mind of the participant' (Reed, 1980: 18).

Historians familiar only with documentary materials have not developed new techniques for sampling and recruiting interviewees, framing questions, recording and transcribing interviews, and analysing transcripts. Instead, they have wisely borrowed from other disciplines – notably sociology, anthropology and linguistics – that are more familiar with these methods. What has been distinctive in the approach of some oral historians has been the *representation* of the interview materials. Some authors, Studs Terkel being the best known in the US and Ronald Blythe being representative of those in the UK, have sought to represent their oral history materials by the minimization of their own mediating presence as historians: the transcripts of their interviewees are presented to the reader without commentary, like a photo archive, to speak for themselves. Other authors (for example, Jung Chang's 1992 history of herself, her mother and her grandmother in the upheavals of twentieth-century China) have reported their interviewees' stories within a dramatic and consciously literary style, mingling memories of the suicide of a classmate with memories of the smell of jasmine blossoms. Both types of representation have been controversial (see below). Further, alongside these realist (Studs Terkel) and literary (Jung Chang) approaches to oral history, there is also a postmodern approach: that of life histories or 'life stories'. Representation in life stories is a consciously joint accomplishment: life stories are 'joint actions assembled through social contexts into texts by authors and readers' (Plummer, 2001: 399).

Examples

Thompson's *The Edwardians* (1975) has become a classic oral history text, an analysis of interviews on the family and work experiences of 459 Britons born between 1872 and 1906. Thompson also initiated the collection and archiving of much subsequent UK oral history work. Jung Chang's *Wild Swans* has already been mentioned. Studs Terkel's best known work is *Hard Times* (1970), his oral history of Americans' memories of the Great Depression; it should be read alongside Frisch's (1972) review of the book. Plummer (2001) summarizes a number of life-story analyses.

Evaluation

It is well known that modern research has confirmed the claims in the Icelandic sagas (which existed as oral stories for 200 years or more before being written down) that Vikings were the first Europeans to settle in North America. But oral historians are rarely concerned to establish the truth status of oral reportage. Rather, oral accounts are valued not for their accurate (or otherwise) depiction of events, but for their reportage of the **narrator's** viewpoint of events, for the access they offer to the participants' perspectives.

However, these participants' perspectives are not transparent and self-evidential. Certainly, they may have other virtues: the collection of oral historical accounts can be empowering for both the narrator and collector, hence the popularity of oral history classes and groups among many local communities world-wide. Nevertheless, there is legitimate critical concern over the representation of oral history as if the accounts spoke for themselves: oral history is not 'the Voice of the People that have not spoken yet'. All published historical accounts, whether or not they include explicit analysis of the narratives, are selected and edited accounts: in effect, they are therefore joint accomplishments between interviewee and interviewer, as is explicitly recognized by Plummer and his fellow 'life-story' analysts.

Associated Concepts: Interviews, Narratives.

Key Readings

Bloor, M. (2000) 'The South Wales Miners Federation, Miners' Lung, and the instrumental use of expertise 1900–1950', *Social Studies of Science*, 30: 125–140.

Frisch, M. (1972) 'Oral history and Hard Times', *Red Buffalo*, 1 (2 and 3). Reprinted 1998. in *R. Perks and A. Thompson (eds), *The Oral History Reader*. London: Routledge. pp. 29–37.

Jung Chang (1992) *Wild Swans*. London: Harper Collins.

Plummer, K. (2001) 'The call of life stories in ethnographic research', in P. Atkinson, S. Delamont, A. Coffey, J. Lofland and L. Lofland (eds), *Handbook of Ethnography*. London: Sage. pp. 395–406.

Reed, J. (1980) 'The Border Ballads', in E. Cowan (ed.), *The People's Past*. Edinburgh: Edinburgh University Student Publications Board. pp. 17–31.

Rowbotham, S. (1973) *Hidden from History*. London: Pluto.

Terkel, S. (1970) *Hard Times*. New York: Pantheon.

Thompson, P. (1975) *The Edwardians: The Remaking of British Society*. London: Weidenfeld and Nicolson.

Phenomenological Methods

Definition

The phenomenological method aims to describe, understand and interpret the meanings of experiences of human life. It focuses on research questions such as what it is like to experience a particular situation. There is a distinction to be made between phenomenology (which is a philosophical school) and phenomenological methods (which is an approach to research).

Distinctive Features

Phenomenology has roots in both philosophy and psychology. The scholar who has been most influential in the philosophy of phenomenology is Edmund Husserl (1859–1938). Husserl emphasized the centrality of the human context in understanding life; that is, researchers and readers of research can understand human experience because they are participants in the human condition. Thus the task of understanding is to retain continuity with what is already experientially evident and familiar to us as humans. Husserl developed the concept of the lifeworld (*Lebenswelt*) which refers to the everyday experiences that we live and which we reflect upon. The notion of the lifeworld is now considered central to phenomenological enquiry. The argument is that concepts (or phenomena) such as 'happiness' only have meaning with reference to the lifeworld. Furthermore, some phenomena in the lifeworld may present themselves as puzzling and much human activity is therefore concerned with enquiry and interpretation.

The main goals of Husserl's phenomenology were therefore first to use the lifeworld as a source of evidence and secondly to describe the essential qualities of a phenomenon so that we can better understand its nature. Husserl's philosophy was influential in sociological theory through the work of Alfred Schutz. But Schutz's method of philosophical enquiry ('eidetic analysis') was not an empirical method. Instead it was in psychology, through the work of Amedio Giorgi and others, that phenomenology was translated into empirical research procedures. Giorgi was concerned that psychologists should focus on the qualitative meaning of experiential phenomena rather than their measurement. Giorgi's methods stressed the need for researchers to gather concrete descriptions of specific experiences and then to search for the 'bare bones' of meanings of a phenomenon that relate to all (or nearly all) cases of its occurrence.

Data collection methods of phenomenological research tend to focus on in-depth **interviews** and **narratives** as these methods are the key to producing a description of the experiences that were lived through. Less frequently lifeworld descriptions may be gathered through other methods such as **diaries, documentary methods** or visual methods. Whatever the method of data collection, the phenomenological researcher becomes a mediator between the voices and experiences of the research respondents and the broader community of interested people. Phenomenological studies typically involve a purposive **sampling** strategy, but may include other strategies such as systematic sampling.

Todres and Holloway (2004) suggest that a good way to ask a respondent to describe a lifeworld experience is to ask questions which will elicit concrete events or experiences. The general approach is therefore to ask 'have you had this kind of experience, and if so how did it occur for you and what was it like for you?' One problem of this approach is that respondents may not know what the researcher means by the phenomenon of interest or, alternatively, may understand what the researcher is asking for but have not had an experience of this kind.

While at one level phenomenology could be seen as a revoicing of an individual's experience, phenomenology is perhaps more useful when the researcher is able to generalize beyond the individual and articulate transferable meanings of what makes an experience what it is. Phenomenology tends to be characterized by rhetorical or self-aware forms of **writing**. Often the purpose is to evoke an aesthetic appeal and engage the emotions of the reader rather than speak to them in an authoritarian manner.

Examples

A phenomenological study by Fow (1996) describes essential features of the phenomena of forgiveness and reconciliation. Fow identifies how one essential feature of the phenomenon is that the individual achieved a change of perspective about a perception of being personally violated. From the cases that he studied, this change of perspective was achieved in three main ways: by identifying with the other, by better understanding the circumstances of the other and by taking the action less personally within a larger philosophical framework.

Evaluation

Advocates of phenomenological methods argue the strengths of the method lie in its clear epistemological position and the centrality of the human individual within the data collection and analysis. Furthermore, the method has become popular in the health and social care arenas, where the need to research the **129** experiences of patients/users has been encouraged. However, as Todres and Holloway (2004) warn, there is a danger of phenomenological methods being used to present research on patients'/users' views rather than on research that is based on the descriptions of their lifeworlds.

As with other qualitative methods, phenomenological methods have been criticized for their poor **generalizability**, that is, the extent to which a researcher's description of the essences of a phenomenon can hold true outside of the context in which they were researched. The **validity** of a phenomenological study can perhaps be best judged on the descriptive adequacy of the research. This might mean that in writing up the study the researcher attempts to communicate the 'thickness' or richness of the experience, providing enough examples to enable the reader to reach the same conclusions while at the same time formulating a level of description that provides more generality.

Associated Concepts: Diary Methods, Documentary Methods, Generalization, Interviews, Narratives, Sampling, Validity (*see* Reliability), Writing.

Key Readings

Creswell, J. (1998) *Qualitative Inquiry and Research Design: Choosing Among Five Traditions.* Thousand Oaks, CA: Sage.

Fow, N.R. (1996) 'The phenomenology of forgiveness and reconciliation', *Journal of Phenomenological Psychology,* 27(2): 219–233.

Giorgi, A. (1985) *Phenomenology and Psychological Research.* Pittsburgh: Duquesne University Press.

*Giorgi, A. (1997) 'The theory, practice and evaluation of the phenomenological method as a qualitative research procedure', *Journal of Phenomenological Psychology,* 28(2): 235–260.

Husserl, E. (1999) *The Essential Husserl: Basic Writings in Transcendental Phenomenology* (ed. D. Welton). Bloomington, IN: Indiana University Press.

Todres, L. and Holloway, I. (2004) 'Descriptive phenomenology: lifeworld as evidence', in F. Rapport (ed.), *New Qualitative Methodologies in Health and Social Care Research.* London: Routledge.

Piloting

Definition

Piloting refers to the conduct of preliminary research, prior to the main study. It provides a structured opportunity for informed reflection on, and modification of, the research design, the research instruments, costings, timing, researcher security and indeed a whole gamut of issues concerning the everyday conduct of the research. Piloting therefore involves the field testing and development of the formal scheme of the research that was initially elaborated to secure research funding and research access.

Distinctive Features

While it is a commonplace that all good research needs to be flexible and developmental in approach, in order to adapt to changing circumstances and to capitalize on emerging analytic themes and understandings, a proper pilot is a formal aid to such ongoing modification and development. Ideally the research timetable should not only allow for the conduct of the pilot, prior to the main study, but also for the proper analysis of the pilot data to ensure that all the potential lessons of pilot work have been fully absorbed. This should pose few problems in most disciplines, but in some anthropological studies travel costs may make it unrealistic for researchers to seek to withdraw physically from the field for reflection between the pilot and the main phase of data collection.

In some fields of quantitative social research, such as randomized controlled trials, it has become accepted practice for the pivotal worth of pilot work to be recognized through a two-phase funding system, whereby an application for the funding of a full-scale trial will only be successful where the applicants have previously conducted and reported on initial pilot work to provide effect sizes for the sample-size calculation, to verify sample recruitment rates, and so on. As Sampson (2004) has pointed out, in qualitative work the value of piloting is often just as great, but is less universally recognized.

There are a number of specific issues in which piloting can be helpful. Piloting can assist in the closer formulation of the forshadowed problems that the study is directed towards exploring. **Access negotiations** may be more successful where gatekeepers and research subjects have an opportunity in the pilot to develop a more informed view of the research project and its implications for them, their work and their lives. In **focus group** research and in qualitative **interviewing**, pilot work allows the researcher to test out different focusing exercises and interview guides, and (crucially) to time the length of those focus groups and interviews and to make modifications when the length is inappropriate. Piloting allows the researcher to develop a better background understanding of the research setting and how the setting is likely to impinge on the conduct of the research. Piloting also alerts the researcher to potential **ethical** issues and to the threats of **dangerous fieldwork**, again allowing remedial modifications in design and procedures to be put in place.

131

Examples

Sampson (2004) contrasts her experiences as a fieldworker on two qualitative research projects, one of which embraced a pilot phase and one of which did not. The latter involved her in shipboard fieldwork (observation, interviews and focus groups) which she felt insufficiently prepared for, not just in respect of prior focused lines of enquiry, but also in respect of the physical demands that the research environment made on her (the 24-hour nature of shipboard work, the sleep-destroying motion of the ship, etc.) and the potential dangers to an isolated fieldworker unable to communicate her concern to the outside world. Whyte's (1955) classic ethnography of Italian-American ghetto life, *Street Corner Society*, contains a detailed account of his initial fieldwork efforts and how these shaped the resulting study.

Evaluation

There is really no doubt whatsoever that pilot work has multiple benefits for qualitative research: these are the benefits that preparedness lends to every endeavour. The only real disadvantage of pilot work is the additional resourcing required.

Associated Concepts: Access Negotiations, Dangerous Fieldwork, Ethics, Focus Groups, Interviewing.

Key Readings

*Sampson, H. (2004) 'Navigating the waves: the usefulness of a pilot in qualitative research', *Qualitative Research*, 4: 383–402.

Whyte, W.J. (1955) *Street Corner Society: The Social Structure of an Italian Slum* (2nd enlarged edn). Chicago: University of Chicago Press.

Postmodernism

Definition

Postmodernism is to be understood as a contrast to the modernist perspective that has dominated western thought since the eighteenth-century Enlightenment, as a rejection of the optimistic assumptions that social reality is graspable and describable in some final or sufficient sense, and that our selves and our social worlds are coherent wholes. Implicit in this contrastive stance is a critique of modernist methodological rigour.

Distinctive Features

The distinctive features of postmodernist methods cannot, by their nature, be exhaustively described. To be true to their nature, they must necessarily be contingent and emergent and even inchoate, just as their begetter, the philosopher Derrida, would sometimes be deliberately and playfully obscure. All this is rather irritating for the earnest student chasing, as a postmodernist critic might have it, the Bubble of Enlightenment. So some minimal distinctive features will be set down here, even though this old-fashioned attempt at representation might be seen by the same postmodernist critic as doomed to failure.

The first principle of a postmodernist methodology is the rejection of all claims to a *scientific* method. Adequate representation of social reality is deemed to be an impossible project and all accounts are necessarily partial, so the pursuit of scientific rigour by various means (establishing comprehensiveness of coverage, avoiding **bias**, demonstrating **validity** and **generalizability**, and so on) is a futile endeavour. It is not that 'scientific' accounts generated by such methods are 'wrong', rather they are held to be simply partial accounts to be set alongside others in a new poly-vocal social science. But since the claims to scientific rigour are viewed as simply 'claims' – techniques to usurp spurious authorial authority – it follows that postmodern methods do not seek to imitate the methodological forms of an allegedly misguided modernism.

A corollary of the rejection of scientific authority is the celebration of alternative accounts of social reality and some postmodernist work is marked by methods which promote an active collaboration between the researcher and the researched, perhaps through publishing an extended single transcript of an interview with a minimal introduction. There is a surprising parallel here with some **oral history** work.

However, overwhelmingly, the methods of choice for postmodernist researchers are those borrowing from poststructuralist literary critics and writers in cultural studies, namely those pertaining to the deconstruction of texts. A text is conceived broadly as any cultural product, films and TV programmes being popular subjects of study. And deconstruction refers to the analytic dissection of the methods of construction used by the author/director of the text to convey meanings, both overt and subliminal. There is a parallel here with **narrative** analysis.

Much postmodernist analysis is self-referential in that it focuses on the methods of construction used by fellow social scientists (to the occasional irritation of the modernist social scientists concerned) to convey meaning and legitimate authorial authority. Lather (2002), drawing on the work of the critic Walter Benjamin, has suggested that through the critical examination of these once-authoritative and now battered 'ruins', the analyst can discern the beliefs that sustained them in their heyday and are only now transparent in their skeletal remains. The postmodernist deconstruction of the authorial 'voice' in social science has been the crucial stimulant of the '**reflexive** turn' in research methods.

Examples
Wacquant (1998) has furnished an extended transcript from an interview with a black ghetto hustler, Rickey, as an example of collaboration between researcher and researched, which is careful to eschew any realist claims for the status of the (carefully edited, and therefore constructed) transcript. Geertz's (1988) analysis of the writing of ethnographic texts is an elegantly constructed deconstruction of the anthropologist's authorial voice from one of the foremost anthropologists of the twentieth century.

Evaluation
Seale's (1999) methods text, *The Quality of Qualitative Research*, begins and closes with an examination of the postmodern challenge to qualitative research methods, taking several postmodern analyses (including Wacquant's article) as extended examples. Seale follows (albeit with occasional departures) the response of the ethnographer, Martyn Hammersley, to the postmodern challenge to ethnographic methods (Hammersley, 1992). Hammersley abandoned with some relief a commitment to naïve realist representation of social reality and to 'author-evacuated texts' (the phrase is Geertz's), but has resisted the view that all representations of reality are equally legitimate and has argued that methodological techniques can assist in the judgement of which partial viewpoints have most plausibility and credibility. Hammersley's nuanced response, termed 'subtle realism', is not of course in contradistinction to the postmodernist position, which would accept subtle realism was one possible response among many in a world with plural social realities.

Associated Concepts: Bias, Discourse Analysis, Generalization, Narratives, Oral History, Reflexivity, Validity (*see* Reliability).

Key Readings
Geertz, C. (1988) *Works and Lives: The Anthropologist as Author*. Cambridge: Polity.
Hammersley, M. (1992) *What's Wrong with Ethnography: Methodological Explorations*. London: Routledge.
Lather, P. (2002) 'Post modernism, post-structuralism and post (critical) ethnography: of ruins, aporias and angels', in P. Atkinson, A. Coffey, S. Delamont, J. Lofland and L. Lofland et al. (eds), *Handbook of Ethnography*. London: Sage. pp. 477–492.

*Seale, C. (1999) *The Quality of Qualitative Research.* London: Sage.
Wacquant, L. (1998) 'Inside the zone: the social art of the hustler in the Black American Ghetto', *Theory, Culture and Society,* 15: 1–36.

Process Evaluation

Definition
Process evaluations are largely qualitative investigations conducted in parallel with quantitative ('outcome') evaluations of policy and practice interventions, particularly but not exclusively in the health services. While the quantitative evaluation focuses on whether or not the intervention is successful, the process evaluation – by focusing on the *processes* by which the intervention is delivered – seeks to answer the question of *why* the intervention has been successful or unsuccessful.

Distinctive Features
Some aspects of a process evaluation can often be addressed in the same survey research instrument as the outcome evaluation, but typically process evaluations will involve a **multi-method** design and be largely qualitative, since the topical focus is descriptive, rather than a matter of hypothesis-testing (Calnan and Ferlie, 2003). Process evaluations should address the efficiency as well as the effectiveness of the intervention in question, and so even when an intervention is shown to be successful in outcome, the process evaluation should contribute information on how the intervention could be further improved.

Examples
Parry Langdon et al. (2003) describe a multi-method process evaluation conducted as part of a randomized controlled trial of a schools-based anti-smoking intervention undertaken across 59 schools. Since the intervention involved training groups of pupils ('peer supporters') to intervene effectively among their peers to prevent smoking uptake and encourage smoking cessation, the process evaluation therefore had to cover the delivery of the training to the volunteer pupils, the conduct of the peer supporters, and their reception by

their peers at key points in the study process. Data had also to be collected on topics such as other coexistent health promotion initiatives, school smoking policies and the perspectives of the school staff. The process evaluation involved in-depth data collection in four 'intervention' schools and four 'control' schools, plus more limited data from all 59 schools.

Evaluation

The inclusion of a process evaluation component has become almost the hall-mark of a good evaluation design in health services research, and is typically advised by bodies like the trials office of the UK's Medical Research Council. But substantial problems remain. Qualitative methods are intensive and costly, but trials are typically conducted on extensive populations and evaluation funds are limited. Process evaluations typically involve sampling of sub-populations rather than research contact with the entire trial population, and so may not always capture the range of responses of the population to the intervention. Further, the different methods in a multi-method design are neither commen-surate nor additive, so the findings that emerge may sometimes be ambiguous, to the particular annoyance of collaborators and sponsors.

Associated Concepts: Multiple Methods.

Key Readings

Calnan, M. and Ferlie, E. (2003) 'Analysing process in healthcare: the methodological and theoretical chal-lenges', *Policy and Politics*, 31: 185–193.

*Parry Langdon, N., Bloor, M., Audrey, S. and Holliday, J. (2003) 'Process evalu-ation of health promotion interven-tions', *Policy and Politics*, 31: 207–216.

Public Participation

Definition

The participation of the wider community (and research subjects in particular) in the research process as more than just research subjects, that is participa-tion in either the planning, oversight, conduct, analysis or appraisal of research, or in some combination of these tasks.

Distinctive Features

Researchers have a duty to facilitate public involvement in the research process, particularly where their research is publicly funded. Some professional associations formally recognize that duty. Thus, the guidelines of the British-based Association of Social Anthropologists state that 'as far as possible anthropologists should try and involve the people being studied in the planning and execution of research projects' (ASA, 1987: 6). Some funding bodies have sections on their grant forms requiring applicants to be explicit about how they plan to involve the public in the proposed research. And many voluntary associations, particularly sufferers' groups like the Breast Cancer Campaign, see the provision of encouragement, advice and support to relevant research projects as an important part of their role.

However, beyond this requirement to facilitate participation, it is claimed that public participation may have the effect of improving the quality of the research, with 'lay experts' providing an extended peer review, that is, providing critical and illuminating commentary on early research findings, in an analogous fashion to the commentary provided by the scientific community through the peer review process (cf. Irwin, 1995). Further still, it is sometimes claimed that, through public participation, research can be transformative and emancipatory for both researchers and public alike. This is the radical agenda of Participatory Action Research (PAR), inspired by the Brazilian educationalist Paolo Freire and taken up in kindred fields of **action research** such as health promotion research. Freire describes the objective of his work as 'conscientization .... the process in which men [sic], not as recipients, but as knowing subjects, achieve a deepening awareness of the socio-cultural reality which shapes their lives and their capacity to transform that reality' (Freire, 1972: 51fn.).

The forms that public participation may take will vary according to the acknowledged objectives. Public participation in the planning and oversight of a project may simply involve community representation on a project steering group. Participation in the conduct of the research may involve the employment of so-called 'indigenous researchers' as focus group recruiters and facilitators, or as interviewers (Baker and Hinton, 1999). Participation in analysis and appraisal may involve the recruitment of lay experts into a **focus group** or **Delphi group**. More ambitiously, attempts to involve the public in deliberations on the policy implications of research have resulted in the development of **'citizens' juries'** (Pickard, 1998) and, more recently (and relatedly), 'deliberative mapping', an innovative method of public consultation which integrates expert and citizen assessments and emphasizes diversity.

137

Examples

An overview of the use of focus groups in the service of public participation in research, summarizing a number of individual studies, is provided in Bloor et al. (2001).

Evaluation

In securing public participation in social research, as in so many things, the devil is in the detail. Public participation is a worthy – even necessary – objective, the difficulty lies in finding forms which will secure that objective. It is important not to fall into the same trap as the artists of the Romantic Movement of the nineteenth century, who sought through their art to access 'true' feelings and 'real' nature: simply opening a research project to public participation will not ensure commentary and judgement from The True Voice of the People. The form that is chosen for that participation will itself shape the expression of the views being sought, and different forms will affect that expression in different ways. For example, public representatives chosen to fulfil a representative function on project steering committees will become increasingly unrepresentative over time as a direct result of their continuing participation in the project. Epstein (1995), studying the involvement of AIDS activists in HIV/AIDS research, has coined the term 'expertification' to describe this process.

Relatedly, some claims about the impact of public participation approaches on the research process may be overblown. While no one can doubt the impact of Freire's original group work among the impoverished peasantry of north-east Brazil, the emancipatory impact of later PAR work in the developed world is less clear: participation in a research project can be a cathartic experience for the participants and researchers alike, but accounts are thin on the ground of how such participation has transformed people's subsequent lives, individually and collectively.

Nevertheless, despite overblown claims and the inevitable structural constraints on the achievement of participation aspirations, there is no doubt that the active engagement of social researchers with critical public audiences will serve both to deepen and extend the analysis, and to sharpen up the implications of the research for policy and practice. Public participation in research, even if not thought to be a natural concomitant of public research funding, is a strong safeguard against a research culture that is politically quietist and self-referential.

Associated Concepts: Action Research, Citizens' Juries, Delphi Groups, Focus Groups.

Key Readings

Association of Social Anthropologists (1987) *Ethical Guidelines for Good Practice*. London: Association of Social Anthropologists.

Baker, R. and Hinton, R. (1999) 'Do focus groups facilitate meaningful participation in social research?', in R. Barbour and J. Kitzinger (eds), *Developing Focus Group Research: Politics, Theory and Practice*. London: Sage.

*Bloor, M., Frankland, J., Thomas, M. and Robson, K. (2001) *Focus Groups in Social Research*. London: Sage.

Epstein, S. (1995) *Impure Science: AIDS Activism and the Politics of Knowledge*. Berkeley: University of California Press.

Freire, P. (1972) *Cultural Action for Freedom*. Harmondsworth: Penguin.

Irwin, A. (1995) *Citizen Science*. London: Routledge.

Pickard, S. (1998) 'Citizenship and consumerism in health care: a critique of citizens' juries', *Social Policy and Administration*, 32: 226–44.

Public/Private Accounts

Definition

The term refers to the distinction between types of responses (or accounts) that are given by respondents depending on how they wish to present themselves to their audience.

Distinctive Features

Researchers should be aware that respondents may modify their biographical presentations of themselves so as to produce a more acceptable or enhanced account of themselves. This is known as a 'public account' and may differ from the 'private account' in terms of reports of behaviour and beliefs and the language in which the account is expressed. West (1990) claims that public accounts serve to affirm and reproduce the moral order. Thus what is said in a public account will be non-controversial, familiar and acceptable to the person listening to the account. For example the often-heard phrase 'I mustn't grumble' is a public account typically given by patients. In such exchanges the speakers may feel that they actually do want to complain about their health but are aware that grumbling about their health is not well tolerated by others. Therefore, in public accounts the social order is maintained and within the fieldwork interaction attention is directed away from any potentially

139

stigmatizing confessions. In contrast, private accounts refer to more personal, honest and reflective accounts derived from the respondents' own experiences.

Having acknowledged that there might be inconsistency between the types of accounts offered by respondents, the social researcher needs to consider which type of account they wish to access and, later on in the research process, whether the data they have collected may be considered to be either a public or a private account. Respondent accounts should be interpreted within the context in which they were produced. For example, the very presence of the **ethnographer** within a setting may influence what the members of that culture say or do. Cornwell (1984) is clear that good **fieldwork relationships** are vital to accessing private accounts. Socio-demographic factors such as age, gender, ethnicity and background are obviously important in aiding rapport between the researcher and respondent but, as Cornwell describes, sharing the same biographical characteristics as one's respondents is not enough to guarantee access to private accounts. **Trust** may need to be built up over a period of time, perhaps with repeated visits to the same respondents. Goffman (1959) has described how, particularly in new and unfamiliar situations, people are unsure of themselves and seek to limit damage to their character by managing information about themselves. The protection of self through the reproduction of a culturally normative account is perhaps particularly important in situations where people are conscious of a difference in status between themselves and their audience.

Cornwell (1984) also notes that public accounts are more likely to be used in response to a direct question. In contrast private accounts are more likely to be given if the interviewee is invited to tell a story. She argues this is because of a subtle shift of power away from the interviewer in favour of the interviewee. The interviewee is therefore diverted away from the interviewer's agenda and focused on their own experiences.

Fieldwork relationships between researcher and respondent are not the only influence on accessing private accounts. The research setting may have a significant effect on the type of response given. For example, respondents being interviewed in a GP surgery may be more likely to produce public accounts than if they were being interviewed at home, perhaps because they might be worried about being overheard or because they feel less empowered and are therefore less likely to speak their minds. The presence of people other than the researcher can also repress private accounts. For example, during **focus group** research or **group interviews** respondents may be more concerned about presenting themselves as socially acceptable to other members of the group (Phoenix et al., 2003).

The term 'public and private accounts' has also been used by researchers to reflect the tension between seeking knowledge and understandings from other people's private lives and then translating them into a format of public knowledge through academic writing. The concern is that an ambiguity arises when researchers seek to simultaneously serve academic demands while also trying to remain faithful to personal and intimate forms of knowledge. This problem has typically been raised among feminist researchers but it is perhaps also relevant in **ethnographic** research (Ribbens and Edwards, 1998).

Examples

Cornwell's anthropological study of families in the East End of London is perhaps the most famous discussion of public and private accounts. The study explored the common-sense ideas and theories about health, illness and health services from 24 people (15 women and 9 men). The study was anthropological in the sense that Cornwell did not explore peoples' ideas about health in isolation but rather in relation to other aspects of everyday life: family, work, community. Cornwell recruited her respondents through informal networks and made repeated visits to them. In her early fieldwork encounters she noted how her respondents produced 'expected' responses to things which they believed to be medically authorized. Over time, as her fieldwork relationships developed, she noted how her respondents gave different accounts regardless of whether the discussion was about work, family, health or the community. For example, at first interview a woman describes her neighbours as helpful and friendly but on the sixth visit the same woman recounts a story of the verbal and physical street fights she had with neighbours. Public accounts of family life typically reflected images of unity with loving relationships between and among the generations. Private accounts of family life, however, drew attention to the conflicts, strains and contradictions between family members. Similarly, when discussing employment, respondents produced public accounts of work as a respectable activity, capable of producing rewards (income, security, satisfaction). Personal accounts of work, on the other hand, emerged from more detailed and specific discussions about respondents' particular job and the meaning that it had for them personally. The resulting private accounts of employment revealed experiences of alienation and constraint.

Duke (2002) provides a methodological and reflexive account of her interviews with drug policy makers within a range of government departments. Within her **access negotiations** she made it clear that she was interested in the civil servants' individual views and experiences rather than the views of the organization or the department. However, she describes that fairly early in her fieldwork it became evident that there was an official line: her task was to recognize this public account and probe beyond it. Duke reflects that she managed to achieve this in some interviews, demonstrated by the fact that some of the respondents requested repeated assurances of anonymity or stressed that they were telling her things 'off the record'. Accessing private

141

accounts was perhaps particularly challenging with this particular occupational group as civil servants are prevented from disclosing information about their work without official sanction. An extreme disclosure could represent a breach of the Official Secrets Act. Furthermore Duke argues that civil servants are socialized to underemphasize their own personal influence within policy making. Interestingly she notes that it was easier to penetrate beyond the official line when asking her respondents to reflect on policies of the previous government.

Evaluation

Acknowledging that respondents may provide differing accounts depending on to whom they are speaking and the context of the question, raises issues about the status of interview data. Accounts may not be viewed in a positivistic sense as simple representations of the world. It cannot be claimed that public accounts are always 'false' and private accounts are always 'true'. Public accounts are given for a purpose, and that representation of the world by the respondent to the researcher should be acknowledged as a valid representation. The skill is for the researcher to be able to acknowledge public accounts for what they are and, if required, to probe beyond into the private beliefs and behaviours.

Associated Concepts: Access Negotiations, Ethnography, Fieldwork Relationships, Focus Groups, Group Interviews, Trust.

Key Readings

*Cornwell, J. (1984) *Hard Earned Lives: Accounts of Health and Illness from East London.* London: Tavistock.

Duke, K. (2002) 'Getting beyond the "official line": reflections on dilemmas of access, knowledge and power in researching policy networks', *Journal of Social Policy*, 31(1): 39–59.

Goffman, E. (1959) *The Presentation of Self in Everyday Life.* New York: Doubleday.

Phoenix, A., Frosh, S. and Pattman, R. (2003) 'Producing contradictory masculine subject positions: narrative of threat, homophobia and bullying in 11–14 year old boys', *Journal of Social Issues*, 59(1): 179–195.

Ribbens, J. and Edwards, R. (1998) *Feminist Dilemmas in Qualitative Research: Public Knowledge and Private Lives.* London: Sage.

West, P. (1990) 'The status and validity of accounts obtained at interview: a contrast between two studies of families with a disabled child', *Social Science and Medicine*, 30: 1229–1239.

Rapid Assessment

Definition
Rapid assessment is a difficult term to define because it has fashionable connotations, with the result that many researchers, using a wide variety of techniques, have sought to claim that their work falls within its ambit. However, broadly speaking, it may be taken to refer to those research approaches which aim to be cost-effective, quick to deliver, explicitly concerned with policy responses, seek an inductive understanding of the situation, and combine qualitative and quantitative methods, tapping a range of data sources. Rapid assessment has been variously and alternatively termed 'rapid rural appraisal' (RRA), 'rapid anthropological procedures', 'rapid appraisal', 'rapid assessment procedures' (RAP), 'rapid assessment methods' (RAM), 'rapid assessment and response' (RAR) and 'rapid assessment techniques' (never abbreviated).

Distinctive Features
Though its applications could extend through many fields, rapid assessment has developed particularly within the public health field and under the stimulus of international agencies, particularly the World Health Organization (WHO) and the United Nations International Drug Control Programme (UNIDCP). In response to a widespread perception among international policy-makers that traditional public health research is of very limited value in developing responses to new public health threats (being too slow, too costly and too remote from possible health interventions), rapid assessment seeks to provide reliable information on the extent of a given health threat, and the feasibility of possible policy responses, within a very short time-scale, typically within three months. Its main uses have been in developing and transitional (former communist) countries, but in principle rapid assessment techniques could be applied in any setting where rigour in relation to cost and use takes priority over exhaustive investigation (Chambers, 1981).

Both quantitative and qualitative techniques of data collection are commonly used in a **multi-methods** design: community surveys and mapping techniques on the one hand, and **key-informant interviews**, brief observation and **group interviews** on the other hand. Rapid assessment emphasizes drawing on deliberately contrasting data sources in order to develop and then extend or check initial hypotheses. Such hypotheses are generated inductively, in contrast to the deductive approach of traditional public health research.

Rapid assessment is explicitly focused on the identification and design of locally relevant intervention programmes. So that, where the policy issue is the prevention of disease spread, rapid assessment aims not just to identify the extent of knowledge and ignorance about mechanisms of disease spread ('Do respondents realise that Lassa Fever is spread by the contamination of human food supplies by rat faeces?'), but also to identify the most effective potential control mechanisms in the local situation (Control of the local rat population? Centralized rat-proof food stores? Use of rat-proof domestic food containers?).

Some writing on rapid assessment emphasizes the potential of this methodology for the **public participation** of local populations in the research process, for the involvement of so-called indigenous researchers in the processes of data collection and analysis, and the resultant 'technology transfer' of research skills. It is certainly true that the best rapid assessment research is undoubtedly conducted with local research partners, and without local partners an external consultant 'parachuted' into an unfamiliar research environment is unlikely to contribute findings of much value, but the extent of research technology transfer that can occur during a single, short-term research project is naturally rather limited. Accordingly, rapid assessment practitioners have emphasized the production of detailed manuals (e.g. Scrimshaw and Gleason, 1992) which should allow local practitioners to conduct rapid assessments without prior research training.

Examples

A study in a developed world setting which used rapid assessment techniques is that of Kelher et al. (1997), where the methodology was used in the planning of cervical cancer screening and treatment facilities for indigenous Australian women. In contrast, a manual on rapid assessment techniques in health-related programmes in the developing world gives examples of studies in Burkina Faso, Cape Verde, Chad, India, Indonesia, Malawi, Niger, the slums of Rio de Janeiro, and elsewhere (Scrimshaw and Gleason, 1992). And Rhodes et al. (1999) report on their experience of using rapid assessment techniques to document and respond to the spread of HIV infection among injecting drug users in Eastern Europe.

Evaluation

No systematic evaluation of the effectiveness and efficiency of rapid assessment has been undertaken. Proponents of rapid assessment techniques, such as Chambers (1981), have taken the view that the argument that rapid assessment is bad science depends itself on an inappropriate view of what science consists of – the piling up of useless mountains of data and an exhaustive concern with accuracy. Instead, Chambers argues for 'optimal ignorance' – the importance of knowing what is worth knowing – and for 'proportionate' rather than exhaustive accuracy. Nevertheless, the impression remains that rapid assessment is second-class science, an impression reinforced by the fact that such techniques are largely confined to studies in developing world populations: where they do occur in developed world studies, they appear to be confined to studies of ethnic minorities.

The overview of rapid assessment techniques by Fitch et al. (2000) takes the cautious view that rapid assessment techniques ought to be used *alongside* more systematic methods of evaluation, rather than as an alternative. In this reading, rapid assessment may play an essential preliminary or **piloting** role in a long-term evaluation and monitoring strategy, where only a limited number of research topics covered by rapid assessment are selected for further and more systematic study.

Associated Concepts: Group Interviews, Key Informants, Multiple Methods, Piloting, Public Participation.

Key Readings

Chambers, R. (1981) 'Rapid rural appraisal: rationale and repertoire', *Public Administration and Development*, 1: 95–106.

*Fitch, C., Rhodes, T. and Stimson, G. (2000) 'Origins of an epidemic: the methodological and political emergence of rapid assessment', *International Journal of Drug Policy*, 11: 63–72.

Kelher, M., Gillespie, A., Allotey, P., et al. (1997) The *Impact of Culture and Ethnicity on Cervical Screening in Queensland*. Report to Queensland Health. Brisbane: Australian Centre for International and Tropical Health and Nutrition, University of Queensland.

Rhodes, T., Stimson, G., Fitch, C., Renton, A. and Ball, A. (1999) 'Rapid assessment, injecting drug use and public health', *The Lancet*, 354: 65–68.

Scrimshaw, N. and Gleason, G. (eds) (1992) *Rapid Assessment Procedures – Qualitative Methodologies for Planning and Evaluation of Health Related Programmes*. Boston: International Nutrition Foundation. www.RARarchives.org

Reflexivity

Definition

Reflexivity is an awareness of the self in the situation of action and of the role of the self in constructing that situation. Reflexivity is thus distinct from

145

reflectivity in its focus on the constitutive role of the self. A famous Max Escher lithograph, 'Drawing Hands', is said to represent reflexivity analogically in its depiction of two hands sketched on paper, each hand holding a drawing pencil with each in the act of drawing the other on to the drawing paper.

Distinctive Features

Reflexivity is particularly associated with the 1980s 'crisis of legitimation' in the social sciences in which the authority of authorship was challenged by writers from divergent traditions, those of feminist scholarship, the post-Marxist writings of Foucault and his followers, and poststructuralist literary critics. Research reports were viewed as deriving their truth status and generalizability, not from their skilful deployment of scientific research methods, but rather from their skilful deployment of authorial rhetorical devices (Geertz, 1988). Postmodern scholarship, in 'deconstructing texts', therefore sought to examine how these authorial devices were effectively employed. Postmodernists have side-stepped the criticism that they are using the self-same devices to make their own claims to authorial authority by both refusing to claim legitimacy (asserting that scholarship should be characterized by dialogue and the encouragement of divergent opinion), and (crucially) by retaining a reflexive awareness of their own authorial practices. 'Author-evacuated texts', Geertz's phrase, are held to be a thing of the past, as each author seeks to communicate to the reader the terms of his or her engagement with the tasks of research and writing.

Yet, although the 'reflexive turn' is synonymous with **postmodern writing**, the constitutive role of the researcher in the setting studied has been long understood. It underlies the preference of many psychologists for controlled laboratory settings, 'uncontaminated' (allegedly) by a co-present observer. And the constitutive power of all actors – researchers included – to socially construct the reality they inhabit was the central analytic preoccupation of **symbolic interactionism** and **phenomenology**, and of much methodological writing: for example, the recognition is found in all qualitative research texts that the research interview is a species of conversation, and that the interviewer is not a neutral information-gatherer, but rather is an active co-participant with the interviewee in the social construction of the research data.

Examples

Seale (1999) discusses examples of recent contrasting attempts by researchers to 'reinstate the author' in a manner consonant with postmodern sensibilities.

Evaluation

As Geertz has commented, it should be a matter of relief that academic scholarship can abandon the pretence that the author is absent from the text. There is an important issue of intellectual honesty here, exemplified in the belated publication of the research diaries of Malinowski (1967), which betray a much more critical view of his native informants than is to be found in his classic text *Argonauts of the Western Pacific* (Malinowski, 1922). The reportage of the author's engagement with the research is a helpful resource to readers in their evaluation of the text.

However, reflexive accounts can be done clumsily. Many a Ph.D. examiner must have sighed to find the candidate's methods chapter begin, yet again, by likening the research process to 'walking down a long dark tunnel'. And worse still, as Atkinson (1992) has pointed out, reflexive accounts can be overdone: no reader, apart from the author's mother, will be engaged by a research report which is too self-referential. There are no guidelines to the production of a faithful and illuminating reflexive account.

Associated Concepts: Phenomenological Methods, Postmodernism, Symbolic Interactionism, Writing.

Key Readings

*Atkinson, P. (1992) *The Ethnographic Imagination: Textual Constructions of Reality.* London: Routledge.

Geertz, C. (1988) *Works as Lives: The Anthropologist as Author.* Cambridge: Polity.

Malinowski, B. (1922) *Argonauts of the Western Pacific.* New York: E.P. Dutton.

Malinowski, B. (1967) *A Diary in the Strict Sense of the Term.* New York: Harcourt Brace.

Seale, C. (1999) *The Quality of Qualitative Research.* London: Sage.

Reliability/Validity

Definition

Reliability is the extent to which research produces the same results when replicated. Validity is the extent to which the research produces an accurate version of the world.

Distinctive Features

Scientific research is typically evaluated using measures of rigour such as reliability, validity and **generalizability**. However, compared with quantitative research, qualitative research has been less concerned with the traditional application of these measures.

Reliability is concerned with the extent to which research findings are reproducible, that is whether a different researcher who replicated the study would come to the same or similar conclusions. It can be argued that reliability is an impossible criterion to achieve in practice as different researchers will always produce different versions of the social world. Strategies to improve reliability include maintaining meticulous records of fieldwork and documenting the process of analysis (in a **research diary** or in analytic memos) so that others can follow the process in the form of an audit trail. Reliability of the data analysis can be improved through the rigorous comparison of coding of the same data by multiple researchers (Silverman, 1993), thereby resolving ambiguities in coding by discussion among the researchers.

When considering the validity of the conclusions of a research project, two types of inferences are involved. The first of these is the internal validity of the study. This is the degree to which the investigator's conclusions correctly portray the data collected. The other inference concerns external validity (also referred to as **generalizability**). This is the degree to which conclusions are appropriate to similar populations and locations outside of the study area.

Strategies to improve validity include **triangulation**, or **member validation**, although these strategies are not without their problems. Some researchers, particularly those working from a conversational analysis and postmodernist perspective, append the original data transcript to the research paper in order to allow readers to reach their own interpretation. Anthropologists have used other measures of validity for their findings following lengthy immersion in the field which enhances the accuracy of their account. These strategies include the ability of the anthropologist to 'pass' as a collectivity member (Goodenough, 1964) and the prediction of native taxonomy classifications by the anthropologist (Frake, 1961). Validity can also be improved by thorough data analysis in which the researcher searches for deviant cases, thereby revising the theory in the light of the data. Denzin (1989) has argued that from a qualitative perspective, validity reflects a need to provide an improved understanding of the research subject rather than improved accuracy.

An alternative (and positivistic) way of distinguishing between reliability and validity is to think of reliability as a measure of precision (the degree to which a research finding remains the same when data are collected and analysed several times) and to think of validity as a measure of accuracy (the degree to which a research finding reflects reality).

Examples

Barrett and Wellings (2002) (discussed in Green and Thorogood, 2004) provide an example of how the reliability and validity of a qualitative study can be maximized in their study of how women use and define the term 'unplanned pregnancy'. To improve the validity of their research the authors provide direct quotes along with the context (for instance the point in the interview) to enable the reader to see and judge how interpretations are made from the data, and they report deviant cases to demonstrate how such cases can still be accounted for in their interpretations. For example they discuss in detail the one case in which a woman reported that she had intended to become pregnant although the pregnancy itself was unplanned. The authors do not report the use of member validation in their research. To improve reliability the authors provide a clear account of the data collection and analytic procedures used. They do not report the use of multiple-coders for the same data but they do report discussion among the researchers to resolve the meaning of individual researchers' interpretations. This study also demonstrates how qualitative research can problematize the validity of survey research. Specifically the authors have concerns about how questions in national and international surveys of pregnancy are interpreted by women.

Evaluation

Advocates of qualitative research argue that it cannot and should not be judged by conventional measures of quality such as validity, reliability and generalizability. They reject the position of naïve realism: the belief that there is one unequivocal social reality which is independent of the researcher and can be reached through the rigorous application of the scientific method. Instead a relativist position is adopted reflecting the belief that there are multiple perspectives of the social world and these are constructed by the research process. Middle ground has been found between the extremes of realism and relativism. These intermediate positions are referred to as 'subtle realism' (Hammersley, 1992) and 'critical realism' (Bhaskar, 1989), amongst other terms. These positions reflect an acceptance that although the social world is perceived from a particular viewpoint, some of these viewpoints are more plausible than others. Consequently qualitative research will still need measures of quality on which to judge plausibility. Lincoln and Guba (1985) have argued that for qualitative research the positivist concepts of validity and reliability may be replaced by criteria of truth value, applicability, consistency and neutrality. But as Seale (1999) points out, terms such as 'truth' do not fit well with the position of relativism which supports the idea of multiple constructed realities rather than the realist view of a single tangible reality. Guba and

149

Lincoln have acknowledged this problem in later writings (Guba and Lincoln, 1989) by providing another criterion, 'authenticity'. Alternative evaluation measures have also been suggested by Hammersley (1990).

Associated Concepts: Generalization, Member Validation (*see* Triangulation) Research Diary, Triangulation.

Key Readings

Barrett, G. and Wellings, K. (2002) 'What is a "planned" pregnancy? Empirical data from a British Study', *Social Science and Medicine*, 55: 545–557.

Bhaskar, R. (1989) *Reclaiming Reality*. London: Verso.

Denzin, N.K. (1989) 'Strategies of multiple triangulation', in N.K. Denzin (ed.), *The Research Act: A Theoretical Introduction to Sociological Methods* (3rd edn). Englewood Cliffs, NJ: Prentice-Hall, pp. 234–247.

Frake, C. (1961) 'The diagnosis of disease among the Subanum of Mindanao', *American Anthropologist*, 63: 113–132.

Goodenough, W. (1964) 'Cultural anthropology and linguistics', in D. Hymes (ed.), *Language in Culture and Society*, New York: Harper and Row. pp. 36–39.

Green, J. and Thorogood, N. (2004) *Qualitative Methods for Health Researchers*. London: Sage.

Guba, E.G. and Lincoln, Y.S. (1989) *Fourth Generation Evaluation*. Newbury Park, CA: Sage.

Hammersley, M. (1990) *Reading Ethnographic Research*. New York: Longman.

Hammersley, M. (1992) *What's Wrong with Ethnography: Methodological Explorations*. London: Routledge.

Hulley, S.B. (2001) *Designing Clinical Research: An Epidemiological Approach*. Philadelphia: Williams and Wilkins.

*LeCompte, M. and Goetz, J. (1982) 'Problems of reliability and validity in ethnographic research', *Review of Educational Research*, 52(1): 31–60.

Lincoln, Y.S. and Guba, E.G. (1985) *Naturalistic Inquiry*. Newbury Park, CA: Sage.

Seale, C. (1999) *The Quality of Qualitative Research*. London: Sage.

Silverman, D. (1993) *Qualitative Data Analysis: Interpreting Talk, Text and Interaction*. London: Sage.

Research Diary

Definition

A research diary is a written record of the researcher's activities, thoughts and feelings throughout the research process from design, through data collection and analysis to writing and presenting the study.

Distinctive Features

The research diary is many things to many people. Some researchers may use a diary to record factual items such as contact numbers of **key informants** or reasons for changes to the research protocol. Others use it more prolifically to record analytical, conceptual or methodological ideas. Others still will be more inclined to use their research diary to express emotions, perhaps their concerns or delights throughout the study.

Coffey and Atkinson (1996: 191) have provided a particularly convincing argument as to the merits of keeping a research diary. They remind us that 'the construction of analytic or methodological memoranda and working papers, and the consequent explication of working hypotheses are of vital importance' and that to do this one must ensure that those 'working hypotheses are documented and retrievable'. By serving as an audit trail of methodological decisions and analytical hypotheses for the research, the research diary can also improve the **reliability** of the study should another researcher wish to replicate it.

Examples

Brownstein (1990) provides a **reflexive** account of a qualitative researcher's experiences of conducting research within a quantitatively orientated government department. The paper is based on his reflections recorded in his research diary, so that the diary itself becomes the data. The author describes his perceived need to prove his own credibility and that of the qualitative method and how he used his social relationships with his subjects outside of the workplace during more informal contact to promote himself and qualitative methods.

Evaluation

Burgess (1981) advocates the use of a research diary to enable the researcher to be **reflexive** about his or her role in the research process and the implications of his or her contact with participants. With the growth of confessional accounts in the **writing** of qualitative research, researchers have been more willing to expose their own subjective biases. Rather than having to prove one's scientific credentials, authority is instead gained by convincing the reader that the researcher's tale is indeed based in real experience.

Associated Concepts: Key Informants, Reflexivity, Reliability, Writing.   **151**

Key Readings

Brownstein, H.H. (1990) 'Surviving as a qualitative sociologist: recollections from the diary of a state worker', *Qualitative Sociology*, 13(2): 149–167.

*Burgess, R.G. (1981) 'Keeping a research diary', *Cambridge Journal of Education*, 11(1): 75–83.

Coffey, A. and Atkinson, P. (1996) *Making Sense of Qualitative Data Analysis: Complementary Strategies.* Thousand Oaks, CA: Sage.

Sampling

Definition
The selection of cases from wider populations.

Distinctive Features
Sampling is the link between the study population and its **generalization** to the wider population. The units of analysis of a sample may be individuals, institutions and communities.

A sample is representative of the population from which it is selected if the characteristics of the sample approximate to the characteristics in the population. Samples might only be representative with respect to characteristics that are important to the study question, although at the beginning of a study the researcher might not know which characteristics are relevant.

There are a wide variety of sampling methods. Miles and Huberman (1994) and Arber (2001) provide a useful typology of sampling strategies. Sampling methods fall into two broad types: probability and non-probability sampling. In probability sampling (random and systematic sampling) cases are selected in accordance with probability theory. The principle of random sampling is that every case in the population has an equal and non-zero chance of being selected to be part of the sample. Cases are selected using some kind of random mechanism such as computer-generated random numbers or random number tables. Systematic sampling requires the researcher to select every nth case (for example, every fifth child on a class register). N is calculated by dividing the population (the entire class) by the desired sample size. Systematic sampling is often easier to perform than random sampling as a random number generator is not required. Probability sampling requires the researcher to obtain a list of all cases in the total population from which the sample is selected. This is referred to as the sample frame and might be a list of all children in a school, or patients on a GP register or all addresses on an electoral register. Probability samples are typically more representative of the total population than other types of samples as selection **bias** is avoided and they are more typically used in survey research than in qualitative methods.

There are variations to random or systematic sampling. Stratified sampling ensures that appropriate numbers of cases are drawn from homogenous subsets of the population. Stratification may be on the basis of variables such as sex, age or ethnicity. Multi-stage cluster sampling involves the initial sampling of groups of cases (clusters) followed by the selection of cases within each of the selected clusters. For example researchers may randomly select general practitioners within an area, and then randomly select patients on the selected general practitioner's list.

Non-probability sampling involves the selection of cases according to reasons other than mathematical probability and includes a range of sampling approaches such as quota, convenience, theoretical and snowball sampling. Quota sampling, a technique popular within market research, involves the population of interest being divided into relevant categories such as age group or ethnicity. Fieldworkers are allocated quotas of types of respondents. The quota size is dependent on the size of the category in the population. Convenience sampling involves the selection of cases on the basis of their availability. This method may be useful when researching hard-to-access populations although clearly there are problems with selection bias. Theoretical sampling (sometimes referred to as purposive sampling) involves the selection of cases on the basis of the researcher's own judgement about which will be the most useful. For example samples might be chosen on the basis of being extreme (maximum variation sampling) or because they are typical of other cases. Theoretical sampling typically involves the selection of cases which are of particular interest to the study in that they confirm or contrast emergent theory thereby making the theory more definitive and useful. Therefore it is a technique often associated with **grounded theory** and **analytic induction**. Researchers may select deviant cases (cases that do not fit the general pattern) in order to tease out reasons why they do not fit the theory.

If the population of interest is particularly hard to **access** and there is no sample frame (for example drug-using populations and homeless populations), researchers might adopt sampling methods such as volunteer sampling or snowball sampling. Volunteer sampling involves respondents presenting themselves to researchers following an advertising campaign. Snowball sampling involves the researcher asking each respondent to suggest other potential respondents.

Qualitative research strategies such as **ethnography** require the researcher not only to think about sampling in terms of who to select but also of when and where data should be collected (Hammersley and Atkinson, 1995). This is known as time sampling. For example, activities in a typical high street will vary over different times of day. Consequently, attempts to represent ranges of people or activities in a given setting will have to take account of temporal structures. Ethnographers who decide to hang around a shopping high street will need to make sampling decisions about when and where to observe, what to observe and who to talk to. These choices are invariably determined by the research question.

A frequently asked question from many qualitative researchers is 'how big should my sample be?' Qualitative research designs typically use small numbers of cases compared with quantitative designs. Some research questions and research designs might use a single **case study** which might be sufficient to study a topic in depth. But even single settings have sub-settings (schools have class-rooms, hospitals have wards, communities have locations) so the researcher must still make judgements about the number of sub-settings. Unlike quantitative research, qualitative research does not estimate sample size so as to determine the statistical significance of its findings, however researchers must collect data from enough points so as to make meaningful conclusions about the phenomenon of interest. One criteria for closure on continued sampling is '**theoretical saturation**', that is when additional data does not provide new insights but rather confirms previous theories. Morse (1994) suggests that between 30 and 50 interviews are required for ethnographies and grounded theory studies.

Examples

Kumar, Little and Britten (2003) used a combination of maximum variety sampling (a form of stratified sampling) and theoretical sampling in their interview study of why general practitioners prescribe antibiotics for sore throats. They used grounded theory to guide their sampling decisions as well as the analysis of the data. The maximum variety sample of 25 general practitioners reflected a range of practitioner characteristics that they felt could influence prescribing (trainer status, gender, qualifications). A further 15 GPs were interviewed in the theoretical sample, the selection of GPs being guided by the emerging analysis. The authors claim that their sampling strategy was powerful because of its ability to capture variation, consistency and contradictions in responses.

Parker, Bakx and Newcombe (1988) used a combination of random sampling and snowball sampling in their study of heroin use in the north-west of England. The research team interviewed 125 heroin users about their motivations and their careers as drug users. Their total sample consisted of both known users, that is heroin users who were known to drug agencies, and hidden drug users who had no contact with drugs agencies. For the known users the research team used a random sample using the drug agencies' client lists as the sampling frame. In order to contact the 'hidden' drug users the team employed snowball sampling in four separate sites, whereby the researcher made contact with new informants by means of a referral chain. The authors discuss how the establishment of good personal relations was crucial to the

155

success of snowball sampling. For example the fieldworker would need to have the similar accent and clothing for them to be considered as 'all right'. Participation in the referral chain was also considered to be dependent on other factors such as the drug users' personal circumstances at the time the request was made, their feelings towards the drug services, boredom, the perception that participation might help them in the future and curiosity.

Evaluation

The main advantages of sampling over researching the entirety of the population (known as census-taking) are that it is quicker and cheaper. More crucially, it is often not possible to study everyone and everything within the population. Such benefits have to be balanced against the fact that researchers run the risk of selecting cases that are not representative of the population, especially in relation to the central research topic.

Although probability sampling does have its place in qualitative research, probability samples are often unachievable or inappropriate. It is therefore often difficult to establish how accurately the study sample reflects the wider population of concern. Rather than aspiring to statistical representativeness or **generalizability**, qualitative researchers are often more concerned with reflecting the diversity within a given population. With theoretical sampling, researchers deliberately seek to include extreme cases which tend to be discounted in samples for quantitative research.

Unlike probability samples where the sample frame must be specified before data collection begins, samples in qualitative research may evolve during data collection and analysis. An initial choice of informants or setting may lead the researcher to select later cases that invite comparisons. Sampling is therefore progressive and theory-driven.

Associated Concepts: Access Negotiations, Analytic Induction, Bias, Case Study, Ethnography, Generalization, Grounded Theory, Theoretical Saturation.

Key Readings

Arber, S. (2001) 'Designing samples', in N. Gilbert (ed.), *Researching Social Life* (2nd edn.) London: Sage. pp. 58–84.

Hammersley, M. and Atkinson, P. (1995) *Ethnography: Principles in Practice.* London: Routledge.

Johnson, J.C. (1990) *Selecting Ethnographic Informants* (vol. 22). Thousand Oaks, CA: Sage.

Kumar, S., Little, P. and Britten, N. (2003) 'Why do general practitioners prescribe antibiotics for sore throat? Grounded theory interview study', *British Medical Journal*, 326: 138.

*Miles, M. and Huberman, M. (1994) *Qualitative Data Analysis: An Expanded Sourcebook*. London: Sage.

Morse, J.M. (1994) 'Designing funded qualitative research', in N.K. Denzin and Y.S. Lincoln (eds), *Handbook of Qualitative Research*. Thousand Oaks, CA: Sage. pp. 220–235.

Parker, H., Bakx, K. and Newcombe, R. (1988) *Living with Heroin: The Impact of a Drugs 'Epidemic' on an English Community*. Milton Keynes: Open University Press.

Social network analysis

Definition

The study of the interconnectedness of individuals. Social network analysis seeks to describe patterns of relationships among actors, analyse the structure of these patterns and explore the effects on people and organizations.

Distinctive Features

Social network analysis is a technique usually credited to Jacob Levi Moreno circa 1934. Moreno was perhaps the first sociologist to use the term 'sociometry' to denote the measurement and analysis of social relationships between groups of individuals. His methods were able to identify informal leaders, social rankings and isolated individuals. In addition to Moreno there were other well-known sociologists using similar techniques including Emile Durkheim, Herbert Spencer and Georg Simmel, all of whom considered that sociology involved the study of the interconnections of social actors. Social network analysis has long been employed by anthropologists (see, for example, Mitchell, 1970) and more recently it has been adopted by disciplines such as economics and marketing.

Social network analysis capitalizes on the premises that the behaviour of individuals is affected by their position in the overall social structure. Consequently, by examining the location, dynamics, cause and consequences of networks, social network analysts hope to draw conclusions about the nature of social behaviour. Networks, usually displayed graphically, consist of a set of nodes which are linked by ties. Analysts typically are interested in measures of the network in terms of its structure (density, centrality etc.) and also its performance (robustness, efficiency etc.) (Scott, 1999).

Freeman (2004) defines social network analysis as having four key features: a structural basis, systematic collection of relational data, graphical images, and

157

mathematical or computational models. In addition, social network analysts also study 'flow' through the networks which may be channels through which almost anything (ideas, values, esteem, friendship, goods or diseases) can travel.

Social network analysis has been traditionally associated with quantitative methods through its obvious links with sociometrics and statistical measures. Quantitative researchers may obtain data, through questionnaires or other means, relating to the connectedness of individuals. In contrast a qualitative researcher who is engaged in social network analysis may draw upon a variety of data derived from interviews, observations or other means, to intensively analyse the subjective meanings that the individuals attach to their social relations and the variety of purposes implied in their networks.

Computer-assisted qualitative data analysis has been advocated by some researchers as a tool to help depict and analyse social networks qualitatively (Lonkila and Harmo, 1999). By using such software, researchers can develop their theory out of the evolving network of codes and display this in a graphical format. This helps the researcher to understand the logic behind the specific configuration of social relations revolving around a particular individual.

Examples

Martínez et al. (2003) present an evaluation of a university computing course through **multiple methods** which combine questionnaires, computer logs and qualitative data generated from observations and focus groups. The authors aimed to evaluate the levels of interaction between class-mates during the course. In doing so, they defined three generic types of social networks: 'direct relationship networks' built from relationships between two actors; 'indirect relationship networks' built from relationships that have been established through a shared object (like the creation and reading of a document); and 'use of resources networks', that relate actors sharing objects (computers etc.). The authors represent the social networks through graphs, or sociograms, which display the actors as nodes of the graphs and the links among them as lines. The authors conclude that the social network analysis indexes and the sociograms are of value for detecting different collaborative patterns that emerge from classroom-based activities, and that both qualitative and quantitative data help to discern these patterns.

Evaluation

Traditionally social network analysis has focused on networks of individuals, but increasingly it is being applied to networks of organizations such as firms, schools or hospitals.

Social network analysis has been criticized for creating static descriptions of a network's structure. As a consequence it is claimed that networks do not represent dynamic entities that evolve under the influence of social forces. Social network analysis has also been criticized for not adequately dealing with the problem of representing both strong and weak links (Watts, 2003). And there is the methodological difficulty that data may not be collectable from all network members, perhaps because of refusals or access problems; so the analyst may face the dilemma of whether to work with incomplete network data, or to abandon analysis on many networks on which he or she has substantial data, which is nevertheless incomplete and therefore possibly misleading.

Associated Concepts: Computer-Assisted Data Analysis, Multiple Methods.

Key Readings
Freeman, L.C. (2004) *The Development of Social Network Analysis: A Study in the Sociology of Science*. Vancouver: Booksurge Publishing.

Lonkila, M. and Harmo, T. (1999) Toward computer-assisted qualitative network analysis, *Connections*, 22(1): 52–61.

Martínez, A., Dimitriadis, Y., Rubia, B., Gömez, E. and de al Fuente, P. (2003) 'Combining qualitative evaluation and social network analysis for the study of classroom social interactions', *Computers and Education*, 41(4): 353–368.

Mitchell, J.C. (ed.) (1970) *Social Networks in Urban Situations*. Manchester: Manchester University Press.

*Scott, J. (1999) *Social Network Analysis: A Handbook*. London: Sage.

Wasserman, S. and Faust, K. (1994) *Social Network Analysis: Methods and Applications*. Cambridge: Cambridge University Press.

Watts, D.J. (2003) *Six Degrees: The Science of a Connected Age*. New York: Norton.

Symbolic Interactionism

Definition
A theory of social action that views actors' behaviour as shaped by the inter-active construction of meaning. Meanings are seen as collaborative, provisional and contingent, and social structures are the emergent and shifting products of such meaning construction.

159

Distinctive Features

Symbolic interactionism is a theory, not a method. But as a theory, its central concern with meaning has led to its identification with qualitative methods. Many of the early members of the 'Chicago School' of sociology, out of which symbolic interactionism emerged, were associated with a range of methods. W.I. Thomas, for example, he of the oft-quoted phrase 'If men [*sic*] define situations as real, they are real in their consequences' (Thomas, 1923), collaborated with Znaniecki in a monumental study of Polish peasant migrants (Thomas and Znaniecki, 1918) that represents the genesis of the **biographic** method. But, as symbolic interactionism developed, the research method that became most closely associated with the theory was undoubtedly **ethnography**. Because actors' meaning-attributions are viewed as provisional and emergent within social settings, it was clearly preferable for data on meaning-attribution to be collected in the actual settings where actors were conducting interpretive work. Thus, social organizations were conceived, not as structures, but as sites of interactions between individuals and groups, and social order was seen as a negotiated order: so the study of organizations was seen as the study of interactional work (Dingwall and Strong, 1985). Symbolic interactionist theory thus became a template for symbolic interactionists' methods.

Examples

Strauss et al.'s (1963) depiction of the hospital as 'a negotiated order' may stand as a classic example of interactionist studies of organizations to set alongside the many studies of subcultures, both occupational (such as Becker et al.'s 1961 study of medical students in training) and deviant (such as Polsky's 1971 study of poolhall hustlers) conducted around the same period. If a single invidious example of symbolic interactionist ethnography is to be selected, then it should be Becker's (1953) study of how jazz musicians become acculturated to marihuana smoking, learning first the technique, then learning to perceive the effects and then learning to appreciate the effects: a study which became a model for studies of drug use over the next 50 years (e.g. Bloor et al., 1998).

Evaluation

Many interactionist studies remain valued descriptions of settings and organizations. Early criticisms of those studies alleged an inadequate representation of power relationships, power hegemonies and structural forces (see the discussion in Meltzer et al., 1975). In more recent years, the development of the sociology of scientific knowledge has led to the view that interactionist studies of work were too focused on social action, on the reportage of conduct and negotiation, leaving largely unexamined the central cognitive or interpretive aspects of work (Bloor, 2001).

The heyday of symbolic interactionism was in the 1960s and the clearest expression of symbolic interactionist theory remains Blumer's 1969 monograph, *Symbolic Interactionism: Perspective and Method.* But symbolic interactionism has continued to be developed, first through Goffmanian dramaturgical theory and social constructionism, and most recently through the work of Randall Collins (2004). Goffman was himself a notable ethnographer (see especially Goffman, 1959) and Collins's chapter on his 'Theory of Sexual Interaction' (Collins, 2004: 223–257) lists a series of empirically testable propositions demonstrating the continuing commitment of theorists in the interactionist tradition to methodic enquiry. Not all sociological theorizing has been so closely linked to empirical study.

Associated Concepts: Biographies, Ethnography.

Key Readings

Becker, H.C. (1953) 'Becoming a marihuana user', *American Journal of Sociology,* 59: 235–242.

Becker, H.C., Greer, B., Hughes, E. and Strauss, A. (1961) *Boys in White: Student Culture in Medical School.* Chicago: University of Chicago Press.

Bloor, M. (2001) 'The ethnography of health and medicine', in P. Atkinson, A. Coffey, S. Delamont, J. Lofland and L. Lofland (eds), *Handbook of Ethnography.* London: Sage. pp. 177–187.

Bloor, M., Monaghan, L., Dobash, R.P. and Dobash, R.E. (1998) 'The body as a chemistry experiment: steroid use among South Wales bodybuilders', in S. Nettleton and J. Watson (eds), *The Body in Everyday Life.* London: Routledge. pp. 27–44.

*Blumer, H. (1969) *Symbolic Interactionism: Perspective and Method.* Englewood Cliffs, NJ: Prentice-Hall.

Collins, R. (2004) *Interaction Ritual Chains.* Princeton, NJ: Princeton University Press.

Dingwall, R. and Strong, P. (1985) 'The interactional study of organisations: a critique and a reformulation', *Urban Life,* 14: 205–231. Republished in G. Miller and R. Dingwall (eds) (1997), *Context and Method in Qualitative Research.* London: Sage. pp. 37–52.

Goffman, E. (1959) *Presentation of Self in Everyday Life.* New York: Doubleday-Anchor.

Meltzer, B., Petras, J. and Reynolds, L. (1975) *Symbolic Interactionism: Genesis, Varieties and Criticism.* London: Routledge & Kegan Paul.

Polsky, N. (1971) *Hustlers, Beats and Others.* Harmondsworth: Penguin.

Strauss, A., Scatzman, I., Bucher, R., Ehrlich, D. and Sabshin, M. (1963) 'The hospital and its negotiated order', in E. Freidson (ed.), *The Hospital in*

Modern Society. New York: The Free Press.

Thomas, W.I. (1923) *The Unadjusted Girl*. Boston: Little, Brown. Reprinted as 'The definition of the situation', in L. Coser and B. Rosenberg (eds) (1964) *Sociological Theory: A Book of Readings*. New York: Collier-Macmillan. pp. 233–235.

Thomas, W.I. and Znaniecki, F. (1918) *The Polish Peasant in Europe and America*. Boston: Richard Badger.

Taxonomies

Definition

Taxonomies are systems of classification used by collectivities to order and make sense of everyday experience.

Distinctive Features

In an argument put most forcefully by Alfred Schutz (1967), but also expounded by the philosophers Husserl and William James, all our knowledge of the world (scientific as well as common-sense thinking) is constructed and mediated by means of typologies: there are no such things as facts, pure and simple, only sense data which are selected and understood according to our own pre-existing schemas of interpretation. These typologies, part idiosyncratic and part learned in families, peer groups and workplaces, may be more or less elaborate depending on our interest-at-hand: in a piece of anthropological lore that has passed into popular consciousness, the Inuit are said to have a wealth of different terms for snow. And our typologies are also purposive, that is, action-orientated. In Schutz's (1970) example, we react differently according to whether we interpret the coiled mass in the corner of the room as a rope or a snake – attached to each typification is a 'recipe for action'.

The elicitation of taxonomies is best undertaken by ethnographers in situations of their use, normally by prediction and seeking confirmation from respondents (Frake, 1962) – a procedure sometimes described as '**member validation.**'

Examples

Thanks to the influence of Boas and other early pioneers, a central concern of anthropology has always been the documentation of indigenous classification systems, with some researchers focusing on specific sub-systems such as ethnobotany or ethnomedicine (e.g. Frake, 1961). **Ethnographers** in developed societies have often followed similar lines of investigation, for example, in documenting experienced bodybuilders' specialist ethnopharmacological knowledge of steroids and ethnonutritionist knowledge of dietary supplements (Monaghan, 2001).

Evaluation

Chomskian linguistics has claimed that the study of syntax and structure should be the core of linguistic study, but anthropologists have continued to assert the inter-dependence of language and culture, and thus the importance of understanding the contextual embeddedness of all communication (Keating, 2001).

Associated Concepts: Ethnography, Member Validation (*see* Triangulation).

Key Readings

Frake, C. (1961) 'The diagnosis of disease among the Subanun of Mindanao', *American Anthropologist*, 66: 113–132.

Frake, C. (1962) 'The ethnographic study of cognitive systems', in T. Gladwin and W.C. Sturtevant (eds), *Anthropology and Human Behaviour*. Washington; Anthropological Society of Washington.

*Keating, E. (2001) 'The ethnography of communication', in P. Atkinson, A. Coffey, S. Belamont, J. Lofland and

L. Lofland (eds), *Handbook of Ethnography*. London: Sage. pp. 285–301.

Monaghan, L. (2001) *Bodybuilding, Drugs and Risk*. London: Routledge.

Schutz, A. (1967) 'Common-sense and scientific interpretation of human action', in A. Schutz, *Collected Papers I* (ed. M. Natanson). The Hague: Martinus Nijhoff.

Schutz, A. (1970) *Reflections on the Problem of Relevance*. New Haven, CT: Yale University Press.

Theoretical Saturation

Definition

The continuation of sampling and data collection until no new conceptual insights are generated. At this point the researcher has provided repeated evidence for his or her conceptual categories.

Distinctive Features

Theoretical saturation is associated with theoretical **sampling** for **grounded theory**, that is, the selection of cases that are most likely to produce the most relevant data that will discriminate or test emerging theories. This process requires a flexible approach to data collection as it progresses alongside data analysis.

Theoretical sampling has the potential to be limitless. This should perhaps be unsurprising as the inductive method of theoretical development suggests that each new case has the potential to offer a slightly alternative insight. However for the purposes of grounded theory, as developed by Glaser and Strauss (1967), the point of theoretical saturation occurs when the researcher sees similar instances repeatedly. Most researchers follow this pragmatic approach to theoretical saturation, ceasing further data collection and analysis when it seems likely that to continue would be almost futile.

Seale (1999) has likened the idea of theoretical saturation to Geertz's notion of 'thick description' (Geertz, 1993). Thick description is a trademark of quality anthropological research in which the author provides rich and multi-layered interpretations of social life.

Examples

There are many published studies which claim to have ended data collection on the basis of theoretical saturation. For example, Fuller and Lewis (2002) researched the meaning of relationships to owner/managers of small firms, and how differences in meaning are implicated in the strategy of the firms. In doing so they conducted in-depth interviews with 36 owner/managers. These were coded using a grounded theory approach and the narrative was analysed for differences in meaning. The research set out to follow a 'theoretical sampling' design whereby interviewees were selected for their perceived 'theoretical relevance' to the study. The authors report that 'the process of interviewing then continued this until it was felt that "theoretical saturation" had been reached, that is, that the research was not discovering anything new'.

Evaluation

In principle the methodological justification for continued sampling until a point of theoretical saturation is reached is convincing, but there are a number of problems associated with its application. One problem is that researchers are often required to stipulate at the research planning stage exactly how many respondents will participate in the research. This information is often required by funding bodies (in order to justify the costs of the study) and perhaps also by ethics committees. Despite this, researchers tend to remain faithful to the number of cases that they identified as being required during research planning, while making claims to have saturated their theory in order to retain methodological credibility. Indeed many journal articles contain the disclaiming phrase 'sampling continued until theoretical saturation was reached', with little evidence of the level of dense theory that was intended for grounded theory. Glaser and Strauss (1967: 63) have argued that 'the inadequate theoretical sample is easily spotted, since the theory associated with it is usually thin and not well integrated, and has too many obvious unexplained exceptions'.

Associated Concepts: Grounded Theory, Sampling.

Key Readings

Fuller, T. and Lewis, J. (2002) '"Relationships mean everything"; a typology of small-business relationship strategies in a reflexive context', *British Journal of Management*, 13(4): 317–336.

Geertz, C. (1993) *The Interpretation of Cultures*. London: Fontama (First published 1973).

Glaser, B. and Strauss, A. (1967) *The Discovery of Grounded Theory*. Chicago: Aldine.

Seale, C. (1999) *The Quality of Qualitative Research*. London: Sage.

*Strauss, A. and Corbin, J. (1998) *Basics of Qualitative Research. Grounded Theory Procedures and Techniques*. London: Sage.

Transcription

Definition

Transcription is a technical typing procedure for representing spoken discourse in text. Undertaken between the research stages of data collection and analysis, transcription is a critical step in the production of scientific knowledge as it captures and freezes in time the spoken discourse that is of interest to the researcher.

Distinctive Features

Qualitative research invariably involves making **audio** or **video-recordings** of social interactions involving communication. These data may be either naturally occurring or produced through the direct intervention of the researcher through, for example, interviews or focus groups. Traditionally, transcribing has been aided through the use of a pedal-operated transcribing machine that allows the transcriber to control the speed, tone and volume of the recorded data as well as having foot-operated play, rewind and forward functions.

Many researchers consider the transcription stage of qualitative research to be tedious, time-consuming and unproblematic. Consequently researchers often delegate transcription to secretarial staff or contract it out to transcribers outside of the research team. Disinterest in transcription as part of the research process is also reflected by the absence of details in empirical research literature. Indeed authors rarely go beyond a general statement that 'data were transcribed'. Although there are obvious time pressures preventing researchers from transcribing their own data, some researchers feel that self-transcription is important as it provides opportunities to engage in early data analysis. The transcription process inevitably involves close listening and re-listening and through this one becomes more familiar with and immersed in the data, thereby gaining a more detailed understanding of the data.

A number of alternative transcription systems have been developed by researchers who work with different theoretical orientations to research (for example, **discourse analysis, conversation analysis** and psycholinguistics). A full review of the principles of contrasting systems can be found in Edwards and Lampert (1993). Essentially such conventions strive to improve the reliability of transcribed data through the systematic and standardized representation of how speech is delivered. For example there are symbols to represent various characteristics of speech production such as pitch, accent, intonation, overlaps, pauses, extensions to and truncations of words and marked changes in volume. The use of conventions permits a more thorough scrutiny of the social interaction that is at the core of linguistic techniques such as discourse analysis and conversation analysis. Perhaps the most comprehensive and widely used convention among conversation analysts is that developed by Gail Jefferson from her work with Harvey Sacks (Sacks, Schegloff and Jefferson, 1974), although there are alternatives to this system (for example, Psathas and Anderson, 1990). A simplified glossary of the most commonly used symbols can be found in Ten Have (1999: 213–214).

Edwards and Lampert (1993) review two general design principles for transcription, namely 'authenticity' (the need to preserve the information in a manner that is true to the original interaction) and 'practicality' (the need to respect the ways in which the data are to be managed and analysed, for example by ensuring the transcripts are easy to read). These two goals are often considered to be in opposition to each other as the inclusion of nuances of the discourse through the inclusion of transcription symbols can distract the reader from the sense of what is being said. For a researcher who is unfamiliar with detailed transcription symbols, not only can the transcript take significantly longer to read but also the reading does not adequately reflect the natural flow of the original speech. A better trade-off between readability and faithful representation of exactly what is heard can be reached if the researcher considers what level of transcription is required for their own research purposes.

Examples

Two examples of how transcribed data are presented in research papers are Shefer et al. (2002) in their focus group study exploring health-seeking behaviour for sexually transmitted infections in South Africa, and Cameron (2002) in a study of the use of metaphors in primary school science education. Both of these papers present a number of transcribed data extracts of participants' talk as well as a table/footnote explaining their transcription conventions. Although transcription symbols denoting main speech characteristics such as pauses, interruptions and 'latching' are included, the transcripts are not overly beset by transcription symbols and hence the reader is easily able to follow the flow of the discourse.

Evaluation

Researchers frequently complain about the cost and time implications of transcription. As a rough guide it may take approximately six hours to transcribe one hour of interview data or ten hours to transcribe one hour of focus group data. These estimates will vary depending on the speed and proficiency of the transcriber, the quality of the audio-recording and the level of detail included in the transcription. Alternatives to transcription have been suggested such as coding directly from the audio-tapes or using real-time observational coding as the data are being produced. Although these alternatives may reduce time and costs, research suggests that these techniques are unreliable and data are not available for later examination and replication (Lapadat and Lindsay, 1999).

Voice recognition software has been explored by some researchers as a quick alternative to transcription. The software is essentially a dictation aid: the researcher speaks words and the software translates those spoken words into written words in a word-processing document. Unfortunately the software is no panacea for qualitative researchers frustrated with transcription. For example the software needs to be 'trained' to the researcher's voice and, until it is adequately trained, the software is likely to make many mistakes of transcription. The fact that the software is trained to one person's voice also means that it is not suitable to transcribe data where there is more than one person speaking (a frequent occurrence for qualitative social research). However, the software may have its uses if, for example, a researcher wishes to dictate hand written fieldnotes and correct them into a computerized document.

Critiques of transcription usually make reference to the fact that transcriptions are not a neutral facsimile of the spoken data but rather a selective process, influenced by the transcription system and the transcriber's individual practices, interests and theories. For example Lapadat and Lindsay (1999: 64) argue that the process of transcription is 'theory laden' and Psathas and Anderson (1990: 77) claim that the transcript itself is 'a version of the data for particular analytic purposes'. These writers are making the point that researchers are selective in their decisions about what to include within the transcript and, in turn, these choices shape how the data are analysed. One example of this, provided by Edwards and Lampert (1993), is the importance of how the transcriber chooses the layout for the transcript. Arranging speaker turns one below another gives the impression of order and symmetry between the speakers, whereas arranging the speech in columns, one for each speaker, gives the impression of asymmetry with the left-most column speaker appearing the most dominant.

Associated Concepts: Audio-Recording, Conversation Analysis, Discourse Analysis, Video-Recording.

Key Readings

Cameron, L. (2002) 'Metaphors in the learning of science: a discourse focus', *British Educational Research Journal*, 28(5): 673–688.

*Edwards, J.A. and Lampert, M.D. (1993) *Talking Data: Transcription and Coding in Discourse Research*. Hillsdale, NJ: Lawrence Erlbaum Associates.

Fielding, N. and Thomas, H. (2001) 'Qualitative interviewing', in N. Gilbert (ed.), *Researching Social Life*. London: Sage. pp. 123–145.

Lapadat, J. and Lindsay, A. (1999) 'Transcription in research and practice: from standardization of technique to interpretive positionings', *Qualitative Inquiry*, 5(1): 64–86.

Peräkylä, A. (1997) 'Reliability and validity in research based on tapes and transcripts', in D. Silverman (ed.),

Qualitative Research: Theory, Method and Practice. London: Sage.

Psathas, G. and Anderson, T. (1990) 'The "practices" of transcription in conversation analysis', *Semiotica*, 78: 75–99.

Sacks, H., Schegloff, E.A. and Jefferson, G. (1974) 'A simplest systematics for the organisation of turn-taking for conversation', *Language*, 50: 696–735.

Shefer, T., Strebel, A., Wilson, T., Shabalala, N., Simbayi, L., Ratele, K., Potgieter, C. and Andipatin, M. (2002) 'The social construction of sexually transmitted infections (STIs) in South African communities', *Qualitative Health Research*, 12(10): 1373–1390.

Ten Have, P. (1999) *Doing Conversation Analysis: A Practical Guide*. London: Sage.

Triangulation

Definition

The systematic comparison of findings on the same research topic generated by different research methods. Such comparisons are often portrayed as a procedure of validation by replication, but the portrayal is misleading.

Distinctive Features

In the natural sciences, the research findings of Scientist A are held to have been validated when Scientist B in a different laboratory is able to repeat Scientist A's original experiment with identical findings. But this validation by replication is not possible in the social sciences because, with the exception of psychological laboratory studies, social science research takes place in natural, everyday settings (streets, workplaces, homes, care institutions, etc.) which will always contain particular and unique features that cannot be exactly reproduced in a second setting, or even in the same setting at a different point in time: history *never* repeats itself. Consequentially, some social scientists have suggested that validation in the social sciences might be achieved by the collection of corroborating findings from the same respondents and on the same topic, but using different methods, the term 'triangulation' being suggested by the analogy with land surveys, where the surveyor gets a fix on his or her position by taking a bearing on two different landmarks.

The term 'methodological triangulation' appears to have been first used by Campbell and Fiske (1959), but was popularized by Denzin in his textbook on qualitative methods (Denzin, 1989), first published in 1970. Denzin writes of four different kinds of triangulation: 'data triangulation', using different data sources to study the same phenomenon; 'investigator triangulation', using different investigators in the same study; 'theoretical triangulation', using different theoretical models in the same study; and 'methodological triangulation', using different methods to study the same phenomenon. But it is the last of these, methodological triangulation, that has received the most attention and it has become almost obligatory for qualitative researchers, in planning their studies, to demonstrate their commitment to methodological rigour by **multi-method** research designs, allegedly capable of **validation** through triangulation. A popular variant form of triangulation is 'member validation', that is checking the accuracy of early findings with research respondents. Although Denzin (then a leading symbolic interactionist and now associated with postmodernist approaches) may not have intended it to be the case, triangulation has become popularly associated with the 'positivist' research paradigm in qualitative research, that is with the view that there is a single objective reality independent of human consciousness which careful scientific methods can reveal to the painstaking investigator. However, the main difficulties associated with triangulation, as it is popularly practised, are largely independent of the difficulties identified with positivist approaches to social science research by constructivist critics.

The main problem with triangulation-as-validation is a simple matter of logic. For any given research topic there will always be one best method by which it may be addressed – broadly speaking, matters of belief may be addressed best by interviews, matters of behaviour may be addressed best by observation and matters of social norms may be addressed best by focus groups. Therefore, triangulation will always involve addressing a research topic using one supplemental method that, for that particular topic, is inferior to another main method. No difficulty arises when the findings from the second, inferior method corroborate those gleaned from the first, superior method, but where the first-method findings are contradicted by the inferior method, then it would be foolish to reject them: the lack of corroboration may simply be due to the inappropriateness of the second method. But any test of validity must be even-handed: a researcher cannot claim to be testing for validity if the test results are only accepted when there is corroboration.

However, in practice, comparison of results obtained by different methods is rarely unambiguous: straightforward juxtaposition of accounts to indicate corroboration or falsification cannot be undertaken because different methods tend to produce accounts couched at different levels of specificity/abstraction. Thus, ethnographic accounts will be highly situated, with lots of 'local colour' – features specific to individual settings – while interview-generated accounts will be more wide-ranging and have a more abstract character. The ethnographic accounts, with their particular focus, may miss out some topic areas covered in the wide-ranging interview accounts. And the interview accounts, being more general, may fail to record variations and exceptions noted in the ethnographic accounts. So no test of corroboration may be possible.

Examples
Bloor's (1997) paper discusses particular examples of his own attempts to compare systematically data collected on the same topic by different methods. One of these attempts involved two different kinds of data on the certification of deaths: depth interviews with a sample of doctors who routinely wrote a lot of death certificates (for example, pathologists, police surgeons and clinicians on geriatric wards), and 'vignettes' describing a number of fictional deaths with a

171

request for the same sample of doctors to write out dummy death certificates for each vignette. Strict corroboration of the interviewee's reported certification practices by the vignettes was not possible. This was partly because the interviews ranged widely over different potentially fatal conditions and it would have been much too tedious and long-winded an exercise for the interviewee to complete vignettes relating to each one of these conditions. And it was partly because, as was implied above, the interviews described fatal conditions in relatively abstract and general terms, whereas the vignettes were naturally much more specific: no match of symptomatology was possible.

Evaluation

Criticisms of triangulation-as-validation have been noted by a number of authors (Blaikie, 1991; Bloor, 1997; Seale, 1999). It is clear that validation cannot be accomplished by corroboration of findings from different methods. But this is not to say that the comparison of data derived from different methods is futile: on the contrary, such comparisons may serve to deepen and extend the analysis. Indeed, it is the stimulus to analysis that such comparisons may provide that has been one of the main reasons for the growth in popularity of research designs which employ multiple methods. Triangulation is admirable, but validation is a chimera.

Associated Concepts: Multiple Methods, Validity.

Key Readings

Blaikie, N. (1991) 'A critique of the use of validation in social research', *Quality and Quantity*, 25: 115–136.

*Bloor, M. (1997) 'Techniques of validation in qualitative research: a critical commentary', in G. Millar and R. Dingwall (eds), *Strategic Qualitative Research*. London: Sage. Reprinted in R. Emerson (ed.) (2001), *Contemporary Field Research: Perspectives and Formulations*. Prospect Heights, IL: Waveland.

Campbell, D. and Fiske, D. (1959) 'Convergent and discriminant validation by the multitrait-multimethod matrix', *Psychological Bulletin*, 56: 81–105.

Denzin, N. (1989) *The Research Act: A Theoretical Introduction to Sociological Research Methods* (3rd edn; 1st edn 1970). Englewood Cliffs, NJ: Prentice Hall.

Seale, C. (1999) *The Quality of Qualitative Research*. London: Sage.

Trust

Definition

Confusingly, the nineties bestseller by the political scientist Francis Fukuyama entitled *Trust* (Fukuyama, 1995), is actually about 'social capital', that is the ability of individuals to work together in groups, associations and organizations, and the impact of social capital on national economic performance. While language dictionaries define 'trust' as *a firm belief* in the reliability or the integrity of a person or thing (as in trust in one's sword), in qualitative research 'trust' refers to an aspired-to property of the relationship between researcher and researched. A relationship of trust between the fieldworker/interviewer/focus group facilitator and his or her collectivity members/interviewees/group members is thought to be a necessary condition for the continuing conduct of the research and for the collection of accurate data.

Distinctive Features

Early qualitative methods writings tended to view trust as fairly durable property of the relationship between the researcher and the researched, so that while the researcher was counselled to pay great attention to the establishment of trust in the initial stages of research (early access negotiations, pilot work, first days in the field, the beginning of the interview or focus group), this was thought to be a matter of less importance once the research was well under way. Trust, once established, was not easily shaken and provided an unproblematic foundation for data collection.

This optimistic view of **fieldwork relationships** was mirrored in the plot of several Hollywood westerns of the period where the hero/cowboy or hero/cavalryman won the trust of the local Indian chief, and the two blood-brothers, White and Red, then successfully preserved the peace of the frontier, despite the shenanigans of the evil medicine-man and the gun-running Whites. In ethnographic fieldwork relationships (as in Hollywood westerns), the establishment of trust relied heavily on sponsorship: most collectivity members would be willing to accept the bona fides of the ethnographer if sponsored by a prominent collectivity member, who in turn often became a **'key informant'** of the researcher. The sponsoring collectivity member is thus one of the various possible research **'gatekeepers'** in **access negotiations**, though by no means all gatekeepers are also collectivity members.

Optimism was duly replaced by pessimism. It was suggested that most collectivity members would look askance at the fieldworker-stranger who came professing friendship across the barriers of education, class, culture and ethnicity, and who sought to distance him or herself from the previous strangers who had ruled/punished/exploited the collectivity in the past. Edgerton (1965), in a trenchant essay on fieldwork relationships between anthropologists and both first-nation Americans and East Africans, observed how tribespeople would 'test' the bona fides of the newly arrived anthropologist by making successive and spiraling demands (such as the request to smuggle liquor on to the reservation), until a refusal was eventually encountered and the essential similarity of the anthropologist with past exploiters was demonstrated to everyone's satisfaction.

But pessimism in turn was duly replaced by a more nuanced approach. Within the **phenomenological** perspective, a degree of trust is an essential feature of everyday social life: for everyday social interaction to be possible, an individual assumes that fellow collectivity members will share at some basic level that individual's 'interpretative framework' (or mental map) of objects, events and collectivities. This assumed reciprocity of perspectives is only provisional – it is open to disruption and revision – but for most purposes a degree of trust between researcher and researched may be supposed, not least because whether critical inspection of the fieldwork relationship occurs depends on the critic's interest in the topic at hand, and most collectivity members will have only a marginal interest in the researcher and the researcher's study.

Examples

The methodological appendix to Whyte's Street Corner Society, an **ethnography** of an Italian-American slum neighbourhood, is a frequently cited example of the role of sponsorship in developing trust between researchers and community members. Whyte's sponsor was 'Doc', a young Italian-American well known in the neighbourhood. Whyte describes his first fieldwork visit with Doc (to an illegal back-street gambling establishment) as follows:

> Doc introduced me as 'my friend Bill' to Chichi, who ran the place, and to Chichi's friends and customers. [...] As Doc had predicted, no one asked me about myself, but he told me later that, when I went to the toilet there was an excited burst of conversation in Italian and that he had to assure them that I was not a G-man [FBI man]. He said he told them flatly that I was a friend of his, and they agreed to let it go at that. (Whyte, 1955: 298)

Johnson's field research in a district welfare office of a US metropolitan public welfare agency (Johnson, 1975) is an example of the variable and contingent character of relations of trust. He describes how the level of trust he established with the social workers in the office varied greatly from individual to individual and also shifted back and forth over time. Johnson coined the term 'sufficient trust' to signify that different levels of trust may be required and accomplishable in different circumstances with different research subjects.

Evaluation

While abuse of trust by researchers is wholly unethical, early methodological writing possibly laid too much emphasis on the central importance of establishing trustworthy research relationships at the outset of the research process. In reality, trust is a relative, not an absolute, entity: there are degrees of trust and not all research requires a high degree of trust from all parties. Furthermore, trust is a variable entity which will change over time, as the purposes of collectivity members change and as the degree of critical inspection by members of the researcher changes. It is not that trust is fragile, but it is the case that trust needs recurrent repair and elaboration as circumstances change: a respondent may be perfectly happy to grant an interview at the outset, but may seek more information on confidentiality in the light of being asked a particularly sensitive question.

Associated Concepts: Access Negotiations, Ethnography, Fieldwork Relationships, Gatekeepers (*see* Access Negotiations), Key Informants, Phenomenological Methods.

Key Readings

Edgerton, R. (1965) 'Some dimensions of disillusionment in culture contact', *South Western Journal of Anthropology*, 21: 231–243.

Fukuyama, F. (1995) *Trust: The Social Virtues and the Creation of Prosperity.* New York: The Free Press.

*Johnson, J. (1975) *Doing Field Research.* New York: The Free Press.

Whyte, W.J. (1955) *Street Corner Society: The Social Structure of an Italian Slum* (2nd enlarged edn). Chicago: University of Chicago Press.

Uses of Qualitative Research

Definition
A concern with applications for research findings generated by qualitative methods, set alongside the implicit belief that research, which is frequently publicly funded and requires some time and effort from respondents, should have some pay-off other than the production of knowledge for knowledge's sake and the furtherance of academic careers.

Distinguishing Features
Since both public and private organizations are prepared to expend considerable sums on consultancy reports, the potential practical value of academic qualitative research to organizational members ought to be considerable (see, for example, Miller et al., 2004). But this potential is rarely realized. To take just one instance of general policy-maker indifference, since Becker's classic 1953 study on 'Becoming a marihuana user', qualitative sociologists have repeatedly depicted the social worlds of drug users in highly policy-relevant terms, including Howard and Borges's (1970) prescient, pre-AIDS, ethnographic study of the social meanings of needle-sharing. Yet all this qualitative drugs research effort bore precious little policy fruit in the developed world. Where policy-makers have sought research evidence, they have preferred quantitative evidence with self-evident **generalizability**. Thus, as Berridge and Strong (1993) pointed out in their contemporary history of British drug policy, the crucial research evidence that contributed to the initiation of the new 'harm minimization' approach in UK drug services was that of a *quantitative* evaluation of pilot needle exchanges.

Unsurprisingly then, qualitative research has usually been judged most useful by policy audiences when it is combined with quantitative methods in a **multiple methods** research design. Such designs include qualitative pilot work as a precursor to survey studies, but also include qualitative work conducted alongside quantitative research, most notably in **process evaluations** – qualitative work occurring within trials and controlled experimental studies designed to show *why* an experimental intervention has succeeded or failed (Parry-Langdon et al., 2003). Process evaluations are an example of what Bulmer

(1982) has called the 'engineering model' of the impact of social research, where the policy value of the research is clear and specific, providing evidence and conclusions to help solve a policy problem. However, beyond the engineering model, we can distinguish a number of different competing arguments about the actual *influence* of qualitative research: the 'enlightenment' argument, the 'reflective practitioner' argument, the 'advocacy' argument, and the 'quietist' argument.

The enlightenment argument (Bulmer, 1982) emphasizes that the opportunities for social researchers to engineer directly changes in policy are limited, but they can influence policy indirectly through processes of personal influence, disseminating the kinds of descriptive accounts and theorizing in which qualitative research is particularly rich. While Bulmer's approach chimes well with empirical studies of policy making (e.g. Rock, 1987), which portray policies as sets of shared tacit assumptions rather than formal programmes, it overestimates the charisma of most researchers and the gregariousness of most policy-makers.

The reflective practitioner argument depicts practitioners as a more receptive audience for research than policy-makers. Schon, in his book *The Reflective Practitioner* (1983), characterizes practitioners as deploying knowledge-in-action in their everyday work, rather than formal scientific knowledge. Qualitative research, in its rich descriptions of practitioner activities (descriptions of knowledge-in-action), thus provides practitioner-readers with an occasion to reflect on their own practices, an occasion to juxtapose them with those described by the researcher (Bloor, 2004), and a spur to change. Further, practitioners can embark on their own qualitative research studies to inform and modify their everyday work practices (Shaw, 1999).

The advocacy argument comes in different shapes and sizes. Becker's (1967) **'Whose side are we on?'** argument calls on researchers to be unashamed about personal and political commitments to underdogs and victims, but to be impartial in the conduct of their research, allowing the possibility that a cherished political hypothesis may be falsified. From a Foucauldian perspective, the research enterprise functions as part of the surveillance society, and the only independent response possible is to lay bare the disciplinary techniques of the surveillance society and stiffen the resistance of those surveyed (Major-Poetzl, 1983). The new 'public sociology' (Burawoy, 2004) seeks to be a radical democratic conscience, appealing directly to lay audiences and bypassing policy-makers and practitioners.

The quietist argument also emerges in different forms. The 'strict constructivist' (Best, 1989) and postmodernist positions are similar in that both would view researchers as having no claim to superior knowledge and thus no wisdom to offer policy-makers, practitioners or laity. But there is a longer

177

standing quietist argument which simply seeks that social science writings be judged on their own terms, like novels, plays and poems, with their value lying purely in the eye of the beholder. Some postmodernist writers have adopted a similar position, reinforced by their deconstruction of the rhetorical devices used to claim authoritative status.

Examples

Goffman's *Asylums* (1961) is undoubtedly the most influential qualitative social science study to have been written. It is a strange blend of conceptual clarity (as in his writings on the moral career of the mental patient), humanitarian concern and dry humour: Goffman's gifts as an essayist in the tradition of Montaigne and Orwell won him a wider audience than merely academic writing could capture. But while the closures of the great nineteenth-century asylums certainly owed something to Goffman's *Asylums* and to other writings like Ken Kesey's 1962 novel (later filmed) *One Flew Over The Cuckoo's Nest*, the closures probably owed a great deal more to other coincidental events – the rise of new pharmacological treatments for mental illness and governments' searches for savings in health-care costs (Sedgwick, 1982).

Evaluation

Since there are, as shown above, a number of different (and sometimes disputed) potential uses for qualitative research, it is no surprise that qualitative research methods can be shown to have both particular pragmatic significance and wider policy value. Qualitative process evaluations have helped to explain why community controlled trials have succeeded or failed. Detailed qualitative descriptions of work practices have led both individuals and workgroups to question and revise their own activities. It is even possible to point (as with Goffman's *Asylums*) to consequent policy changes, though such instances are rare and other causal elements are likely to be more potent than the research report. There are also 'uses' for qualitative research beyond pragmatic explanation and policy stimulus: the experience of the research process itself can be life-enhancing for the reflexive researcher, and sometimes enjoyable too for the respondent – feeling listened to, having enjoyed telling your story, feeling that you have participated in something that might make a difference, helping someone with their studies, etc. However, with one class of exception, qualitative research findings are perceived to be less useful than quantitative research findings because of their problematic **generalizability**. The one class of exception here is **rapid assessment** techniques, which although largely qualitative in nature (key informant interviews, group interviews, short observation, etc.), have been explicitly developed for maximum policy utility, albeit usually for use in developing countries where survey methods would be unfeasible or uneconomic.

Associated Concepts: Generalization, Multiple Methods, Process Evaluation, Rapid Assessment, 'Whose Side Are We On?'

Key Readings

Becker, H. (1953) 'Becoming a marihuana user', *American Journal of Sociology*, 59: 231–242.

Becker, H. (1967) 'Whose side are we on?', *Social Problems*, 14: 239–247.

Berridge, V. and Strong, P. (1993) *AIDS and Contemporary History*. Cambridge: Cambridge University Press.

Best, J. (ed.) (1989) *Images of Issues: Typifying Social Problems*. Hawthorne, NY: Aldine de Gruyter.

Bloor, M. (2004) 'Addressing social problems through qualitative research', in D. Silverman (ed.), *Qualitative Research: Theory, Method and Practice* (2nd edn). London: Sage.

Bulmer, M. (1982) *The Uses of Social Research*. London: Allen and Unwin.

Burawoy, M. (2004) 'For public sociology', presidential address, American Sociological Association, annual meeting, San Francisco, 15 August 2004.

Goffman, E. (1961) *Asylums*. New York: Doubleday.

Howard, J. and Borges, P. (1970) 'Needle-sharing in the Haight: some social and psychological functions',

Journal of Health and Social Behaviour, 11: 220–230.

Kesey, K. (1962) *One Flew Over The Cuckoo's Nest*. New York: Victory Press.

Major-Poetzl, P. (1983) *Michel Foucault's Archaeology of Western Culture*. Brighton: Harvester.

Miller, G., Dingwall, R. and Murphy, E. (2004) 'Using qualitative data and analysis – reflections on organizational research', in D. Silverman (ed.), *Qualitative Research: Theory, Method and Practice* (2nd edn). London: Sage.

Parry-Langdon, N., Bloor, M., Audrey, S. and Holliday, J. (2003) 'Process evaluation of health promotion interventions', *Policy & Politics*, 31: 207–216.

Rock, P. (1987) *A View from the Shadows: Policymaking in the Solicitor-General's Office*. Oxford: Oxford University Press.

Schon, D. (1983) *The Reflective Practitioner*. London: Temple Smith.

Sedgwick, P. (1982) *Psycho Politics*. London: Pluto Press.

*Shaw, I. (1999) *Qualitative Evaluation*. London: Sage.

Video-Recording (and Video Analysis)

Definition
The use of video to record social life. Social scientists who use video are not just concerned with the activities and interactions of human bodies but also with how subjects interact with physical artefacts. Researchers may use the recorded images and sound either as a resource for analysis or for the documentation and representation of those actions to other audiences.

Distinctive Features
Video-recording as a method of data collection and means of data analysis has allowed significant methodological improvements to the study of non-verbal behaviour. As with **audio-recordings**, video-recording is seen to be more reliable than real-time observation and note-taking as it allows for repeated examination of the data and consequently data are not limited by the problems of selective attention or recollection.

　　The use of video as a research method came relatively late to the disciplines of sociology and education. The technology has received more attention within anthropology, but even here it has tended to be used as a form of representation rather than as a resource for analysis. Psychologists have also been among the first to use video within experimental research designs, usually for the purpose of observing behaviours such as compliance. Interest in using video as a method of data collection and analysis is linked with the techniques of **ethnomethodology** and **conversation analysis** which are concerned with the social organization of face-to-face interactions within organizational settings. In particular, analysis has focused on how subjects produce actions and respond to the actions of others through facial gestures, gaze, bodily posture and artefacts as well as through talk (Heath, 1997). Thus, video analysis has demonstrated how any single utterance may be accompanied by a gesture that influences co-participation within the conversation and allows researchers to take the visual, as well as the vocal, aspects of the interaction seriously.

　　Just as the minidisc and later the digital voice recorder have replaced cassette tapes in audio-recording, so too has the video been superseded by digital cameras and recorders. Despite technological advances, video-recorders remain simple enough for amateurs to record and edit data. Video analysis progresses through a process of **indexing**, in much the same way as a researcher might analyse audio data that have been transcribed. The simplest method of indexing is through the use of mechanical counters which are built into the equipment. Themes or codes are assigned to sections of data a bit like numbering pages in a transcribed text. Computer-compatible time coding is more sophisticated. The computer plays back the recorded actions (either in real time or slow or fast motion) and the observer allocates appropriate codes for the data while the computer registers the corresponding videotape time-code.

Examples

Lomax and Casey (1998) explore how midwifery consultations are interactionally accomplished at home following the recent birth of a baby. The collection of the video-data is remarkable in itself as inevitably such consultations are of a sensitive nature and may include physical examinations. The authors adopt a reflexive approach to their data, stressing that the researcher is unavoidably part of the social world that is being studied. They argue that data generated by video is neither an accurate representation of social life nor so contaminated that the data is unusable. The authors also exploit additional data produced by the presence of the video. Insights into how midwives differentiate between different parts of their professional duties, and manage body taboos, are gained by analysing how the midwife influences when the camera is turned off and on. Midwives also considered that some aspects of the consultation, such as the greetings and explanations of the purpose of the consultation, did not require recording, consequently playing down the importance of talk compared with technical care.

A study by Rich and Patashnick (2002) explores the use of video diaries to produce visual illness narratives. The method involved participants constructing their own video diaries of their experiences of living with and managing their chronic medical condition. The video diaries were then subsequently coded and analysed, with the assistance of **computer-assisted qualitative data analysis**, particularly through an examination of the participants' spoken accounts and the social setting in which they recorded themselves.

Heath and Luff (1993) offer a short example of how an analysis of both visual and vocal behaviour is important when studying the accomplishment of social interaction. Using video recordings collected from a London Underground control room, the authors demonstrate how a transcript of the audio data alone does not explain how one controller's request to 'tell him to go' can be fully understood by another controller. Specifically, the request does not explain who the 'him' is and why he should go. Analysis of the video data provides a clue as to how the action can be carried out as it illustrates that, just before the request is made, both controllers are orientated towards the CCTV screen displaying an image of Oxford Circus. Thus the second controller is able to make sense of the request in the light of their shared orientation towards the same object.

Evaluation

There are some clear advantages of video-recording research participants. Its principal advantage is perhaps that the technology records actual behaviour rather than reported behaviour. It enables collection of minute details of social life that would not be possible by unaided human observation. Furthermore it enables other researchers to analyse data once the researcher collecting the data has left the field. Despite these advantages, video data has not been used extensively in sociological research. One suggestion for this is the practical, ethical and theoretical difficulties associated with using videos in natural settings (Lomax and Casey, 1998). As with audio-recording, people may not act naturally in the presence of a video-recorder, casting doubt on the authenticity and spontaneity of supposedly naturally occurring data. Strategies to validate it have included using a **covert** approach (such as hiding the video-recorder behind a screen), the application of **multiple methods**, or member validation techniques.

A further **ethical** problem is that maintaining participants' anonymity proves even more difficult with video than with audio-recordings. Researchers should ensure that they have secured permission to reproduce images of their research subjects within any representations of the research data.

Associated Concepts: Audio-Recording, Computer-Assisted Data Analysis, Conversation Analysis, Covert Research, Ethics, Ethnomethodology, Indexing, Multiple Methods.

Key Readings

Ball, M.S. (1992) *Analyzing Visual Data.* Newbury Park, CA: Sage.
Banks, M. (2001) *Visual Methods in Social Research.* London: Sage.
Bauer, M. and Gaskell, G. (2000) *Qualitative Researching with Text, Image and Sound: A Practical Handbook.* London: Sage.
Dowrick, P.W. and Biggs, S.J. (eds) (1983) *Using Video: Psychological and Social Applications.* Chichester: Wiley.
Emmison, M. (2000) *Researching the Visual: Images, Objects, Contexts and*

Interactions in Social and Cultural Inquiry. London: Sage.

Heath, C. (1997) 'The analysis of activities in face-to-face interaction using video', in D. Silverman (ed.), *Qualitative Research: Theory, Method and Practice.* London: Sage. pp. 183–200.

Heath, C. and Luff, P. (1993) 'Explicating face-to-face interaction', in N. Gilbert (ed.), *Researching Social Life.* London: Sage. pp. 306–327.

Lomax, H. and Casey, N. (1998) 'Recording social life: reflexivity and video methodology', *Sociological Research Online*, 3(2). http://www.socresonline.org.uk/socresonline/3/2/4.html

Rich, M. and Patashnick, J. (2002) 'Narrative research with audiovisual data: video intervention/prevention assessment (VIA) and NVivo', *International Journal of Social Research Methodology: Theory & Practice*, 5(3): 245–261.

Vignettes

Definition

A technique, used in structured and depth **interviews** as well as **focus groups**, providing sketches of fictional (or fictionalized) scenarios. The respondent is then invited to imagine, drawing on his or her own experience, how the central character in the scenario will behave. Vignettes thus collect situated data on group values, group beliefs, and group norms of behaviour. While in structured interviews respondents must choose from a multiple-choice menu of possible answers to a vignette, as used in depth interviews and focus groups, vignettes act as stimulus to extended discussion of the scenario in question.

Distinctive Features

The scenarios must carry sufficient detail to allow the respondent to visualize the scenario as an actual event or situation. Because the elaboration of the requisite detail is rather time-consuming for the interviewer and rather fatiguing for the interviewee, the number of different vignettes used in interviews is usually rather limited (four to six being typical). So topic coverage with the vignette technique is frequently not very extensive. However, rather more vignettes can be used if the interviewee's response to Vignette A is used as the basis for a more developed scenario (Vignette B), the response to which is then the basis for a third scenario, etc., etc. (see Hughes, 1998 for an example of these developmental vignettes). In the latter case, less time is expended in

183

repetitious detail and the interviewee's interest is engaged by the unfolding of the scenario across successive vignettes.

Vignettes need not be narrated by the interviewer. Sometimes artwork or photos are used (Benderlow, 1993). Jenkins (2006) has used an interactive computer program for the presentation of developmental vignettes. Whatever the format, vignettes need to be carefully piloted. Since the vignettes often present decision choices or moral dilemmas, they need to explore different options in an even-handed manner.

Examples

The developmental vignettes used by Hughes (1998) explored needle-sharing and unprotected sex scenarios with drug-using ex-prisoners, taking the same fictional characters through relationship changes, prison sentences, and so on. Respondents were encouraged to relate the vignettes to their own personal experiences with prompts such as: 'Have you ever found yourself in a similar situation?'

Evaluation

Developmental vignettes allow for the possibility of vignettes having a central rather than an auxiliary place in depth interviews. While vignettes should not be thought of as matches for real-life experiences and responses to vignettes as reportage of behaviour in real-life situations, they are a useful guide to group norms and beliefs. They are also a valuable non-threatening way to introduce discussions with respondents on sensitive topics (Neff, 1979).

Associated Concepts: Focus Groups, Interviews.

Key Readings

Benderlow, G. (1993) 'Using visual imagery to explore gendered notions of pain', in C. Renzetti and R. Lee (eds), *Researching Sensitive Topics.* London: Sage.

*Hughes, R. (1998) 'Considering the vignette technique and its application to the study of drug injecting and HIV risk and safer behaviour', *Sociology of Health & Illness*, 20: 381–400.

Jenkins, N. (2006) 'More than skin deep? A study of young people's leisure injuries'. PhD dissertation, Cardiff University.

Neff, J. (1979) 'Interaction versus hypothetical others: the use of vignettes in attitude research', *Sociology and Social Research*, 64: 105–125.

'Whose Side Are We On?'

Definition
The title of Howard Becker's much-referenced presidential address to the Society for the Study of Social Problems in 1966 (Becker, 1967) and a question which neatly encapsulates a number of long-running concerns in social research – concerns over political **bias**, methodological rigour and the audiences for social research.

Distinctive Features
Becker's initial standpoint is that it is impossible to undertake research that is 'uncontaminated' by personal and political sympathies. It is an argument that owes much to Gouldner's (1962) earlier analysis of Max Weber's writings, indicating that – although objective scientific standards should govern the conduct of scientific research – the choice of research topic and the interpretation of the implications of the findings are infused with personal values. Moreover, in the course of qualitative research in particular, the researcher often falls into a deep sympathy with the subjects being studied.

In a world in which it is impossible (so Becker argues) not to take sides, the sociologist often finds him or herself on the side of the underdog – the prisoner, the mental patient, the factory worker, the ghetto dweller. But this affiliation is disputed (not least by colleagues) and shamefaced, because it contradicts what Becker calls the 'hierarchy of credibility' which assumes that superordinates (prison governors, psychiatrists and the rest) know best. Becker calls for researchers to acknowledge their personal and political commitments and not be shamefaced about these, but also to be on their guard against **bias** and self-censorship in the *conduct* of their research: 'whatever side we are on, we must use our techniques impartially enough that a belief to which we are especially sympathetic could be proved untrue' (Becker, 1967: 246).

Examples
Clearly, the best encapsulation of the 'Whose side are we on?' question is Becker's own. But Hammersley (1994) discusses at length the issue of commitment

in educational research, drawing on examples of research studies which drew critical fire for their failure to support political shibboleths, such as the view that white teachers with racist attitudes disadvantage black pupils in class-room interaction.

Evaluation

The cry of the political left (and of some **feminist** writing) has long been that the aim of research should not be to describe the world, but to change it. And Becker's question has been posed rhetorically by some leftist and feminist writers who have overlooked Becker's old-fashioned determination to preserve both the value-neutrality of research techniques and the possibility that a cherished (and revolutionary) hypothesis may be falsified. The falsification of a cherished hypothesis may pose particular difficulties for **action researchers** and those embracing **public participation** in the research process.

The hijacking of Becker's work has drawn criticism from Silverman who has written about the disabling 'rhetoric of sides [...] often associated with a style of research which is unable to discover anything because of its prior commitment to a revealed truth' (Silverman, 2001: 260). From a slightly different standpoint, Hammersley and Atkinson (1995: 20) argue that much qualitative research has a very limited social function (whether it be in defence of, or in opposition to, the status quo) and has a right to be judged on its own terms, rather than in respect of its presumed social function.

Nevertheless, Becker's question continues to resonate. The 2004 presidential address of Michael Burawoy at the American Sociological Association annual meeting addressed the conference theme of 'public sociologies' whereby social researchers seek to engage directly with wider public audiences, declaring that sociology should be both a mirror and a conscience of society (Burawoy, 2004). Implicitly, social scientists continue to be strongly concerned with exploring the nature of their own commitment.

Associated Concepts: Action Research, Bias, Feminist Methods, Public Participation.

Key Readings

*Becker, H.S. (1967) 'Whose side are we on?', *Social Problems*, 14: 239–247.

Burawoy, M. (2004) 'For public sociology', presidential address, American Sociological Association, annual meeting, San Francisco, 15 August 2004.

Gouldner, A. (1962) 'Anti-minotaur: the myth of a value-free sociology', *Social Problems*, 9: 199–213.

*Hammersley, M. (1994) *The Politics of Social Research*. London: Sage.

Hammersley, M. and Atkinson, P. (1995) *Ethnography: Principles in Practice* (2nd edn). London: Sage.

Silverman, D. (2001) *Interpreting Qualitative Data: Methods for Analysing Talk, Text and Interaction* (2nd edn). London: Sage.

Writing

Definition

The process of reflection, communication and presentation of research and knowledge through text. Writing is often mistakenly considered to be the process that happens at the end of a research project in which we tell our audience about our findings. Writing should be a method of enquiry, the means by which we come to know about the social world and our relationship to it (Richardson, 2000).

Distinctive Features

The style of a piece of qualitative writing will depend on the topic of social life with which the researcher is concerned, his or her method of research and the purpose of the writing (for example whether the aim is to describe, reflect or persuade). A typical writing style for empirically based qualitative research is one which follows a general pattern of introduction, methods and/or theory, results (organized around main themes and categories) and conclusion/discussion (which often includes implications for policy). This format is usually found in the journals of disciplines closest to the scientific model of research. There are many alternatives to this basic form of qualitative writing. Some articles may have little or no data and instead their main purpose is to present theoretical or methodological debates or review literature. They are often typified by a presentation of an accepted position or view, followed by an alternative.

The 'literary turn' is a movement within the social sciences that typifies the more expressionist or evocative forms of writing. Writing in this style is more reflexive and represents the author's emotions, feelings and relationships. This movement has opened up opportunities for researchers to present their work in many different forms including poetry (Richardson, 1994), reflective narratives of personal experiences (Elwyn, 1997), fictional stories (Rowland, 1991) and intentionally 'messy' or indeterminate texts that may use multiple authors (Lather, 1997).

Ethnography has a unique style of writing because, as **reflexivity** is an essential part of the ethnographic process, ethnographic writing tends to be very personal. Ethnographic writing combines personal narrative with 'thick description' – the result of sustained immersion in the culture which reflects the richness of the data. Van Maanen (1988) distinguished three main types of ethnographic writing that are also applicable to research generated from other qualitative methods. These three styles can be summarized as realist tales, confessional tales and impressionist tales. Realist tales are characterized by the author's absence from the text so that observations are presented as facts and the experiences are presented from the viewpoint of the members of the culture being studied (see **naturalism**). Confessional tales are written in a personal style with the author expressing his or her role and experiences. They are often characterized by honest descriptions of successes and failures in gaining access to and maintaining fieldwork relationships with members of the culture. Finally impressionist tales are characterized by a narrative in which the author represents the events of the culture to the reader thereby inviting the reader to experience what the author him or herself has experienced.

The writing of **fieldnotes** in a **research diary** is an important aspect of the research process, particularly for ethnographic research. Research diaries or journals should record the researcher's observations, methodological notes, theories, hypotheses and hunches, and personal notes such as feelings and anxieties. Writing fieldnotes helps the process of expanding ideas and developing creative writing skills.

There are a number of texts for social scientists (particularly directed at the student market) which help with the often difficult issue of how to actually sit down and produce a piece of academic writing (see for example Becker, 1986; Wolcott, 1990; Woods, 1999). These texts offer practical advice for common problems such as how to get started and overcoming the paralysing fear of others reading your work. In addition to these student survival guides there are texts that deal with the technical aspects of writing such as grammar and style (for example see Dummett, 1992). The importance of knowing one's audience and writing for that audience is another frequent feature of texts on qualitative writing (see for example Richardson, 1990). The same research may need to be presented in different formats and styles depending on whether the audience are colleagues in one's own discipline, academics from other disciplines, policy makers or the general public.

Examples

Lowton's (2002) paper in the *Journal of Advanced Nursing* is an example of an empirically based qualitative study that follows the standard format most closely aligned with the natural sciences. She presents a thematic analysis of her qualitative data from 31 relatives of individuals with cystic fibrosis. The paper opens with background data on the prevalence and consequences of cystic fibrosis, then states the research aims which are to explore the perceptions and experiences of carers. Details of the study sample and data collection are then discussed in the methods section, which is then followed by the study findings presented through two main themes: notions of 'expert care' and the significance of the relationship with the patient. The conclusion of the paper has policy recommendations as she makes a plea for higher levels of social and nursing support for carers.

Palladino (2002), writing in the journal *Social Studies of Science*, offers a theoretical discussion paper which traces the historical development of a clinical test for a hereditary form of colon cancer – familial adenomatous polyposis. In his paper Palladino suggests a revision of the relationship between power and knowledge presented by theorists such as Foucault and Rabinow. The paper is opened by a quote from the *Sunday Times* about the development of a pre-natal test for colorectal cancer and its implications for 'designer babies'. The author then reflects on the report, suggesting that patients and their families are increasingly presented as passive objects of professional intervention. Palladino then reconstructs the historical development of evidence for a colorectal cancer gene using extracts of physicians' written accounts, and concludes by suggesting that the relationship between physicians and their patients can be characterized more by negotiation than power.

Evaluation

During the 1970s and 1980s the social sciences were said to have been experiencing a 'crisis of representation'. The authority of written texts, and their authors, was being challenged on the basis that they excluded the 'other', that is, those people whose lives are the subject of the research. The problem of representation of others and their experiences was a particular concern for feminist scholars who were mindful of the power differentials between researchers and subjects. In addition, written texts were said to be experiencing a 'crisis of legitimation', that is, the validity of accounts was being questioned. With the literary turn has come an appreciation that social science writing cannot present one objective reality and that our knowledge can only be partial. New forms of writing therefore tend to be more relativist than realist, maintaining that there is not one truth but a multiplicity of perspectives. In consequence some have felt the traditional form of research writing to be misplaced and boring (Richardson, 2000). The expressionist writing that has emerged in the 'literary turn' has sometimes been criticized for being too self-indulgent in that, at times, it can say more about the author than the subject matter. The response to this charge is usually that written texts should be self-knowing, engaging and evocative in order to be authentic and believable.

Associated Concepts: Biographies, Ethnography, Fieldnotes, Naturalism, Reflexivity, Research Diary.

Key Readings

Atkinson, P. (1990) *The Ethnographic Imagination: Textual Constructions of Reality.* London: Routledge.

Becker, H.S. (1986) *Writing for Social Scientists: How to Start and Finish your Thesis, Book or Article.* Chicago: University of Chicago Press.

Brown, R.H. (ed.) (1992) *Writing the Social Text.* New York: Aldine de Gruyter.

Dummett, M. (1992) *Grammar and Style: For Examination Candidates and Others.* London: Duckworth.

Elwyn, G. (1997) 'So many precious stories: a reflective narrative of general practice based care, Christmas 1996', *British Medical Journal*, 315: 1659–1663.

Fairbairn, G.J. and Winch, C. (1996) *Reading, Writing and Reasoning: A Guide for Students.* Buckingham: Open University Press.

Flick, U. (1998) *An Introduction to Qualitative Research.* London: Sage.

Geertz, C. (1988) *Works as Lives: The Anthropologist as Author.* Cambridge: Polity.

Jackson, A. (1987) *Anthropology at Home.* London: Tavistock.

Lather, P. (1997) 'Drawing the line at angels: working the ruins of feminist ethnography', *International Journal of Qualitative Studies in Education*, 10(3): 285–304.

Lowton, K. (2002) 'Parents and partners: lay carers' perceptions of their role in the treatment and care of adults with cystic fibrosis', *Journal of Advanced Nursing*, 39(2): 174–181.

Palladino, P. (2002) 'Between knowledge and practice: on medical professionals, patients and the making of the genetics of cancer', *Social Studies of Science*, 32(1): 137–165.

Richardson, L. (1990) *Writing Strategies: Reaching Diverse Audiences.* London: Sage.

Richardson, L. (1994) 'Nine poems: marriage and the family', *Journal of Contemporary Ethnography*, 23(1): 3–13.

*Richardson, L. (2000) 'Writing: a method of inquiry', in N. Denzin and Y. Lincoln (eds), *Handbook of Qualitative Research.* Thousand Oaks, CA: Sage. pp. 923–948.

Rowland, S. (1991) 'The power of silence: an enquiry through fictional writing', *British Educational Research Journal*, 17(2): 95–113.

Van Maanen, J. (1988) *Tales of the Field: On Writing Ethnography.* Chicago: University of Chicago Press.

Wolcott, H.F. (1990) *Writing up Qualitative Research.* London: Sage.

Woods, P. (1999) *Successful Writing for Qualitative Researchers.* London: Routledge.

Index